Financial Literacy of Women Entrepreneurs

Financial Literacy of Women Entrepreneurs

Dr. P.N. Harikumar
Dr. Reshma Rachel Kuruvilla

ABHIJEET PUBLICATIONS
NEW DELHI 110002

ABHIJEET PUBLICATIONS
4658-A, First Floor, Ambika Bhawan,
21 Ansari Road, New Delhi 110002
Phone: 011-23259444
E-mail: abhijeetpublication@gmail.com
www.abhijeetpublications.com

FINANCIAL LITERACY OF WOMEN ENTREPRENEURS

First Published 2021

ISBN 978-81-953707-5-7

PRINTED IN INDIA

Published by J.K. Singh for Abhijeet Publications, New Delhi-110002, Lasertypeset by Abhijeet Typesetters, New Delhi and Printed at Milan Enterprises, New Delhi.

Contents

List of Abbreviations

ANOVA	Analysis of Variance
CII	Confederation of Indian Industry
CIPHET	Central Institute of Post-Harvest Engineering & Technology
Df	Degree of freedom
GST	Goods and Services Tax
IRDAI	Insurance Regulatory and Development Authority of India
MANOVA	Multivariate analysis of variance
OECD	Organisation for Economic Co-operation and Development
P	Probability
RBI	Reserve Bank of India
SEBI	Securities and Exchange Board of India
SGST	State Government Service Tax
Sig.	Asymptotic Significance
UK	United Kingdom
US	United States
USA	United States of America
USD	United States Dollar

1

Introduction and Design of the Study

1.1 Introduction

Women were looked upon as a source of power in the olden days, but now women are given an inferior position in the present patriarchal family hierarchy. Serious gender bias has become a casual thing for the women right from her childhood. School dropout, Incidences of malnutrition, child marriage, dowry harassments etc, are common examples of the difficulties faced by the womenfolk during her lifetime. Dropping male female ratio in our country has also become a matter to be concerned at. All these taboos jointly contribute to the poor status of women in our society. If the status of women has to change, female involvement in economic activities and monetary contribution to the family too has to change. Traditionally, women were involved in household management alone. Ever increasing requirement to supplement the family income and increasing opportunities for entrepreneurship has attracted many women to come to the forefront of entrepreneurship. Conventionally, woman has been performing the role of a supervisor of household activities and that too will no doubt empower her to run a business professionally and successfully. The appearance of women on the new arena as entrepreneurs is a noteworthy development in the upliftment of women for establishing them an abode in the society. Therefore, it is extremely important to see that the women are not lagging behind in entrepreneurial development. Lack of knowledge and competency in financial matters can turn up as a difficult problem for the growth of women owned enterprises.

Finance is a major requirement for every business need. A proper balance between risks and profitability is the main aim of every business person while maximizing the assets and networth of the business. For this, proper allocation and use of funds is needed. Without proper utilization of funds, prosperity of the business will be at risk. Proper utilization requires proper knowledge on financial terms. Survey conducted by Standard & Poor's Financial Services LLC (S&P) postulates that less than 25 per cent of adults are having sound financial literacy in South Asian countries. It also augments that though India is home for 17.5 per cent of the world's population, almost 76 per cent of India's adult population is not capable to understand the Fundamental financial concepts. Women are not an exception in this regard. Cultural traditions and sociological taboos have kept women inactive for quiet a long period of time. Deficiency in the levels of financial knowledge is a major pullback factor for many entrepreneurs especially women entrepreneurs.

Financial literacy is not exactly about the knowledge of financial matters but it is about having the set of skills and knowledge which will influence a person's awareness, behavior, and attitude in the personnel management of finances with all of their available limited financial resources. Research done earlier has indicated that firms managed by financially literate entrepreneurs has performed better than their counterparts who were financially illiterate since better tools of risk management and financial strategies have been adopted by the financially literate entrepreneur. Proper financial literacy is required for evaluating the various investment avenues available in the market and for utilizing the credit options particularly available for women. If proper financial literacy is there, then that will be of benefit for the woman entrepreneur in proper management of her business which will indirectly benefit the society and the economy at large in the long run. Financial literacy has gained so much importance since globalization, because new avenues of investments and credit availability emerge very often and the ordinary laymen who are not directly linked with commerce and management area otherwise won't know much about the complicated financial markets.

Generally women tend to live longer than men and hence lack of financial literacy can turn out to be more costly, because awareness of financial terms and services can instill confidence, self-esteem and courage to step up and lead a successful personal and professional life. If the skills and talents of women are properly utilized, it can make India stand in a distinguishable position among other world countries because women are a major source of power and resource for development with huge potential.

1.2 Statement of The Problem

The dawn of 21st century has come with greater trials and tribulations and lesser stability in every domain of social life. Right through history, women have been an equal economic partner to men, besides her biological and social roles. In the present world of business and entrepreneurship men and women are participating in large number. Today, more and more women are seeking economic opportunity and self-determination by creating their own enterprise, especially in food processing industries with which they are traditionally related.

Food processing means different forms of value addition made to agricultural or horticultural produce and it includes various processes such as sorting, grading, packaging which are expected to enhance the shelf life of food products to make it marketable to outsiders for earning revenue. The food processing industry provides connections and synergies between agriculture and industrial sector. In terms of consumption, production, export and growth prospects, the Food Processing Industry sector in India is one of the largest among the various industries. India's food processing sector includes a large range of products, vegetables; fruits, meat products, fisheries, milk products, alcoholic beverages, plantation, grain processing and other consumer product groups. Women can play a major role in the overall development of every country as they constitute half of the human resources of every nation, particularly for a developing country like India. The economic wealth of a country is said to be seriously dwindling if about half of the nation's human resource is neglected. Across the globe, it is calculated that approximately one third of all the businesses are owned by women. Based on the global statistics, all over the world the number of female business owners continues to increase progressively which is changing the shape of global economy.

Studies show that, the women entrepreneurship position in select States of India is above 30 per cent on an average. Number of women involved in making money has increased over the year's in India. As per the World Bank Report 2010-2011 and WAWE Conference Report 2009-10, the women work participation rate in India has been increased from 14.2 per cent to 31.6 per cent in a gap of 4 decades from 1970 to 2011. Increasing women involvement in money making has brought about perceptible changes in the socio-economic conditions of women. The food processing and conservation solutions are cost-effective and are easy to implement. They have been particularly effective at enhancing and diversifying livelihoods.

Statistics has revealed that huge importance has been given by governments for the food processing sector and the women entrepreneurs'. More often, complex decisions have to be taken by the entrepreneurs in managing their businesses from its grass root levels. Equipping the entrepreneurs with the financial skills can help them in having an improved understanding of the financing options and in the utilization of the plethora of various financial services available in the market which can be made benefitted.

Only if businesses develop, society and the economy at large can grow along with it. Therefore it has a pivotal role in our nation's economic progress. This study will help analyze the awareness level on various banking products and services offered to women entrepreneurs in specific and the impact of financial literacy among women entrepreneurs'. This will raise the following questions.

1. Are the women entrepreneurs managing food processing industrial units located in Kerala knowledgeable about common financial terms?
2. What are the attitude and behaviour of women entrepreneurs managing food processing industrial units located in Kerala towards financial matters?
3. What is the impact of financial knowledge on investment and credit decisions of women entrepreneurs managing food processing industrial units located in Kerala?

1.3 Objectives of the Study

The objectives of the study are:

1. To identify the determinants of financial literacy of women entrepreneurs.
2. To measure the awareness level of financial matters among women entrepreneurs managing food processing industrial units.
3. To analyze the financial attitude and financial behaviour of the women entrepreneurs managing food processing industrial units towards financial matters.
4. To measure the impact of financial literacy level on investment and credit decisions of women entrepreneurs managing food processing industrial units.

1.4 Conceptual Model of The Study

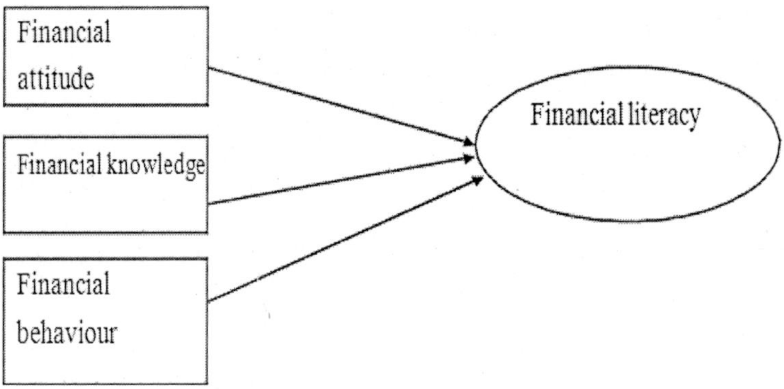

1.5 Hypotheses

Following hypotheses are framed to achieve the research objectives:

Ho1. There is no significant relationship between the demographic variables of women entrepreneurs managing food processing industrial units and their financial knowledge level.

Ho2. There is no significant relationship between the demographic variables of women entrepreneurs managing food processing industrial units and their financial attitude levels.

Ho3. There is no significant relationship between the demographic variables of women entrepreneurs managing food processing industrial units and their financial behaviour.

Ho4. There is no significant impact of financial knowledge level on investment decisions of women entrepreneurs managing food processing industrial units .

Ho5. There is no significant impact of financial literacy level on borrowing decisions of women entrepreneurs managing food processing industrial units .

Ho6. There is no significant difference in the utilization of funds among women entrepreneurs according to the nature of activities undertaken in the food processing industrial units.

H07: There is no significant effect of financial attitude on financial behaviour of the respondents.

1.6 Significance of the Study

Increased Awareness on financial matters has become the need of the hour for everyone ranging from homemakers to business houses. People have been managing day to day finances from the olden days by themselves but recent developments have made financial education and awareness increasingly important for financial well-being. Even for the average family to decide on balancing its budget, when deciding about buying a home, and for planning the necessities of life, financial awareness has become essential. But now more and more complex financial instruments have emerged and have made the entire financial market difficult to manage. People are offered a variety of instruments for saving their surplus funds and for making the borrowals at a much flexible interest rates. Risk and responsibility for the financial decisions taken will have a major impact on a person's future life. Therefore awareness of financial products and services has huge importance in a person's life. In the case of a business person, number of financial transactions undertaken and financial decisions taken increases manifold more than in the life of an ordinary person. Food processing sector has huge value for Kerala considering the environmental friendly nature of the food processing industry, market potential of the sector and the consumption pattern of economy in Kerala. Therefore, a study on the financial literacy of women entrepreneurs has huge significance.

1.7 Scope of the Study

Industrial growth in the past was on the basis of industrial policy followed by the government. Policy changes have to be brought in by the policymakers according to the changing business environments. Population density is a matter of concern for Kerala government compared to other Indian states, when it comes to the matter of formulating industrial policy in Kerala. Otherwise, industries in Kerala should not cause a problem for the locales of the region through pollution. Industrial units should be responsible and should try to promote the social cause of being environment friendly and should try to have minimum levels of pollution. Agro based food processing industries which create minimum quantity of wastages can be a solution at this point of time. Moreover, traditionally for over a century, Kerala was used as an exit point for the export of spices from our country. Geographical peculiarities and situation of the Western Ghats have led to the promotion of ports like Vallarpadam and Vizhinjam in Kerala. These ports will encourage more entrepreneurs to sell of their good quality harvests to foreign land for foreign currencies. If this is to be utilized, Kerala has scope in the development of India's economy through the food processing sector. If Government promotes the export of agro food processing units, then that has the capacity to bring in huge revenue for the country and to be a solution for the increasing unemployment problem without creating troubles for the environment. Higher rates of educational literacy among the households and skill development have improved the conditions of entrepreneurs. But over all these, despite all the efforts from the government and conditions favouring food processing sector, if proper knowledge on financial matters accompanied by favourable financial attitude is not there, it might create problems in the management of funds for the business units leading to shut down of units within a short while. Considering the importance of financial literacy, deliberate plans should be framed to evaluate the financial literacy position of women entrepreneurs in food processing sectors to suggest measures to promote financial literacy and its usage among the women entrepreneurs in food processing sector.

1.8 Methodology of the Study

Nature of the Study

The study is descriptive in nature. The study attempts to describe the financial literacy among the women entrepreneurs in Kerala who are engaged in food processing industrial units. It analyzed the financial literacy variables of the respondents after categorizing financial literacy into financial knowledge, financial attitude, and financial behaviour.

Collection of Data

The study is based on both primary data and data collected from published sources. Secondary data required for the study is collected from journals, government reports, magazines, books, and websites and so on. Primary data of this study are to be collected from the women entrepreneurs managing food processing industrial units located across Kerala through a well structured interview schedule. Respondents will be chosen at random from each of these areas.

Period of Data Collection

A pilot study was conducted among 50 women entrepreneurs in Kerala who are engaged in food processing industrial units selected at random with an interview schedule during Nov 2018. After examining the reliability of the questionnaire, final interview schedule was prepared and provided to women entrepreneurs in Kerala who are engaged in food processing industrial units from December 2018 to May 2019.

Research Instrument

Interview schedule was used in collecting the data from the women entrepreneurs engaged in food processing industrial units after a pilot study to test the reliability of the variables after discussion with a statistician.

Population

Women entrepreneurs engaged in food processing industrial units located across Kerala were the population of the study.

Sampling method

Simple random sampling is adopted for the selection of sample respondents. Sample size determination for the above population was done using the table published by Daryle W Morgan and Robert V Krejcie. Sample size of the study is determined as 620. Period of the study covers from November 2018 to May 2019.

Data Analysis

Data analysis is done using statistical tools like Manova, Mann Whitney U test, Friedman test, MDS, Regression, and Kruskal Wallis test.

1.9 Statistical Tools Used for the Study

➢ ***Kruskal-Wallis H Test***

Kruskal-Wallis is a rank-based nonparametric test that can be utilized to decide whether there are measurably huge contrasts between the two groups of an independent variable and a continuous variable. This tool was used to identify the food processing industrial unit having the highest difficulty in managing the finance on the basis of their industrial activity.

➢ ***Mann Whitney U Test***

Differences between two independent groups can be compared using a Mann Whitney U test with a dependent variable which is either continuous or ordinal. Mann Whitney U test was used to identify the food processing unit which utilized funds mainly for dividend payment. It was also used to identify the differences between the types of industry in managing the cash flows of the organization.

➢ ***Canonical Discriminant Analysis***

Canonical Discriminant analysis probes the differences between groups on the features of the cases, pointing to the factor which contributes in group separation. This multivariate reduction technique was used to identify the financial products, financial services and financial terms having the highest awareness among women entrepreneurs engaged in food processing industrial units.

➢ *Friedman Test*

Friedman test is a simple non parametric test which compares between two or more number of variables to identify the most prominent factor. Lower mean ranks in Friedman test indicate more preference. Respondents are asked to mark their preference and based on the ranks given, mean scores were calculated to comprehend whether mean rank obtained is significant for the test or not. In this study, Friedman test was utilized in identifying the problems faced by the women entrepreneurs engaged in food processing industrial units in managing their finances and also to identify the most utilized financial activity in the business.

➢ *MANOVA*

Manova is nothing but ANOVA using more number of dependent variables. Differences in the two or more vectors of means are tested using MANOVA unlike ANOVA which tests for contrasts between the means of two groups. MANOVA was used in our study to evaluate the association of demographic variables of the women entrepreneurs engaged in food processing industrial units with financial knowledge, financial attitude, and financial behaviour.

➢ *Linear Regression*

Statisticians use linear regression as a tool to explain the relationship of a dependent variable with an independent variable. Linear models predict the value of a dependent variable based on the data collected on an independent predictor variable. Impact of financial knowledge on the borrowing and investment decisions among women entrepreneurs engaged in food processing industrial units was undertaken with linear regression. Influence of financial behaviour towards various financial activities according to the attitudes of respondents was also evaluated using linear regression.

1.10 Pilot Study

A pilot study was conducted by using the preliminary questionnaire circulated among 50 Women Entrepreneurs. The collected data from 50 respondents were studied in detail with variance reported, to incorporate changes in the preliminary questionnaire. Thus, the reliability analysis was done on the responses pertaining to the Financial Literacy of Women Entrepreneurs based on 98 statements recorded on a seven-point scale. The classical Cronbach Alpha Model for reliability was used. The procedure was started with all the statements considered and by sequentially eliminating those statements whose elimination must improve the Alpha value. The final value obtained for each variable, against the number of statements under this study, is presented in the following Table.

TABLE 1.1: CRONBACH ALPHA FOR THE VARIABLES UNDER STUDY

Sl. No.	*Variable*	*No of Statements*	*Cronbach's Alpha*
1.	Knowledge about financial concepts	4	0.760
2.	Financial attitude towards budgeting	5	0.770
3.	Financial attitude towards Investment	9	0.790
4.	Financial attitude towards financial planning	9	0.702
5.	Financial attitude towards record maintenance	4	0.786
6.	Financial attitude towards savings	7	0.796
7.	Financial attitude towards borrowings	4	0.726

8.	Financial attitude towards fund utilization	6	0.718
9.	Financial attitude towards spending	7	0.795
10.	Financial behaviour towards budgeting	4	0.880
11.	Financial behaviour towards investment	5	0.737
12.	Financial behaviour towards financial planning	8	0.799
13	Financial behaviour towards record maintenance	3	0.706
14.	Financial behaviour towards savings	8	0.730
15.	Financial behaviour towards borrowings	5	0.741
16.	Financial behaviour towards fund utilization	4	0.852
17.	Financial behaviour towards spending	6	0.794

1.11 Limitations of The Study

- In this study, the researcher considered only women entrepreneurs, so the results may not be justified to all the entrepreneurs.
- This study is related with Kerala, so the result may not be justified to other states.
- Study has been restricted to financial literacy of the women entrepreneurs; other aspects have to be considered for improving managerial effectiveness.

1.12 Operational Definitions Financial literacy

Financial literacy is the ability to understand about funds and to make informed decisions about its proper usage and management. Financial literacy can be measured using basic money management, financial planning and investment knowhow of a person.

Financial Attitude

Financial attitude is a psychological measure which projects as to how a person would feel about an event, person, or an object which is used as a tool to determine the future choice of an investor in financial decisions and to plan for the future market movements.

Financial Behaviour

A resultant product which would be available based on the financial attitude of a person that can explain the choices of investors by viewing the investors as rational decision makers.

Investment decisions

Decisions taken by the entrepreneur on the utilization of surplus funds saved from the business activity or from personal finances are called an investment decision.

Borrowing decisions

Decision to run or manage a business unit with funds rose from others without running into the credit risk issue.

Savings

It is the amount deferred without spending for conserving funds to meet the needs that will arise in future for the entrepreneur or for his business needs or for some contingencies.

Spending

It is an act of utilizing money for meeting the needs.

Budgeting

Budgeting means formulating plans which will determine in advance about the future expenses and incomes of a business which will give guidance for the control of income and expenses.

Financial planning

Financial planning refers to the job of deciding in advance about the means and ways to achieve the targeted goals of the organization without failure.

Utilization of funds

It is an activity which ensures proper health of the business by being vigil from planning phase.

Financial Record maintenance

It means the maintenance of proper records of the organization like cash book, journals, ledger, financial statements, and various returns prepared on behalf of the company to give evidence about the financial transactions happening in the organization on a future date.

Financial concepts

Commonly followed principles, procedures, and practices in the practice of accounting are called as financial concept.

Financial terms

Financial terms are commonly used terminologies during business transactions which give a better understanding of the financial statement evaluation and analysis.

Financial products

Financial products refer to new instruments developed that aid in saving, getting insurance coverage, investing or in accessing finance with the help of an external party.

Financial services

Financial service refers to economic activity developed and provided by persons in the finance industry that aid a person in the management of financial matters.

1.13 Chapter Scheme

The research report will be organized and presented in six chapters:

Chapter 1: Introduction and design of the study

This chapter includes Introduction, Statement of the problem, Objectives of the study, Hypothesis of the study, Conceptual Model, Purpose of the study, Scope of the study, Significance of the study, Limitations of the study, and Chapter scheme.

Chapter 2: Review of Literature

Various reviews collected on the research topic are presented in this chapter. Reviews have been collected on the topics financial literacy, variables of financial literacy and about entrepreneurship, Research gap was identified after review of earlier studies on this topic.

Chapter 3: Overview about Financial literacy and Conceptual framework of the study

This chapter gives an overview about gender inequality, importance of entrepreneurship, about financial literacy and its variables, determinants of financial literacy, financial attitude, and financial behaviour and on the importance of food processing sector

Chapter 4: Analysis of the Study

This chapter is framed to explain the data analyzed and to interpret the results from such analysis which meets the objectives of the research.

Chapter 5: Summary of Findings, Suggestions and Conclusion

A consolidated summary of the findings recommendations and appropriate suggestions and conclusion of the study is pointed out in this chapter.

REFERENCES

1. Barte, R. (2012). Financial Literacy in Micro Enterprises: The Case of Cebu Fish Vendors. *Philippine Management Review*, 19, 91-99.
2. Bonte, W. a. (2012). Financial literacy, information flows, and caste affiliation: Empirical evidence from India., *Journal of Banking & Finance*, 36, 3399–3414.
3. Meier, S. a. (2012). Discounting financial literacy: Time preferences and participation in financial eductaion programs, *Journal of Economic Behavior and Organzation*.
4. Ramaswamy D., e. a. (2013). A Study of the Level of Awareness of Financial Literacy among Management Undergraduates, *Proceedings of 3rd Asia-Pacific Business Research Conference*. Kuala Lumpur.
5. Servon Lisa J., a. R. (2008). Consumer Financial Literacy and the Impact of Online Banking on the Financial Behavior of Lower-Income Bank Customers. *The Journal of Consumer Affairs*, 42(2), 271-305.
6. Behara, S.R. and Niranjan, K. (2012). Rural Women Entrepreneurship in India,. IJCEM *International Journal of Computational Engineering & Management*, 15(6).
7. Hisrich, R.D.et.al. (2007). Entrepreneurship. The McGraw-Hill Companies. 6th ed.
8. JayaKumar, P. and Kannan, J. (2014). Challenges and Opportunities for Rural Women Entrepreneurs.*Economic and Business Review*, 2(1), 35-39.
9. Kumbhar, V. (2013). Some Critical Issues of Women Entrepreneurship in Rural India. *European Academic Research*. 1(2).
10. Pharm and Sritharan (2013). Problems Being Faced By Women Entrepreneurs in Rural Areas.*The International Journal Of Engineering And Science* (Ijes). 2(3). 52-55.

11. Senthilkumar, Vansantha and Varadharajan, (2012). Role of women entrepreneurs in Prambular District (Tamilnadu). *Asian Academic Research Journal of Multidisciplinary,* 1(1).

12. Sharma, A., Dua, Hatwal, V. (2012). Micro Enterprise Development and Rural Women Entrepreneurship: Way for Economic Empowerment. Arth Prabandh: *A Journal of Economics and Management*. 1(6).

13. Sharma, P. (2013). Women Entrepreneurship Development in India. *Global Journal of Management and Business Studies,* 3(4), 371-376.

14. Singh, A.(2014). Role of Women Entrepreneurs in India: A SWOT Analysis. *International Journal of Management and Business Studies,* 4(2), 231-238.

15. Aduda, J., Mogutu, P. O., & Githinji, M. W. (2012). The Relationship between Credit Scoring Practices by Commercial Banks and Access to Credit by Small and Medium Enterprises in Kenya *International Journal of Humanities and Social Science* 2(9), 1-11.

16. AL-Omiri, & Drury, C. (2007). A Survey of Factors Influencing the Choice of Product Costing Systems in UK Organisations. *management Accounting Research* UK, 18(4), 26. doi: 10.1016/J.MAR.2007.002.

17. Mbogo, M. (2011). Influence of Managerial Accounting Skills on SME's on the Success and Growth of Small and Medium Enterprises in Kenya. *Journal of Language, Technology and Entreprenuership in Africa,* 3(1).

18. Szchta, A. (2002). The Scope of Management Accounting Methods in Polish Enterprises. *Management Accounting Research,*13(4), 18.doi: http://dx.doi.org/10.1006/mare.2002.0198

19. Fox, J., Bartholomae, S. and Lee, J. (2005), 'Building the Case for Financial Education , *Journal of Consumer Affairs,* vol. 39, pp. 195-214.

20. Sandra Huston (2010), Measuring Financial Literacy, *The Journal of Consumer Affairs,* vol. 44, pp. 296-306.

21. Beal, D.J. and Welch, C. (2002), "Financial literacy among Australian University students", *Economic Papers,* Vol. 22 No. 1, pp. 65-78

22. Hogarth, J.M. (2002), "Financial literacy and family and consumer sciences", *Journal of Family and Consumer Sciences*, Vol. 94, pp. 14-28.
23. Worthington, A.C. (2005), "Financial literacy in Australia", paper presented at AFA *ANZ Conference Proceedings*, Melbourne, 3-5 July.
24. Abraham Ansong, Michael Asiedu Gyensare (2012). Determinants of University Working-Students' Financial Literacy at the University of Cape Coast, Ghana, *International Journal of Business and Management*, 7(9), 126-135.
25. D'Souza, S., & Pandey Dimple. (2016). A study on lack of financial literacy amongst women entrepreneurs. *Journal of Research, viii*(2), 34–46.
26. K.C.Sushma, An Analysis of Entrepreneurship Development in Women through EDP Trainings (Unpublished thesis).
27. Nagendra Kumar Jha: Development of Women Entrepreneurship – Challenges and Opportunities, Ninth AIMS International Conference on Management, Jan 1-4, 2012.
28. Statistics on Women in India 2010, :National Institute of Public Cooperation and Child Development, New Delhi, 2010, p. 356.
29. Rathore, B.S. and Dhameja, S.K. 1999. Entrepreneurship in 21st Century. Rawat Publications, Jaipur, p. 31.

2

Review of Literature

2.1 Introduction

Economic growth of a country is possible through entrepreneurship. Entrepreneurs generate jobs for themselves as well as for others in the society who cannot raise money to set up an establishment themselves. Statistical data published by the Government of India says that though the number of persons involved in business activities is growing, number of women entrepreneurs is not presenting an uptrend. Kumbhar V (2013) also discusses the challenges faced by women entrepreneurs of rural areas in India and is of the opinion that lack of work life balance, freedom in financial decisions, patriarchal society, inability to bear risk, lack of financial literacy, and lack of self-confidence contribute a lot in the poor performance of women entrepreneurs. Gender based barriers may be the limiting factor which is pulling the women entrepreneurs from behind the legs. Karim (2001) conducted a study on the women entrepreneurs in Bangladesh and he came to a conclusion that financial problems were the most common problem faced by women entrepreneurs of rural areas. It was therefore felt as a need to investigate as to whether financial education could possibly bring a change in the economic conditions of women entrepreneurs. This part of the study contains important observations of researchers as a result of various research activities carried out in the area related to women entrepreneurship, financial literacy and women empowerment.

Pradeep Khandwala (1988)[1] is of the view that inefficient management is the primary reason for sickness .Though secondary factors like raw material shortage, marketing problems of the products manufactured, limited availability of funds, competition etc. contribute in a big way for sickness, it is the entrepreneur's actions which ultimately decides the future of an enterprise. If governments and the financial institutions which provide funds are vigilant during project appraisal phase, sicknesses can be brought down in a big way. Continuous and cautious monitoring of units should be done after the implementation of project. Attractive incentives should be given to those units functioning effectively. There should be separate mechanisms to provide professional solutions for the problems of sick units in a speedy manner.

Sue Birley et.al, (1989)[2] evaluated whether there are any differences caused by the gender on taking up entrepreneurial roles. Marital status can bring lot of changes in a woman's life. He also examined whether social and cultural roles have caused some changes in the lives of females. It was observed that marital status does not influence a person's confidence levels, but parenthood is found to influence. The change brought in by motivation was almost indifferent among both the genders, but women exhibited a higher level of self-confidence than men. Prior experience and environmental factors are also found to influence a person's business choice.

Literature reviewed revealed that increasing financial literacy is a means to financially empower people and improve their quality of life (**Knapp, 1991; Voydanoff, 1990)**[3].

Penrose (1995)[4] emphasized that prior experience with a particular task reduces the need for cognitive attention to do similar tasks in future. Hence, entrepreneurs with past experiences or knowledge in similar business are more exposed to uncertain exercises of trials.

Chen and Volpe (1998)[5] conducted a survey of 924 college students of U.S. from thirteen different colleges to investigate their personal financial literacy; the relationship between financial literacy and student's characteristics such as gender, experience and impact of financial literacy on student's opinions and decisions. The survey tried to examine the personal financial literacy of the U.S. college students across the four prime areas: general knowledge, savings and borrowings, insurance and investments. The analytical tool used by them was Analysis Variance (ANOVA) technique to show the variations in the levels of financial literacy among subgroups of students. Additionally, a logistic regression model was used to investigate the financial literacy levels of students across different demographic factors. The students participated were classified into two subgroups using the median percentage of correct answers of students with higher scores than the median were classified as having relatively more knowledge and students with scores equal to or below the median were classified as having relatively less knowledge. The financial literacy, a dichotomous variable was used as the dependent variable in the logistic model and the independent variable were represented by the demographic characteristic variables. This study observed that personal finance skills and knowledge needs to be improved, with the overall median percentage of correct scores was 53%. The survey results were indicative that the most poorly answered questions were those involving investments, knowledge, savings and borrowings while the best answered questions were those on general knowledge. The demographic variables used in the analysis were academic discipline, class rank, gender, race, nationality, years of work experience, age and income. It was also found that those students with a non-business majors, women, and students in a lower class rank, under the age of 30 and had little work experience have lower levels of knowledge. It was also found that the participants with better financial knowledge identified more efficient options, while in their decision making concerning personal financial issues, they reacted more effectively. This study concluded that students with less knowledge were more likely to hold wrong opinions and make incorrect financial decisions and college students were not knowledgeable about personal finance. The low level of knowledge may limit their ability to make informed decisions. The study also concluded that the level of an individual's financial knowledge tends to influence attitudes that in turn affect the individual's financial behaviour. It was also noted that there was a lack of personal finance education in the education system which led to the persistent found financial literacy in American public.

CRIC Discussion paper (2000)[6] through their wok entitled "Defining the Role of Knowledge- Intensive Business Services in the Economy", points out that only a knowledgeable entrepreneur will be able to improve his business performance and survive in a competing global market. The study also explains that only knowledge can equip an entrepreneur to invest in their various fields based on their suitability. Investment for knowledge updation among the entrepreneurs will be an asset for the enterprise in the long run. Properly trained individuals will be able to attract new customers and capture business based on the trainings acquired by the individual.

Volpe et al. (2002) Volpe, R. P., Kotel, J. E. & Chen, H. (2002)[7] in extension of the previous studies, they surveyed 530 online investors of U.S. to examine their investment literacy and the relationship between the literacy and online investor characteristics. (E.g. education, gender investing experience and other factors). The study had sample unit as online investors with the view that the advent of online investment has significantly impacted an investor's decision making process by providing immediate access to a large volume of financial information, lower transaction charges, and quick decision execution. This approach opens the possibility of reaching investors outside of one geographical region .To determine the survey's coverage of investment topics, they reviewed 35 financial websites that offered educational information on investing. They also included 20 online brokers websites .The final questionnaire included questions on the investment concepts such as effect of distribution from a mutual fund on its net asset value (NAV), blue chip stock terminology, compounding of interest, beta as a volatility measure, capital gain tax rate, portfolio diversification, stock splits, financial ratio analysis, appropriate asset allocation strategies and the relationship between interest rates and bond prices. The analytical tool used was analysis of variance (ANOVA) to determine the differences in investment knowledge among participants. Further to analyze how various factors impacted investor's level of knowledge, the logistic regressions was used. The results of the study found that online investors answered about 50 per cent of the questions correctly which indicates a deficiency in the knowledge of investment concepts, despite the large amount of educational information and research available to online investors .It was also found that investors of 50 years of age or older were more knowledgeable than those who were younger which was found consistent with the previous study undertaken by Volpe and Chen,

1998. Compared to men, women had lower levels of knowledge about investment alternatives. Investors with graduate degrees were more knowledgeable than those with some high school or college education and online traders were more knowledgeable than those who had not. The results of this survey indicated that online investors should improve their knowledge about basic investment concepts and tools. It was concluded that online investors knowledge of investment is insufficient and needs to be improved in the future. Online investors who takes decision by self, should be able to comprehend about various investment choices and should be able to evaluate the appropriateness of each and every investment choices according to their requirements.

Moore, D. (2003)[8] Conducted a survey for Washington State DFI's to know about the financial literacy among the residents of Washington state and stated that the degree to which an individual exhibits financial information, financial experience, and positive defensive financial practices predicts the degree to which they would be all the more financially proficient. A focus group data was integrated with the survey group to comprehend data about the experiences in connection with mortgage transactions. Differences between the survey group and focus group with respect to financial behaviors, knowledge, attitudes, opinions, and mortgage loan experiences were analyzed to reach on a consensus. Author has the perception that financial experience and practices can influence the financial knowledge levels of the individuals.

Andrew Worthington (2004)[9] made an attempt to predict the financial literacy levels of Australians based on socio demographic variables. Financial literacy levels of individuals from the perspective of economic and financial characteristics were also studied. Author has not studied about the relationship of financial literacy with financial behavior, financial knowledge and financial results but has limited the study only within the boundaries of socio demographic and economic variables. It was observed in the study that financial literacy of individuals vary in relation to the socio demographic and economic variables. Aged people tend to be more financially literate than the younger generation of Australians. When it comes to gender of the respondents, Females exhibited lower financial literacy levels compared to males. Educated and professionals are found to have good financial literacy scores compared to unemployed ones and people with poor educational background. People who have taken mortgage loans multiple number of times are found to have higher financial literacy levels than those who have taken it less number of times.

Joo & Grable (2004)[10] conducted a study aimed at determining factors that influence financial satisfaction. The survey results posit that educational level, financial literacy, risk, financial activity, financial ability, and financial pressures have a direct impact on financial satisfaction. The results showed that in high levels of knowledge and financial skills, the strengthening of the financial behaviors leads to higher levels of financial satisfaction. Therefore, their study indicated that financial literacy had a direct effect on financial well-being.

Sanjib Chowdhury et.al (2005)[11] thinks that males are found to exhibit better confidence in dealing with finance than females. Perception of the people about their levels of financial knowledge is seen to influence the confidence levels of the individuals irrespective of their gender. This is seen in the entrepreneurial self efficacy of the entrepreneur. Women are found to exhibit better confidence levels in dealing with finance, if education is provided to them. But impact of education in influencing the confidence levels was not seen among the males as it is seen in females. So if a person's entrepreneurial trait has to be polished, mere education or knowledge support won't suffice, but the persons perception about the financial skills achieved has to be improved. If perception improves, entrepreneurship also will improve.

Campbell, J. Y. (2006)[12] focused on the study about household finance. Campbell describes the study on household finance as a difficult matter because household behavior, being a qualitative factor is difficult to evaluate, and will vary according to the judgment of the respondents. Though there is a minority which is creating the mistakes in financial management, majority of the respondents invest effectively. This is evident from the diversification, participation, and mortgage refinancing done by majority of the respondents. Low levels of education and low income was traced from the households which made mistakes. Evidence was available which suggests the dependence of people who are poor and uneducated on others for developing a strategy for managing their finance.

DeVaney, Anong, and Whirl (2007)[13] found in their studies the likelihood of hierarchy of saving motive. As per the study it was found that once the lower level of saving motive is fulfilled then the individual pushed to the next level. The various levels of saving motive have been identified, at the base the physiological saving, followed by safety saving, security saving, saving for self-esteem and at the top was saving motive of self actualisation, all these levels were just the replica of Maslow's need hierarchy theory. But they added one another level showing no saving. It was also inferred that young households tend to move from no saving to physiological saving and then next all levels as predicted above. But older households tend to move from security saving motive to saving for the luxuries. The various studies on saving motives suggest that there is large number of variables influencing saving decisions of the households. Amongst them income growth, demography, inflation rate, interest rate, unemployment, tax structure are the most common ones.

Report prepared by Australian government titled Financial Literacy among Marginalized Women (2007)[14] gives valuable information as to how women, and especially marginalized women, have access to and make informed financial choices. Women living in urban, and remote areas of Australia were given due attention. Community organizations, family support services, migrant resource centre's and internet were reported as helpful sources of financial advice for some women. For some respondents, Financial counselors and Paid financial advice has helped but a few others found the advices of these experts as creating confusion and unreliable. Physical, Social, Educational, Financial and Cultural barriers prevented marginalized women in accessing financial information. Financial literacy needs among marginalized women were also studied by the researchers. Report did not limit its area within the boundary of Australia, but also reviewed other overseas experiences in financial literacy education focusing on the approaches of USA and Canada and points out that improving levels of financial literacy amongst marginalized women will improve their ability in making informed financial choices and will enhance their economic status and well-being.

Robert Kaestner and Lisa J. Servon (2008)[15] observed a demonstration by a major bank to comprehend whether availability of information and knowledge of internet along with financial education can help individuals belonging to poor households in urban to perform better with respect to financial matters. It was noted that if properly implemented, qualitative trainings can have positive effect on individual's financial literacy scores and that there is a positive association between the financial literacy, financial knowledge and availability of modern communication technologies.

Stephen L. Mueller et.al (2008)[16] in line with many other researchers was on the track of evaluating the forces for certain people to take up entrepreneurial roles. Entrepreneurial self-efficacy is the area which has developed lot of research interest. It was found in many studies that men have higher entrepreneurial self-efficacy compared to women. But now due to the lack of empirical support, influence of other factors was studied. Authors studied on the differences in gender-roles as a possible influencing factor of the variations in entrepreneurial self-efficacy. A complex and multifaceted result was obtained after the study indicating that feminine and masculine traits were required in the initial stages of business development, but strong masculine traits are required in the later stages of business development for persuasion and giving leadership.

Kayla Allen, & Victoria Kinchen (2009)[17] is of the opinion that , Americans depend too much on debt for their living and this is the reason for the large numbers of insolvency suits filed in 2008. Study was done among the college students in America who are the future of America to know about the personal finance management skills and habits. Researcher makes an attempt to know about the reasons for financial misconduct and on measures for improving financial stability. Apart from the primary objectives, several secondary research objectives were also there. In addition, the study sought to discover college students' patterns concerning checking and savings accounts; checking credit scores bill payments, and use of a monthly budget. This study suggests training for strong personal financial management skills about the credit terms, investing, budgeting, and development of long term financial goals which will help students to live without financial instability. Efforts should be made to educate students about the reinforcement of financial management skills during college. Otherwise society may have to deal with a generation of Americans who will financially overextend themselves, resulting in further mortgage foreclosures and bankruptcies.

Lewis Mandell and Linda Schmid Klein (2009)[18] examined the differences in the impact of a personal financial management course among 79 high school students. Matched sample design was adopted for the study which identified students who have attended the personal financial management course and those who have not taken the course. Author observes that there existed no difference when it comes to financial literacy levels of those who have attended the personal financial management course and those who have not taken the course among the respondents. He draws attention to the fact the personal financial management courses have not increased the savings habit or appear to exhibit a better financial behavior than those who have not taken the course. Author thinks that this discrepancy in the results can be because of the fact the 79 respondents chosen for the study are high school graduates who are not having any regular earnings and these courses might help the respondents in later stage of life when they have to handle funds. But the study also exhibits a positive relationship between the financial literacy scores and financial behaviors of those with a full-time college education.

Sandra J Huston (2009)[19] is of the opinion that measuring financial literacy is important to understand the impact of education on a person's financial choices. Author thinks that financial education can be used as a variable in measuring the variations in financial performances. This will help in the identification of the impact of financial education on a person's financial choices and the barriers that he might have come across in making financial choices. Roadblocks that affected financial literacy research are also mentioned by the author. This article can be used as a road map for those who want to pursue research in financial literacy since all the limitations related to financial literacy and available instruments which can be used in measuring the financial literacy levels have been mentioned well in the paper.

Huston (2010)[20] in a study measuring financial literacy showed that a person who is financially literate, and has the understanding and the ability to utilize the knowledge, may not exhibit predicted manners or growth in financial well-being because of certain impacts. Such influences could come from cognitive biases, family, economic, self-control problems, community and institutional factors.

Norman, A. S. (2010)[21] conducted an observation on the spending of households. Author asserts that people who complain of insufficient funds are the ones who are illiterate in wise spending. Only a person who spends wisely will be having savings in his hands. People usually spend a lot on mobile phones, fuel, and food and for maintaining the repute. If money is not utilized carefully, nothing will be left back. Investments will be possible, only with savings. A financially literate person would be careful with his funds and won't waste them unnecessarily. So author thinks giving proper financial education can improve the savings of households and thereby his investments and wealth in the long run. In the paper, author explains about the importance of financial knowledge, challenges and problems in attaining financial knowledge, suggestions and recommendations to improve the existing levels of financial education of a person.

Oseifuah, E. K. (2010)[22] evaluated the financial literacy levels of the youth and its impact on entrepreneurship in South Africa. Financial knowledge, financial behaviour, financial attitude, mathematical and computer literacy were the variables used in the test to measure the financial literacy of youth. It was found that the financial literacy levels of the youth in South Africa seem to be above average. It was observed that the youth in Africa had good knowledge about the existing interest rates, tax issues and insolvency, but lacked the knowledge about stock market participation. Enriching students with financial knowledge from the primary schools can contribute in a big way in polishing the entrepreneurship skills of the youth. Development of entrepreneurial skills will bring development for the individual as it will improve his living conditions.

Shim, Barber, Card, Xiao and Serido (2010)[23] found that, while some students were seeking to learn in managing their finances better, others are engaged in risky behaviors and doesn't care much about the finance and its shortage as a resource. According to the authors, a better understanding of the reason for the occurrence of such behavior is a necessity for better financial control and management among the students. Disparity in the values may be obtained by analyzing the students' socioeconomic and demographic profile, having in mind its influence on financial literacy.

Willian J Gale et.al (2010)[24] analyzed the meaning of financial literacy and the effectiveness of financial literacy among American households. Author opines that private actions and public policies can influence the savings behaviour of the people. Private sector also has a big role to play along with the public sector in creating an atmosphere to promote financial literacy. Benefits need not be considered from the viewpoint of beneficiaries only, but also of the family members and related ones of those beneficiaries too since they will be benefitted indirectly. Authors are of the view that financial education could not bring in a positive change in the financial behavior of the respondents. Efforts should be needed to integrate existing policies of savings with the initiative towards gaining the achievements to improve.

Frances M. Amatucci et.al (2011)[25] explored the factors contributing to the success of women entrepreneurs though their article "Financial self-efficacy among women entrepreneurs". According to the author, women entrepreneurship is growing globally increasing the importance of study on the factors which lead into its success. Many studies have been undertaken on the relationship of demographic aspects with women entrepreneurship but socio psycho factors of women were not considered much by the authors. Financial self efficacy was measured among nascent experienced and aspiring women entrepreneurs to evaluate whether age and racial differences have an effect on a person's success. Author suggests the requirement for advanced research about women entrepreneurs and their confidence in dealing with matters related to financial management. It also recommends the need for support from the part of policymakers to the women entrepreneurs to improve their Financial Self efficacy levels.

Lusardi & Mitchell (2011)[26] studied about the relationship of financial literacy with planning for retirement and expressed that people who are having better experiences with financial matters exhibit better possibility of having plans for retirement. According to them, women across the globe are found to possess low levels of financial literacy and are aware about their poor status. But there are old aged people who consider them to have better knowledge about finance, but have a lack of financial knowledge than their perceived levels. This is because of the ever changing financial markets which keep on changing every now and then. These changes in financial markets happen as per the changes in the needs and demand of the public.

Lusardi and Mitchell (2011)[27] undertake an evaluation of the previous literatures existing about financial literacy. Since majority of the population is not aware even about the basic concepts of inflation, interest compounding and risk diversification, there is only a slight chance for the persons to have a change in his decision making behaviour as a result of the short term training on financial literacy. He opines that it is not easy to measure how a person process the financial information that he has received from various sources though it is important to measure the financial literacy of people within a limited time frame ofresearch.

Nunoo and Andoh (2011)[28] studied about the role played by financial literacy in promoting the utilization of financial services among the small and medium sized entrepreneurs in Ghana. Small and medium sized entrepreneurs are looked upon as something very important in the development of both developed as well as developing countries. Earlier there was reluctance in lending to the small and medium sized enterprises because it was viewed as a risky area but time evolved and small and medium sized enterprises turned out as a major contributor of national income. Opening up opportunities for the small and medium sized enterprises would lead to the development of a better financial market system. So now there are lot of financial products and services being provided to the entrepreneurs. Logistic regression was used in predicting the relationship between financial literacy as an endogenous variable with the utilization of plentiful financial services and products. Financial skills, financial knowledge, and financial confidence were evaluated as determinants of financial literacy. It was concluded after the study that there is a positive connection of financial literacy and the financial education of individuals.

Rosnani Jusoh (2011)[29] explored the business competencies which were required in successfully managing the business. Authors are of the view that entrepreneurs are in need of training that can support their business activities. Though entrepreneurs are moderately skilled in certain areas, study confirms the need for the updating of knowledge related to the business to make the business more robust and competitive. Only those who are trained will be able to compete in this era of globalization making use of technology at its best. Then only an entrepreneur will be able to sell the right product at the right place and in the right time. Entrepreneurial skills training is required in areas where the entrepreneurs are finding it difficult to get trained like financial management skills, accessing source of funds, to improve creativity and innovation, creation of a business account, developing advertising skills, and in fixing the right price for the product.

Barte (2012)[30] investigated the financial skills of fish vendors in Cebu City. Capitalization sources of the fish vendors were also studied along with their financial skills. Relationship between income of the fish vendors and their financial skills was evaluated in the study with cash management, Record keeping, profit and loss analysis, credit access as the variables and came to the conclusion that financial skills were very low among the fish vendors in Cebu City of Philippines. It was understood that due to the lack of financial skills many of them depended on informal loans with high interest rates. High interest rate loans are seen to adversely damage the income and growth of the business houses which access such loans. Authors recommend proper education, low cost funding, better facilities and regulations like micro banking which facilitate the custodianship of money, and improved linkages with advocate organizations which support the vendors for their prosperity.

Heena K. Bijli (2012)[31] in her study explored the money management practices followed by women SHG members belonging to a MFI called Grameen Koota in Karnataka. Eight target groups were adopted for the study. Purposive sampling was followed for data collection. Poor knowledge level of the women members regarding the significance of savings, capital formation, cash flow management, and account keeping were the obstacles in the growth of their units. A Financial literacy module was advised in the study by the author for improving the economic independence of the SHG members. Purpose behind the Financial Literacy Modules was to suggest ways to reduce the liabilities of the members, to help the members in having an increase in the SHG members' assets, and ultimately to increase the net-worth of the individuals in the long run. Qualitative changes can be brought into the lives of SHG members through measures of economic empowerment. Increased knowledge sharing among the support groups, information dissemination, and guidance in the practice of financial planning can help improve the economic conditions of the members.

Kimwolo, A. K., 2 Saina, C.K., 2 Cheserek, G.J. (2012)[32] in their article " Effects of Credit Training Skills on Sales Performance among Women Entrepreneurs in Elgeiyo Marakwet County, Kenya" made an attempt to study about the success of training organized by Kenya Women Finance Trust (KWFT) about credit and to know whether the training has improved the performance of women managed micro-enterprises in terms of sales figures; It also examined the effectiveness of financial skills on the functioning of micro-enterprises. The importance of planning and management skills is advocated by the study. The study updates the knowledge database of researchers, supplements useful knowledge for the Kenya Women Finance Trust policy makers contribute to scholars and researchers in the field of microenterprises and provide enough support for the governments in formulating policies with regard to the challenges faced by the women managed micro-enterprises.

Marty Gillen and Diane N. Loeffler (2012)[33] has conducted a pilot study among undergraduate and graduate social work students to understand their knowledge levels and awareness on financial matters. It was pointed out by the authors that students were not found to possess the required skills necessary to take a financial decision. This is a matter of concern for the academicians. Authors mention that adding basic financial literacy skills along with the social work curriculum can indirectly help the beneficiaries handled by social work students.

Roman Graf (2012)[34] in his study "Financial literacy and financial behavior in Switzerland" examines the condition of German speaking adult population of Switzerland about their financial literacy. Comparison studies were also done across the country. Inflation, interest rates and risk were the variables studied by the author. During the study association of financial knowledge with behavior of individuals was studied and author points out that those who have sufficient financial knowledge are found to possess investment plan and retirement saving options. Consumption behavior indebtedness and financial knowledge levels of the respondents were not found to be associated with each other. 20 per cent of the respondent population was unaware about inflation. But this was observed to be a better position than that found in the other developed countries. Financial literacy gap between developing countries and developed country like Switzerland was also pointed out by the author during the study after the comparison was undertaken. Author invites attention of the policymakers of Switzerland to focus on this area further because deprived sections of the society exhibited poor financial literacy levels and financial literacy levels are found to bring in a positive change in the financial behavior of respondents.

Sobhesh Kumar Agarwalla et.al , (2012) [35], piloted a survey titled "A Survey of Financial Literacy among Students, Young Employees and the Retired in India" .The study was an attempt to scrutinize the financial literacy level of young working adults, retired and students in India who form three important demographic groups. Moreover, study targeted to know about the investment behavior of the two groups i.e. working adults and retired. The retired and employed were asked questions related to financial behavior, knowledge, and attitude. 2,967 respondents was questioned, out of which 983 were employees, 1001 were students, and 983 were pensioned off. The retired and employed people were interviewed about their financial knowledge levels as it is customary for them to be acquainted with the financial matters in managing household and personal finances. The results showed that high knowledge on financial matters is not very common among Indians. It was observed that

1. Basic principles of household finance and money matters such as inflation rate, compound interest, impact on prices and returns are not well understood.
2. Positive financial attitude was noticed in the attitude towards consumption and saving habits among Indians.

3. Positivity was observed in the financial behaviour of Indians. Performance of employed and retired was very high with regard to financial behaviour .The retired and employed borrowed less and were dependent on their savings. The found positive financial behaviour was appeared to be associated with higher financial knowledge.
4. Financial knowledge levels were seen to be better among men than women. It was seen that financial knowledge was more extensive among comparatively wealthy and educated people.
5. The financial attitude and behaviour was found to be slightly better among women compared to men. Education and background of the respondents had no influence on their financial attitude.
6. Retired people started their preparations for retirement from the beginning of their career by making regular savings. Most of them claimed to have estimates about their funds requirement after retirement. And the preferred options for savings were the assets which were safe.
7. Most of the respondents were not dependent on financial advisers and relied too much on advertisements for their choice of investments. The lack of knowledge about financial products limited the divergence of portfolios for investments across the various asset classes.
8. Compared to the global standards, respondents performed very poor with respect to the levels of financial knowledge. This happened mainly due to the poor quality of the Indian primary education system.

Attom (2013)[36] perceive cash management as an important factor leading to the success of business ventures. Cash management means the management of finance related to the handling, collection, and usage of cash. It extends to the level of assessing cash inflow and outflow of the organization and maintaining a balance between market liquidity and investments of the venture. Cash management practices and cash control procedures followed by micro and small-scale enterprises and its association with business performance was explored by the author. An improper financial management and improper utilization of cash available was the reason for slowing down the prosperity of the businesses. Lack of cash budgets due to lack of knowledge about preparation was viewed as a possible reason for this misfortune practice in businesses. Sensitization and training of micro and small-scale business owners on cash management practices and capacity building trainings were recommended by the researcher.

Ayodele, K.O. (2013)[37] explored the relationship between Demographics, locus of control and entrepreneurial self-efficacy as the determinants of entrepreneurial intention among the adolescents residing in the Ogun state of Nigeria. It was pinpointed that self-efficacy of the entrepreneur would lead a person to start up a business venture and will take the business in the path of progress towards growth. In this paper self-efficacy means the belief about the skills of the entrepreneur himself and the over confidence to deal with the troubles of the business in the long run. Conceptual as well as theoretical aspects of self-efficacy were dealt with in the paper.

Research was done on the previous literatures about the scales which were used in measuring self-efficacy **Ben-Caleb, Egbide, Faboyede, Olusola Samuel, Fakile and Adeniran Samuel** has **(2013)**[38] have done a research on the empowerment of SMEs as a key poverty alleviation

strategy in Nigeria. The study says that though SMEs

constitute major stake of all productive activities in Nigeria, the same has not contributed much towards the economic progress of the Country. The reasons for this were inadequate funds, constrained access to financial institutions, poor infrastructural facilities, regulatory constraints, financial indiscipline and restricted market. The research also touches the potentials of SMEs in poverty alleviation, which are faster economic growth which helps effective eradication of poverty, removal of bias against labour intensive production, employment of more low skill labours and linkage to small and less sophisticated suppliers. The researchers are of the opinion that inadequate finance is the most influential inhibitor to SMEs development in Nigeria till date. It was concluded by the researchers that the under development of any nation, particularly one like Nigeria to a large extent is because of non exploitation of the SMEs in the particular nation.

Bimolata Devi (2013)[39] made an attempt to study about the financial management practices followed in certain women owned enterprises by collecting a sample from 400 women entrepreneurs operating 5 different businesses i.e., Tailoring, Embroidery, Jewellery making, Kids Care Centre , and Beauty Parlour in Thoubal district of Manipur and Imphal West. Stratified random sampling was adopted as the sampling technique. Data was collected using questionnaire cum interview methods. The main objective of the study was to identify the sources from where the entrepreneurs are availing the financial requirements economically, identify the investments made by the entrepreneurs and its factors influencing the decision to invest, and to study whether they follow proper control of the available finance. Author concludes that if sufficient finance, favourable environment, infrastructure and more than anything knowledge of financial management if provided to the entrepreneurs can lead to the success of an enterprise and can benefit society at large.

Gupta, A. et. al (2013)[40] explained the meaning of financial inclusion and financial literacy. They also studied about the relation of financial inclusion and financial literacy with various demographic variables of a population and to see how it has affected them. 90 respondents were adopted as samples for the study. CRISIL Inclusix score was used to determine the financial inclusion of the population. Multiple regressions were the tool used in analysis and could find that educational background, occupation, and household income are found to have significant influence in the financial literacy and financial inclusion of a person. Low levels of financial inclusion in rural areas may be the reason for poor financial literacy scores in rural areas compared to the better scores in urban areas. It can be concluded that financial literacy of a person is complimentary with the financial inclusion in his place of living.

Meta Brown (2013)[41] studied about the influence of financial education on the debt behavior of the youth in U.S. For a large number of people, financial literacy education has a noticeable impact on the natural tendency of youth in having a credit report. Equifax-sourced FRBNY Consumer Credit Panel along with the state-level curriculum variation was used in studying the effects of economic, financial and general level quantitative training on debt during the early stages of a person's life. Decreased debt use, perceived creditworthiness, and decreased delinquency in multiform was observed in the case of mathematics graduates. But there was no clarity whether the content of maths training is appropriate. Research done also highlights that higher income and a decreased level of risk aversion is associated with economic education. The calculated effects of economics education on debt vary substantially from those of financial education and mathematics education. Study concludes that schooling reforms have just helped in the growth of quantitative skills, but it did not have any direct measure on the quantitative skills or financial literacy of a person.

Njoroge, R. M. (2013)[42] examined the association of Entrepreneurial Success with financial literacy in Nairobi County Kenya. Understanding the meaning of the term inflation, understanding the meaning of the term risk, interest rates, time value of money, money illusion, financial markets and risk diversification were evaluated as variables to correlate between the successes of enterprise with financial literacy. Increase in the growth of revenue was evaluated along with the tenure of existence of the establishment and number of employees to measure the functioning of the business. 79 respondents were surveyed to reach into a conclusion that there is a positive correlation between the successes of a business establishment with the financial skills of the entrepreneur.

Nwibo, SimonU. et.al (2013)[43] is of the opinion that where the entrepreneur had no previous relevant experience, the management of the venture tends to diminish. Managers of agribusiness undertakings need to be knowledgeable in sales, production, and finance. In fact, lack of knowledge or experience is responsible for inability of entrepreneurs to recognize investment opportunities that abound in their business environments. Prior business experience augments task based efficiency, and prompts an individual to seek for similar type of task in his/her job searching process.

Richard Disney (2013)[44] conducted a study based on the survey data taken from a sample of households in UK based on the consumer credit availed by the family. Authors analyzed the relationship that existed between financial literacy and consumer credit portfolios. Financial literacy of those customers who depended on consumer credit was poor compared to others who don't depend much on credit. Respondents were given a list of credit product types and were asked to state which product types were held by them or anyone in their household and about the current revolving balance in each type of consumer credit product. Authors were of the opinion that people who got poor marks in their survey had awareness about their lack of knowledge about finance and they were ready to admit the fact that they lacked the confidence in interpreting the credit terms. Results of the analysis showcased those households with heads who were poor on the financial literacy questions hold a greater share of high cost credit in their portfolios and thereby exhibited higher portfolio-weighted average APRs. Studies further add that there is less chance for the family heads with poor financial literacy to acquire information relating to finance from financial pages in a newspapers.

Sanja Ajzerle et.al (2013)[45] studied about the relationship between debt usage and financial capability of Australian citizens. In the article, authors have taken the effort to explain the terms financial knowledge and financial capability with clarity to give an insight into the topic under study. Authors are of the view that with liberalized financial regulations, debt usage among all sectors of the society increased manifold. Debt has the capacity to increase the asset volume of an individual. But if not used judiciously, it can create a tarnishing effect for the borrowers. Financially capable individuals make use of debt effectively and are found to increase their asset base with increased debt usage. It was observed by the authors, in the study that financially capable individuals are found to enjoy taking financial decisions. But people who had low education, low income and older age are found to have lower financial capability than the other demographic categories. Such people are less likely to borrow debts effectively and even if debt was taken, their behavior does not assure a judicious usage. Therefore, this area should be of a matter of concern for the government. Government should concentrate its efforts on improving the quality of financial decision making by its citizens rather than in creating awareness.

Suchanphin Suwanaphan (2013)[46] explored the influence of personal financial literacy among academic support employees working in a university. According to the author, bad financial decisions are a result of lack of knowledge about finances. For most of the respondents, revenue was not sufficed to cover up all their expenses. Credit cards were the source of debt for most of the respondents. Savings were used primarily by the university staff to meet contingencies or for creating wealth. Spending and saving practices followed by the university staff also was explored.

Sucuahi, W.T. (2013)[47] investigated the financial management proficiency of the chosen small scale business owners in Davao City. 100 small scale business owners doing business in Davao city were the sample for the study. Savings skills, Record keeping skills, Financing and budgeting skills were adopted as the variables for the study. It could be noted that the extend of finance related education among the owners of smaller scale business units were moderate pointing out a sign of improper management of their financial resources. Multiple regression analysis was used and it could be understood that the influence of education is meaningful in the financial literacy levels of the small scale business owners in Davao City.

Swarn Chatterjee et.al (2013)[48] aims to find out the position of financial literacy in different countries. A cross national survey was conducted to find out if cultural and national differences could bring about an impact on the financial literacy of its citizens. Canada, UK, Italy and US were selected for the study. Logistic regression analysis was the tool used in the study to reach into a conclusion. Influence of socio demographic variables was different across the countries. Considering the cultural and regional differences of its citizens, author thinks it judicious to develop a financial literacy tool individually for every country rather than developing a single instrument for all the countries taken together, but individually if it is not being done, author highlights the requirement of a standardized broader scale to assess the financial literacy levels across international borders.

Taft, Hosein, Mehrizi & Roshan (2013)[49] explored the meaning and details about the concepts financial literacy, financial well-being, and financial concerns of business owners and revealed that higher financial literacy leads to greater financial well-being making it easy to manage the business. Financial concerns will disappear with the improvement of financial literacy levels. Thus, for financial comfort to be achieved financial literacy is needed.

Wise (2013)[50] Evaluated the quantitative relationship between new venture failure, loan repayment and the financial literacy of young entrepreneurs after a training was given through the micro credit training programmes. Author thinks that failure of new ventures happens as a result of lack of sufficient knowledge on financial matters. Therefore, training was given to the young entrepreneurs to improvise their financial skills. An improved knowledge of the entrepreneur in the analysis of financial ratios and financial statements will create an increase in the number of times the financial statements are generated in an enterprise, which in-turn will result in more loan repayments on time and a decreased rate of venture shutdowns. Thus financial skills gained through the micro finance education programme were successful.

Akande, O., & Oluwaseun, Y. (2014)[51] aimed to identify the influence of a proper budgeting system on the improvement of Entrepreneurial Business performance based on the perception of Small business entrepreneurs in Lagos state of Nigeria. Budgeting has been depicted to be critical and fundamental to Business Financial execution. Small business houses are very important for every country's economy. Author focused on the extent to which budgetary controls has exerted influence on the financial execution of independent projects as it deserves special investigation for developing economies like Nigeria. This research examines the comprehensiveness of the budgetary practices being followed in business units. Research progressed through multi stage sampling technique and was able to conclude that there is a significant relationship between small business financial performance and budgeting practices being followed. Availability of a clear financial goal in mind in line with the budgeted figures is a requirement for designing a good business strategy for the business unit.

Joseph Kurwo Chelimo and Isaac Ole Sopia (2014)[52] studied about the effect of book keeping in the growth of small and medium enterprises particularly in Kabarnet Town of Kenya. The findings show that of the 75 per cent of the SMEs who maintained business records, 25 per cent indicated that they always used business records to assess their profits, 15 per cent Often used, 30 per cent Sometimes used, 20 per cent Rarely used and 10 per cent Never used. 75 per cent of the respondents believed that book keeping helped to ascertain the financial position of SMEs compared to 25 per cent who disagreed.

While asked about whether book keeping improves the growth of SMEs, only 9 per cent of the respondents agreed the same. The study says that majority of the traders in Kabarnet Town uses single entry book keeping system. The study has also proven that there is a direct relationship between growth, book keeping and profitability ofSMEs. If properly maintained, bookkeeping could result in increased profitability and expansion of business of the SMEs in Kabarnet Town. Researchers concluded by recommending that the SMEs in the subject town may appoint skilled clerk/ officials to maintain proper books of accounts in order to financially succeed in their businesses.

Dahmen, P., & Rodríguez, E. (2014)[53] assessed the financial literacy skills of the business owners who came for a business incubation in US. Small, medium and micro enterprises are very important for the growth of every economy. Fall of a business unit cannot be viewed as something that will affect the individual independently, but as something that will affect the country. Therefore, Florida business development centres assessed the financial literacy of the owners of small business units and found that most of the owners don't review financial statements or do the financial ratio calculations of their business units due to lack of knowledge in financial matters. More than 50 per cent of the owners of small business units had troubles with excessive debt issue and had difficulty in managing the cash flows without liquidity crunch. Loss of revenue was also a matter of concern for the business houses. Relationship between financial illiteracy and difficulties in financial management was traced out by the author in the study.

Fatoki, O. (2014)[54] Studied on the The Financial Literacy of Micro Enterprises in South Africa and observed that book-keeping, Financial planning, Financial analysis ,Financial control, business terminology, understanding of the various sources of funding, information on financial matter, risk-management skills and use of technology were the variables adopted to evaluate financial literacy. Low financial literacy levels were found among the owners indicating the need for attention. Most of the business owners had working knowledge about banking. Knowledge on banking was there among the business owners because the business houses were constantly in touch with the banks for their business purposes. Knowledge on financing using equity was deficient among the business owners. Information about taxes, interest rates, and exchange rates was found deficient among the business owners.

G., Samkin, E., Pitu, & M., Low. (2014)[55] made an attempt to point out the financial literacy skills required to maintain a small business in New Zealand. Study was done on a sample of 18 respondents. Dealing with debtors, Pricing, taxation and recording, receiving income, managing payments, usage of accounting software were used during the study as variables to identify the skills required for managing finance. It was understood that learning English and Mathematics at higher secondary school was important to make it easy for Studying accounting and the financial aspects of business.

Kamal Gupta and Jatinder Kaur (2014)[56] conducted a study to assess the awareness level of financial matters among the micro entrepreneurs of Kangra district of Himachal Pradesh. Data was collected using a structured questionnaire. Respondents were questioned to know about the Familiarity with Financial Institutions, Awareness Regarding Loan and Credit Products, Record Keeping of Funds by Micro Entrepreneurs, Information Sources that Influence the Decisions of Micro–Entrepreneurs, Factors Contributing to the Choice of Micro Entrepreneurs in Taking a Bank Loan. Results of the study showed that micro entrepreneurs in Kangra district possess low financial skills which were clearly revealed from the poor cash management, deficient record keeping practices, low awareness regarding different financial products and improper saving habits. Author observes that improper financial management due to lack of financial literacy has lead to the low income and growth of the firms. Author recommends government to include programmes targeted at micro entrepreneurs to make them aware about the different alternatives available for their benefits.

Michaela Krechovská (2014)[57] observes that access to credit cards, personal loans, and other payment options have become easy these days leading to an increase in the spending and consumption pattern of people and debt levels of people have increased manifold. 10 Questions from the standardized questionnaire framed by OECD was adopted to verify the financial literacy in the Czech Republic, Poland, Slovak Republic and Hungary among the university students of the area. Questions were related to inflation; investment risks; evaluation of data from a graph; compound interest; terminology and products of the financial market; and household reserve fund. Author is of the view that it is vital to continue to devote attention to include financial education in university teaching with the use of teaching methods which are suitable for improving financial literacy among individuals.

Musah, A., & Ibrahim, M. (2014)[58] explored the relationship between business performance of SMEs and record keeping from a study which was done in Ghana. Sales growth, Profitability, capital injection and increases in the number of employees was seen as the base for measuring business performance. Record keeping was the variable adapted to measure financial literacy. Business performance doesn't improve with record maintenance alone. - Factors such as access to finance, improved relationship with customers, access to internal and international markets and use of better technology has to be pursued simultaneously along with Record keeping.

An improvement of performance can be visualized when owners of SME's begin to maintain records to monitor their daily activities.

Xiao et. al (2014)[59] Investigated into factors which result in financial independence of young adults. Young adults will be in between the age group 18–23. Psychological, economic and family factors were hypothesized as factors contributing to the financial independence of young adults in America. Educational attainment, income, work status and assets were found to be positively related with financial independence of the young population. An individual who has attained financial independence was comparatively seen more among those people who got education than those who had never gone to college. Ability to manage monetary matters, self confidence in dealing with finance and problem solving skills were found to have positive association with independence of the individual on matters relating to finance. Income levels of the parents, stocks held by the parents and financial assistance received from the parent reduced the independence of the individuals. Study suggests educators to develop training programmes according to the differences in the levels of education received by the people.

Ani Caroline Grigion Potrich et al. (2015)[60] is of the opinion that financial literacy has an influence on the lives of a person from the monetary point of view since it can make the person more assertive and informed about his decisions. This study was done in Brazil. Relationship of financial literacy levels of the person and his socioeconomic and demographic variables were evaluated in the study. Multivariate analysis techniques were applied on the descriptive statistics collected. Financial literacy levels were measured on the basis of three constructs financial attitude, financial behavior, and financial knowledge. During the preliminary analysis, author asserts that most of the respondents were having low financial literacy level. He is of the opinion that parental educational levels and occupation has no impact on a person's financial literacy. Author added that women, who have lower educational level and dependent family members, and having, lower individual and family income levels are having increased probability for being with the low financial literacy levels. So he suggests the policy initiatives to consider women with lower individual and family income levels as well as educational levels while framing the policies for improving the financial literacy of persons.

Brown, E. (2015)[61] explained that gender has a potential of creating differences in the financial attitude and thinking of individuals. Pilot data for the study was taken from the OECD survey done in 12 countries. Causes and consequences of this kind of differences were studied through the literatures surveyed. It was found from the study that females performed better than males in the knowledge of finance and their confidence levels with respect to finance was found to be low compared to males. In this point, authors make it a point to affirm the need for quality training programmes focusing on woman's financial literacy needs to better their conditions.

García, M. and Adame, M. (2015)[62] evaluated the various factors which are responsible for the success of SME. The idea behind this work was to find a connection between the traits of businesses and its owners and competitiveness of the SMEs (Small and Medium Enterprises) functioning in México City. Data for the study was collected through field work from 400 companies. Chi square was used to find the correlation between the variables under study. Legal personality of the firm was found to have a close association with the competitiveness of the firm. Education was found to create a significant influence on the competitiveness of the firm globally. Sexual orientation of the entrepreneur, age, size of the SME and the kind of establishment are also found to have association with the global success of a firm.

James Berry (2015)[63] financial literacy among youth in Ghana was evaluated using a control experiment. Two programmes were offered to the students to put a stop for child labour. One of the programme offered both financial and social education to students whereas HMB program offered only financial education. Children were invited to participate in the club and, were introduced to the importance of money, savings and spending, planning and budgeting, personal finances, and entrepreneurship. Students were then provided with a locked money box in both the programmes. Results showed that both programs positively influenced the savings behavior of children. When children were given financial education accompanied by social education, children worked less compared to the control group. Though financial education alone encouraged students to work more, there was no significant difference in the effects of the two treatments on child labour.

Jelena Titko et al. (2015)[64] through their paper evaluated the financial literacy level of Latvian citizens. Financial literacy was measured using an instrument developed on the basis of a conceptual model of financial literacy developed after scrutinizing the available pre-existing literature. Numerical skills, knowledge of financial concepts, ability to plan for future, knowing financial products, debt literacy and budgeting, and knowing of the financial markets and instruments were the variables under study. Tools developed by the authors and results analyzed by the authors in the paper could be of help for other investigators. Data collected was analyzed using the software SPSS. Questions relating to "borrowings" were answered correctly by most of respondents indicating that Latvian citizens have acquired a certain type of knowledge during the financial crisis that occurred.

Joseph Crispus Ndungu Karanja et al. (2015)[65] thinks that operating at minimum cost is significant for attaining competitive edge over the competitors for an SME unit. This requires the expertise of a qualified management accountant. But in most of the cases, this doesn't happen. Authors of the article evaluated the various determinants behind the usage of modern management accounting techniques, and about the preferences and adoption levels of modern management accounting techniques such as Just in Time method (JIT) target costing and Activity based costing (ABC), as well as other non-conventional methods for improving the performances of the enterprise.

Md. Monirul Islam et.al (2015)[66] studied about the gender gap in literacy rates across India. Authors analyzed the spatial pattern of the literacy rates and about the gender gap that exist in India with the help of secondary data collected from various sources. They are of the opinion that gender gap in literacy rate is a major obstacle in the path of development for the world especially for developing countries like India. Gender gap occurs when one section of the population is discriminated on the basis of gender continuously which ultimately affects the country's economy negatively. Improvement in the total literacy rates is showing a reduction in the gender gap among the population. Compared to other parts of the country, North Eastern states and the southern states are having better conditions in respect to the literacy rates of the general population, especially with respect to the gender gap. Reasons for the gender gap in literacy can be traced to the differences in schooling conditions provided for both the gender when studied separately.

Muraga and John (2015)[67] explored the performance of youth-led enterprises from the basis of financial literacy. Financial literacy training was given in the areas related to debt management, budgeting, banking services and record keeping which was then compared with the variables to evaluate the Performance of the organization like profitability, growth in market size, number of employees, accumulated assets, and compliances with government regulation. Among the variables, Record keeping literacy was the factor which affects the least when performance is considered. Debt management literacy was the most affected factor in the performance of the organization. Performance of the business houses is positively correlated with the financial literacy of the leaders of the organization.

OECD report (2015)[68] reports about a research on the financial and risk management challenges of SMEs done by SME Chamber of India along with MCX- SX .According to the research, SMEs are facing a tough time with increasing consolidation with Mergers and Acquisitions [M&A], rising cost of production and cost of capital which ultimately increases the cost of operation. The study envisages the need for a dedicated exchange platform with which SMEs can raise cheaper capital and can explore the niche markets of SMEs. Recent years have seen the emergence of numerous SME exchanges playing a significant role in investment markets not only in North America & Western Europe but also in many developing economies in the world. In spite of challenges like lack of financial resources, management skills, little research and development, competition from cheaper market etc. there exists enormous opportunities for the SMEs. The researchers are of the opinion that there is a strong need for a healthy financial system to overcome the growing currency risks faced by this sector. The same will not be a matter of concern as many exchanges as mentioned above are providing assistance in efficient management of risk associated with volatility in exchangerate.

Bediako (2016)[69] carried out this investigation with a target to study about the role played by sound financial statements in the development of SME units. Challenges faced by SME in the preparation of financial statements were also analyzed. The single entry bookkeeping system is followed by the SME in the preparation of sales day book. It was pointed out that requirement of a learned expert accountant for the preparation of accounts makes the financial statement preparation a costly affair. Only if financial statements are prepared properly, owners can use the financial statements to monitor, analyze and evaluate the policies being followed in the enterprises. Formal financial institutions will be willing to give credit only to establishments which are regularly recording the transactions. Survey revealed that there is a strong relationship between accurate financial statement preparation and the growth of SME. If financial transactions are not entered properly, financial statements will give a false picture of the financial condition of the business.

Dr. Garima Baluja (2016)[70] studied about the factors which influences the financial literacy among women living in India, interventions undertaken by government in improving the financial literacy among women and has explored new ways to enhance the levels of financial literacy among the women. Physical barriers, Cultural barriers, psychological, and financial barriers prevented many women in improving their financial literacy levels. Lack of Independence, culture, lack of women centric financial schemes, lack of accessibility, lack of information on existing financial services and requirements, less lucrative benefits, lack of basic education, and lack of financial resources as the factors influencing the financial literacy levels of women in India. Financial Literacy and Credit Counseling Centres, Beti Bachao Beti padhao Yojana, Sukanya Samridhi Yojana (Girl Child Prosperity Scheme), Pradhan Mantri Jan-Dhan Yojana, and Establishment of NCFE were the government interventions for promoting financial literacy. Financial education programs, training, better technology, E-learning, cultural change, more benefits to women and establishment of women oriented universities were suggested to enhance the financial literacy levels.

EndalcachewBayeh (2016)[71] through her paper "The role of empowering women and achieving gender equality to the sustainable development of Ethiopia" mentions about the role of empowering women and achieving gender equality in the sustainable development of Ethiopia. Qualitative methodology was employed by the researcher utilizing secondary sources for data collection. Women was used very less compared to men as a participant of the labour force and hence has contributed very little to the economy of the country. Unless and until women are empowered and equality across gender is attained, women cannot play their part in social, economical , political, and environmental scenarios and the country will not be able to achieve sustainable development. Since women shares 50 per cent of the total population, ignoring women cannot be tolerated at any cost. And hence author invites the special attention of policymakers in empowerment of women for attaining sustainable progress for the country's economy.

Geoffrey Kimunduu et al. (2016)[72] tried to establish the relationship of the influence of financial literacy on financial performance of small and medium enterprises in Kiambu County, Kenya. Primary data was collected with the help of a questionnaire from enterprises located in Ruiru Sub County of Kenya. Influence of financial literacy on the financial performance of small and medium sized enterprises in Ruiru Sub County, was measured using a 5 point Likert scale. Qualitative data obtained was later converted into meaningful form using analysis with the help of SPSS software. Study concludes that training given for personal saving; entrepreneurship skills, book keeping and training for providing information on various financial services could be accounted for the changes in the financial performance of small and medium enterprise. He also observes the skills of an entrepreneur to positively influence the sales volume to a great extent. The author recommends the awareness generation to be done among the entrepreneurs managing the SMEs on the importance of participating in financial literacy training programmes.

Lisa Farrell, et al (2016)[73] focused on financial self-efficacy of a person rather than focusing on improving the financial knowledge of people. Self-efficacy means a person's belief about his traits, and skills. Authors examined whether an individual's financial behaviour was a predictor for the independent variable self-efficacy. Survey was conducted among Australian women to reach into a result that financial risk preferences, education, age and household income are seen to have the capacity to explain self-efficacy of the women entrepreneur. Women who have higher self-efficacy levels are found to hold more financial products related to savings and investments and there is minor possibility for them to hold debt instruments. A psychometric instrument used in psychology was adopted in conducting this study.

Lokhande, M. A. (2016)[74] stated that due to changing financial markets and financial system, individuals who have little or no knowledge on finance would find it tough to invest their hard earned money. Rules and regulations are undergoing amendments very frequently and the investor without sufficient knowledge on finance would end up in troubles. A survey was done based on gender among 300 respondents belonging to a village in Maharashtra to know about the awareness levels and about the factors which are considered in taking an investment choice. Safe investment options were preferred by the investors over risky avenues. There was no difference in the preferences based on the gender of the respondents.

Marco Trombetta (2016)[75] studied about the financial literacy levels among a sample of self- employed entrepreneurs in Spain. Questions related to financing and the financial reporting of the business were asked to the respondents during the study. Basic financial literacy levels of the respondents in Spain were also quite low, though it was slightly better than the results which were found in previous studies. It was observed that there was no significant differences between the level of financial literacy of non-entrepreneurs and entrepreneurs but entrepreneurs seem to have a slightly better basic financial literacy level, if they already had an entrepreneurial venture in the past. Micro and small entrepreneurs in Spain tend to exhibit a debt aversive nature irrespective of their financial literacy levels. Author further suggests future research to be carried out for understanding the relation between financial literacy and entrepreneurship in a coordinated way at an international level to provide valid conclusions about the topic.

Richard Josua Christian Yap et.al (2016)[76] has done a study on married individuals to know about the impact of financial attitude and knowledge on a person's behavior and its effect on financial satisfaction of that individual. 200 couples were surveyed to collect the responses for the study. Financial attitude and financial knowledge were taken as independent variables and the effect was analyzed using multiple regression techniques. Financial behavior was both a dependent variable and an independent variable in measuring financial satisfaction. Authors think that high level of financial satisfaction could be achieved through having a positive financial attitude and through imbibing financial knowledge.

Robert Amoah (2016)[77] studied about the impact of financial literacy on African Americans. Everyday across the globe many new and complicated financial products and services are entering into the markets making it tough for people to take important economic decisions for retirement, savings, insurance and investing. This study intended to assess the financial knowledge of African Americans. Statistical tools like T-test and Annova were used in the study. Study revealed the participants to exhibit a lower level of knowledge about personal finance. It also points out that formal financial education has a positive impact on the personnel financial knowledge. Financial education in finance and economics is expected to bring in a positive social change implications that can improve the person's economic well -being and would contribute to a healthy economy of the country.

Stanzin Mantok (2016)[78] through his research paper "Role of Women Entrepreneurship in Promoting Women Empowerment" investigated to identify the impact of women entrepreneurship in bringing women empowerment. Author focused on women entrepreneurship as the only factor contributing to the empowerment and development of skills in women. A total of 169 women entrepreneurs located in Gujarat were surveyed from among small and medium sized enterprises (SMEs). Structural equation modeling (SEM) and confirmatory factor analysis (CFA) were applied for analyzing the relationship between women entrepreneurship and women empowerment. It was noticed from the study that women empowerment is positively interconnected with women entrepreneurship and thus requests policymakers to promote women entrepreneurship.

Xiao Carol Cui (2016)[79] in his paper "Calisthenics with Words: The Effect of Readability and Investor Sophistication on Investors' Performance Judgment" requests the financial disclosures of firms to be given in "plain English" so that it would be more convenient and understandable by the persons reading it. Financial literacy has a big role in making it understandable for the investors. And levels of financial literacy can influence the decision-making of an informed person. When the disclosure is easy to understand and read, persons with higher financial literacy make more negative decisions than those people with low financial literacy and vice versa. He also draws out details of past research that signifies the importance of high readability in influencing investor judgments of firm performance.

Adele Atkinson (2017)[80] in his working paper with title "Financial education for MSMEs and potential entrepreneurs" points out MSMEs as an important tool for the nation's development because of its capacity to generate employment opportunities for the masses. MSMEs are also looked upon as a major contributor to the GDP. In spite of all these MSME are having trouble in accessing finance, dealing with tax burden and regulatory hurdles. Author suggests financial education as a tool for solving all the problems in managing an MSME business.

Da Silva et.al (2017)[81] assessed the relation between social inclinations, money related proficiency and inter temporal choices. Social inclination is an important aspect which will create a benefit for the society due to the actions of the individuals. Survey was done among the university students to know about their pro social orientation levels and its influence on financial literacy. It was observed that university students generally have good pro social orientation which is a good indication for the prospects of the country. Pro social character was found to be the highest among the senior students than the juniors. Gender differences in pro social orientation could not be seen among the sample respondents. Relationship between Pro social orientation and financial literacy levels could not be established with the survey. Spearman coefficient of correlation was calculated and it was decided that those who were pro social were observed to be more patient than others who were not pro social.

Dr J Gajendra Naidu (2017)[82] in his study "Financial literacy in India: An overview" assessed the level of financial literacy in India based on the review of previous literatures. Secondary literature analysis formed the basis of his study. He thinks that financial awareness, financial knowledge, financial attitude and behaviour are the skills required for achieving financial success. It can be found that rapid growth of the economy and complicated financial markets made it complex for the people to take the right financial choices in the absence of proper financial literacy. He is of the opinion that women and youngsters in India who make up the deprived category in India are having low financial literacy levels in India and therefore he suggest new initiatives for improving financial literacy among such people.

Dr. Harsha Vijaykumar Jariwala (2017)[83] Financial literacy level of retail individual investors (RIIs) located at Gujarat was assessed during the study . Performance test was the tool used to measure the financial literacy levels. Median percentages of correct answers obtained from the sample were utilized to categorize the financial literacy level and the investors were classified into two sub groups. From 385 respondents, 40.78 per cent of the respondents had higher financial literacy levels and 59.22 per cent of respondents were having relatively low financial literacy levels. Binomial logistic regression method was used to measure the effect of investors' socio-economic and demographic variables on financial literacy. Investors gender, monthly income, age, type of workplace activity, stage of life cycle, years of investment experience and number of times shop around, are found to influence the financial literacy of the respondents. Present Education level of the respondents was not found to be a predicting factor of financial literacy. In this scenario, educating the respondents about the personal finance would be a good idea.

Husniyati Ali (2017)[84] studied about the success of small and medium enterprises and its relationship with financial literacy. 100 entrepreneurs from SMEs have been taken for the study. Along with purchasing, allocating, and distributing the resources efficiently, entrepreneurs should be able to understand the business management in terms of costing, budgeting and accounting. Authors observed that in order to be able to manage the financial matters, and to remain in business, financial literacy was mandatorily required. It is important for them to acquire the necessary skills to understand the financial matters like costing, budgeting and accounting of the day to day matters to be able to sustain in the long run. Budgeting was identified as the main factor which the entrepreneurs wanted to learn.

Nadia Asandimitra & Achmad Kautsar, (2017)[85] studied about the financial self-efficacy on women entrepreneurs success. The study was done based on the opinions from 45 respondents who were women entrepreneurs managing SME located in the East Java area. She tried to relate self-efficacy of the women entrepreneur with the proper financial management of firms. It can be noticed from the research paper about the significant importance of women entrepreneurs in contributing for the development of the economy of developing countries. Business development by women can decrease the poverty levels of a country and can drive the social transformation leading to women empowerment. Influence of working experience, education, business age, age, number of employee, and financial self-efficacy on the success of women entrepreneurs were explored during the study using multiple regression analysis techniques .Results of the study shows that age of business and the age of women entrepreneurs has an influence on the success of SMEs. Positive association of self-efficacy and the success of SMEs can also be seen from the study.

Ritu Yadav (2017)[86] explained the role played by women entrepreneurs in the upliftment of rural areas. Only if enterprises establish, people will get income from employment and living conditions of people will get better. Income and jobs generated through entrepreneurship can give education for the employees as well as his family members leading to progress of the country. This paper focused on women entrepreneurs in particular to understand if any progress has been achieved in the status of women. Neglecting half of the population would be problematic for the county's growth and prosperity. Future possibilities of women entrepreneur as well as the initiatives by government for the welfare of women were studied in the paper.

Sezgin, H. F. et.al (2017)[87] studied about the contributions required for economic growth of a country. He pointed out human capital, financial development, technological progress, institutional development, trade openness, and capital as the major contributories for the economic growth in the long run. He evaluated the impact of financial literacy on the savings habit of a person using a logistic regression analysis done among the Usak University staff. He concluded by saying that financial literacy, income level, educational level and age positively affected the personnel savings of the persons while risk tolerance levels of the entrepreneurs influenced the person in a negative manner. So the author suggests the policymakers to consider about the measures to improve the financial literacy of individuals for getting a micro level benefit for the individual and a macro level benefit for the country's economy.

Negou Ernest (2018)[88] through this paper analyzed the impact of sound accounting on the going concern status of very small organizations in the Kumba region. 150 respondents were chosen at random through stratified sampling. Survey was used to gather the required information from the respondents. It was noted that proper bookkeeping positively influences the going concern status of the small establishments in the Kumba municipality as it facilitates the businesses to identify their problems and to suggest optimum solutions. Shortage of time was the most challenging issue faced by business houses. Most of the enterprises employed an accountant to record the transactions using a single entry system. If a person is not hired from outside, owners should take the training in the preparation of accounts. It would be better for the entrepreneurs to learn accounting procedures to avoid being cheated.

Venkataraman (2018)[89] conducted an analysis of the factors determining financial literacy with the help of structural equation modeling based on a study on the salaried class working in Bangalore .Confirmatory factor analysis was also used in analyzing the data. Financial attitude, behavioral, influence and financial knowledge were the prominent factors identified based on the survey of pre existing data and analysis was performed to find out the most significant factor. Out of the factors, study reveals that financial knowledge and influence determined the financial literacy levels of a person. Author suggests for initiatives like role plays, financial literacy programs, and case studies from practical investments to develop skills on better financial planning and improvement of financial knowledge.

2.2 Research Gap

Financial literacy studies have not been done in developing countries like India to study about variables which influence the financial literacy among individuals in general and entrepreneurs in particular. It appears from the studies done in the past, in foreign countries that, gender is an important aspect which creates a bias between the people and women are always considered as inferior to men across the globe and are usually denied opportunities and favourable conditions unlike men. In India, though there is discrimination according to the gender, number of women involvement in politics, business, and technology has seen a rise. It was felt important to identify the status of financial literacy prevailing among women entrepreneurs involved in food processing sector in Kerala and to study about the association of financial literacy variables with various demographic features of the respondents to suggest measures for improving the financial literacy for giving better living conditions for women and for the community as a whole.

REFERENCES

1. Pradip N. Khandwalla: Fourth Eye. Excellence Through Creativity: 1988. Allahabad: Wheeler. 2nd ed., 423 pages. (1991). *Organization Studies*, 12(2), 328– 328. https://doi.org/10.1177/017084069101200220
2. Sue Birley, (1989), "Female Entrepreneurs : Are They Really Different?" Journal of Small Business Management, Vol. 27, No. 1, (January) 32-37.
3. Knapp, J. P. (1991). The benefits of consumer education: A survey report. Yipsilanti, MI: Eastern Michigan University, Consumer Education Center.

4. Penrose, E.T. (1995). The Theory of The Growth of The Firm (3rd edition). *Oxford: Oxford University Press* [with new Foreword by Edith Penrose].

5. Chen, H. and Volpe, R. P., (1998). An analysis of personal financial literacy among college students. *Financial Services Review* , 7 (2), 107-128.

6. Howells, J. (2000). Innovation and Services: New Conceptual Frameworks,

7. Volpe, R. P., Kotel, J. E. & Chen, H. (2002). A survey of investment literacy among online investors. *Financial Counseling and Planning*, 13(1), 1-13.

8. Moore, D. (2003), Survey of Financial Literacy in Washington State: Knowledge. Behavior, Attitudes, and Experiences, *Technical Report* 03–39, Social and Economic Sciences Research Center, Washington State University.Google Scholar

9. Worthington, A. C. (2006). Predicting Financial Literacy in Australia, *Financial Services Review*, 15(1), 59-79.

10. Joo, S.-h., & Grable, J. E. (2004). An Exploratory Framework of the Determinants of Financial Satisfaction. *Journal of Family and Economic Issues*, 25(1), 25-50.

11. Chowdhury, Sanjib and Endres, Megan Lee, Gender Difference and the Formation of Entrepreneurial Self-Efficacy (2005). *Entrepreneurship in a Diverse World*, Vol. , 8 pp 2005. Available at SSRN: https://ssrn.com/abstract=1497806

12. Campbell, J. Y. (2006), Household Finance, *NBER Working Paper No. 12149*, Cambridge, MA: National Bureau of Economic Research, Google Scholar

13. Devaney, S., Anong, S., & Whirl, S. (2007). Household savings motives. Journal of Consumer Affairs, 41(1), 174-186.

14. "Commissioned by the Australian Government Office for Women in the Department of Families, Community Services and Indigenous Affairs", *Report prepared by Australian government* , *Financial Literacy among Marginalised Women* (2007), p 54-55.

15. Robert K. and Lisa J., Consumer Financial Literacy and the Impact of Online Banking on the Financial Behavior of Lower-Income Bank Customers, *The Journal of Consumer Affairs*, Vol. 42, No. 2, 2008.

16. Mueller, Stephen & Conway Dato-on, Mary. (2008). Gender-Role Orientation as a Determinant of Entrepreneurial Self-Efficacy. *Journal of Developmental Entrepreneurship* (JDE). 13. 3-20. 10.1142/S108494670800082X.

17. Allen, Kayla and Kinchen, Victoria, Financial Management Practices of College Students (2009). *Global Journal of Business Research*, Vol. 3, No. 1, pp. 105-116, 2009. Available at SSRN: https://ssrn.com/abstract=1555194

18. Mandell, Lewis and Schmid Klein, Linda, The Impact of Financial Literacy Education on Subsequent Financial Behavior (2009). *Journal of Financial Counseling and Planning*, Vol. 20, No. 1, 2009. Available at SSRN: https://ssrn.com/abstract=2224231

19. Huston, S. J. (2010). Measuring financial literacy. *Journal of Consumer Affairs*, 44(2), 296-316. http://dx.doi.org/10.1111/j.1745-6606.2010.01170.x

20. Huston, S.J. (2010b). Determining Financial Literacy: Developing and Refining a Financial Literacy Assessment Instrument. *Consumer Interests Annual*, 56.

21. Norman, A. S. (2010). Importance of financial education in making informed decision on spending, 2(October), 199–207.

22. Oseifuah, E. K. (2010). Financial literacy and youth entrepreneurship in South Africa. *African Journal of Economic and Management Studies*, 1(2), 164-182. doi:10.1108/20400701011073473 4

23. Xiao, Jing Jian & Shim, Soyeon & Serido, Joyce. (2010). Financial Education, Financial Knowledge and Risky Credit Behavior of College Students. *Working paper* 10.2139/ssrn.1709039.

24. G. Gale, William & Levine, Ruth. (2010). Financial Literacy: What Works? How Could It Be More Effective?. *SSRN Electronic Journal*. 10.2139/ssrn.1758910.

25. Frances M. Amatucci, Daria C. Crawley, (2011) "Financial self efficacy among women entrepreneurs", International Journal of Gender and Entrepreneurship, Vol. 3 Issue: 1, pp.23-37, https://doi.org/10.1108/17566261111114962

26. Lusardi, Annamaria & Mitchell, Olivia S., 2011. "Financial literacy around the world: an overview," *Journal of Pension*

Economics and Finance, Cambridge University Press, vol. 10(04), pages 497-508, October.

27. Lusardi, Annamaria & Mitchell, Olivia S (2011)"Financial Literacy and Retirement Planning in the United States" *Journal of Pension Economics and Finance*, October 2011, vol. 10(4), pp. 509-525.

28. Andoh, F. K., Nunoo, J., & Darfor, N. K. (2011). Sustaining Small and Medium Enterprises through Financial Service Utilization: Does Financial Literacy Matter? *Journal of Business and Enterprise Development*, 5(1), 74–94.

29. Jusoh, Rosnani & Ziyae, Babak & Asimiran, Soaib & Abd Kadir, Suhaida. (2011). Entrepreneur Training Needs Analysis: Implications On The Entrepreneurial Skills Needed For Successful Entrepreneurs. *International Business & Economics Research Journal (IBER)*, 10. 10.19030/iber.v10i1.933.

30. Barte, R. (2012). Financial Literacy in Microenterprises – The Case of Cebu Fish Vendors. Philippine, *Management Review*, 19, 91 -99.

31. Heena K. Bijli (2012) Financial Literacy: An Essential Tool for Empowerment of Women through Micro-finance, *Studies on Home and Community Science*, 6:2, 77- 85, DOI: 10.1080/09737189.2012.11885370

32. Kimwolo, a K., Saina, C. K., & Cheserek, G. J. (2012). Effects of Credit Training Skills on Sales Performance among Women Entrepreneurs in Elgeiyo Marakwet County, Kenya. *Journal of Emerging Trends in Economics and Management Sciences*, 3(6), 945–950.

33. Gillen, M. & Loeffler, D.N. (2012) Financial literacy and social work students: Knowledge is power. *Journal of Financial Therapy*, 3 (2), p. 28-38.

34. Graf, R. (2012). Master Thesis Financial Literacy and Financial Behavior in Switzerland, University of St. Gallen, School of Finance.

35. Sobhesh Kumar Agarwalla, Samir Barua, Joshy Jacob and Jayanth R. Varma (2012), A Survey of Financial Literacy among Students, Young Employees and the Retired in India, *IIMA*, study supported by citi foundation, June

36. Attom, B. E. (2013). Cash management practices by micro and small-scale enterprises at Kasoa in the central region

of Ghana. *Asian Journal of Business and Management Sciences,* 3(2), 1-12. Retrieved from www.ajbms.org.

37. Ayodele, K. O. (2013). "Demographics, entrepreneurial self-efficacy and locus of control as determinants of adolescents' entrepreneurial intention in Ogun state, Nigeria", *Journal of Educational Research and Studies,* 1(2): 12-16.

38. Ben-Caleb, E., Faboyede, O.S. & Fakile, A.S(2013), Empowering Small and Medium Scale Enterprises in Nigeria: A Key Poverty Alleviation Strategy, *International Journal of Business and Management Invention,* 2 (5) PP.06-12

39. Devi, L. B. (2013). Financial Management In Women Owned Business Enterprises In Manipur (A Case Study Of Imphal West And Thoubal Districts), *International Journal of Social Science & Interdisciplinary Research,* 2(7), 83–89.

40. Sinha, S. B., & Gupta, A. (2013). Financial Inclusion and Financial Literacy/ : A Comparative Study in their interrelation between selected urban and rural areas in the state of West Bengal, *,IOSR Journal of Economics and Finance (IOSR-JEF)* ,67–72.

41. Meta Brown, John Grigsby, Wilbert van der Klaauw, Jaya Wen, Basit Zafar (2013) Financial Education and the Debt Behavior of the Young, *The Review of Financial Studies,* Volume 29, Issue 9, Pages 2490–2522, https://doi.org/10.1093/rfs/hhw006

42. Njoroge, R. M. (2013). Relationship between financial literacy and Entrepreneurial Success in Nairobi County Kenya (*MBA Dissertation,* University of Nairobi).

43. Nwibo, S., & Okorie, A. (2013). Determinants of Entrepreneurship Among Agribusiness Investors , *European Journal of Business and Management,* 5(10), 115– 124.

44. Disney, R., & Gathergood, J. (2013). Journ al of Banking & Finance Financial literacy and consumer credit portfolios, *Journal of Banking and Finance,* 37(7), 2246–2254 https://doi.org/10.1016/j.jbankfin.2013.01.013

45. Ajzerle, Sanja; Brimble, Mark; and Freudenberg, Brett, Is Financial Capability Related to the Effective Use of Debt in Australia?,Australasian Accounting, *Business and Finance Journal,* 7(3), 2013,107-126. doi:10.14453/aabfj.v7i3.7

46. Suchanphin Suwanaphan, 2013. "Personal Financial Literacy of Academic Support-Employee in Chiang Mai University," Active Citizenship by Knowledge Management & Innovation: *Proceedings of the Management, Knowledge and Learning International Conference* 2013, ToKnowPress.

47. Sucuahi, W.T. (2013). Determinants of financial literacy of micro entrepreneurs in Davao city. *International Journal of Accounting Research*, Vol. 1(1), 44-51.

48. Nicolini, G. , Cude, B. J. and Chatterjee, S. (2013), Financial literacy, *International Journal of Consumer Studies*, 37: 689-705. doi:10.1111/ijcs.12050

49. Taft, M.K., Hosein, Z.Z., Mehrizi, S.M., and Roshan, A. (2013). "The Relation Between Financial Literacy, Financial Well-being and Financial Concern". *International Journal of Bussiness and Management*, Vol. 8 No. 11, pp. 63-75.

50. Wise, S. (2013). The Impact of Financial Literacy on New Venture Survival. IJBM *International Journal of Business and Management*, 8(23). doi:10.5539/ijbm.v8n23p30

51. Akande, O., & Oluwaseun, Y. (2014). Influence of budgeting system on Entrepreneurial Business performance: Perspective of Small business Owner in Lagos state Nigeria, *Journal of Business and Management*, 16(6), 58–64. www.iosrjournals.org

52. Chelimo, Joseph Kurwo, and Isaac Ole Sopia, (2014), Effects of Bookkeeping on Growth of Small and Medium Business Enterprises in Kabarnet Town, Baringo County, Kenya, *International Journal of Science and Research*, Vol. 3, 432-437.

53. Dahmen, P., & Rodríguez, E. (2014). Financial Literacy and the Success of Small Businesses: An Observation from a Small Business Development Centre. Numeracy, *Scholar Commons*, 7(1). doi:10.5038/1936-4660.7.1.3

54. Fatoki, O. (2014). The Financial Literacy of Micro Enterprises in South Africa, *Journal of Social Science*, Vol 5, No 20, 40(2), 151-158.

55. G., Samkin, E., Pitu, & M., Low. (2014). Identifying the Financial Literacy Skills Necessary to Run a Small New Zealand Business, *E-Journal of Business Education & Scholarship of Teaching*, 8(1), 44-66.

56. Kamal Gupta, Jatinder Kaur(2014) A study of Financial Literacy among Micro Entrepreneurs in District Kangra, *International Journal of Research in Business Management,* 2(2):63-70.

57. Krechovska, M & Tausl Prochazkova, Petra. (2014). Enhancing entrepreneurial education activites: New challenges for SMEs development. *Actual Problems of Economics*. 158. 262-271.

58. Musah, A., & Ibrahim, M. (2014), Record Keeping and the Bottom Line: Exploring the Relationship between Record Keeping and Business Performance among Small and Medium Enterprises (SMEs) in the Tamale Metropolis of Ghana, *Research Journal of Finance and Accounting,* 5(2), 107-117.

59. Xiao, J. J., Chatterjee, S. and Kim, J. (2014), Financial independence of young adults. *International Journal of Consumer Studies*, 38: 394-403. doi:10.1111/ijcs.12106

60. Caroline, A., & Potrich, G. (2015). Determinants of Financial Literacy/ : Analysis of the Influence of Socioeconomic and Demographic Variables *,**, 362–377. https://doi.org/10.1590/1808-057x201501040

61. Brown, E. (2015), *OECD Working Papers on Finance,* Insurance and Private Pensions No . 14 Empowering Women Through Financial Awareness and Education Angela Hung , Joanne Yoong, (July).

62. García, M. and Adame, M. (2015) The Characteristics of the Businesses and Entrepreneurs and Their Relationships with the Competitiveness of the SMEs in México. *Open Access Library Journal,* 2, 1-15. doi: 10.4236/oalib.1101555.

63. James Berry, Dean Karlan, M. P. (2015). The impact of financial education for youth., *Tinbergen Institute Discussion Paper*. https://doi.org/10.1016/j.econedurev.2019.101918

64. Titko, J., Ciemleja, G., & Lace, N. (2015). Financial Literacy of Latvian Citizens/ : Preliminary Survey Results. *Procedia-Social and Behavioral Sciences,* 213, 12–17. https://doi.org/10.1016/j.sbspro.2015.11.396

65. Crispus, J., Karanja, N., Mwangi, E., & Nyaanga, P. (2015). Adoption of Modern Management Accounting Techniques in Small and Medium (SMEs) in Developing Countries/: A Case Study of SMEs in Kenya ., 1–15.

66. Islam, M.M. and Mustaquim, M(2015): Gender Gap in Literacy: A Study of Indian Scenario, in Ismail, M. et al., (eds.), *Life and Living through Newer Spectrum of Geography*, Mohit Publications, Delhi, pp. 188-202.

67. Muraga, K.P., & John, N. (2015), Effects of Financial Literacy on Performance of Youth Led Enterprises: A Case of Equity Group Foundation Training Program in Kiambu County, *International Journal of Social Sciences Management and Entrepreneurship*, 2(1), 218-231.

68. OECD. (2015). New Approaches to SME and Entrepreneurship Financing. In New Approaches to SME and Entrepreneurship Financing. https://doi.org/10.1787/9789264240957-en

69. Bediako, Israel Kofi Nyarko, and Matthew Brains Kudo, (2016), Assessing the effects of sound financial statement preparation on the growth of small and medium-scale enterprises, The *International Journal of Business & Management*, 4, 104.

70. Baluja, G. (2016), Financial Literacy Among Women in India/ : A Review, *Pacific Business Review International*, (Vol. 9), October.

71. EndalcachewBayeh (2016), The role of empowering women and achieving gender quality to the sustainable development of Ethiopia, *Pacific Science Review B: Humanities and Social Sciences*, 2 (1), 37-42, https://doi.org/10.1016/j.psrb.2016.09.013

72. Geoffrey Kimunduu, Otieno Erick, Adam Shisia, (2016), *International Journal of Economics Commerce and Management*, Vol. IV, Issue 11, 416-433, UK http://ijecm.co.uk/

73. Lisa Farrell; Tim Fry and Leonora Risse, (2016), The significance of financial self-efficacy in explaining women's personal finance behaviour, *Journal of Economic Psychology*, 54, (C), 85-99.

74. Lokhande, M. A. (2016). A Study of Investment Awareness and Pattern of Savings and Investment of Rural Investors, *Indian Journal of Finance*, Vol IX, Issue 7, July 2015). https://doi.org/10.17010//2015/v9i7/72351

75. Trombetta, M. (2016). Accounting And Finance Literacy And Self-Employment/ : An Exploratory Study., pages 1-32,*IE Business School – IE University*, May.

76. Ilmu, J., Josua, R., Yap, C., Komalasari, F., & Hadiansah, I. (2016). The Effect of Financial Literacy and Attitude on Financial Management Behavior and Satisfaction, *International Journal of Administrative Science & Organization,* 23(3).

77. Robert Amoah(2016) , "Assessing the Level and Impact of Financial Literacy on African Americans", *A Thesis Report* for Walden University.

78. Stanzin Mantok , (2016) " Role of Women Entrepreneurship in Promoting Women Empowerment ", *International Journal of Management and Applied Science (IJMAS),* pp. 204-207, Volume-2,Issue-9, Special Issue-1.

79. Cui, X. (2016). Calisthenics with Words: The Effect of Readability and Investor Sophistication on Investors' Performance Judgment, International Journal of Financial Studies, 4(1), 1. doi:10.3390/ijfs4010001

80. Atkinson, A. (2017), "Financial Education for MSMEs and Potential Entrepreneurs", *OECD Working Papers on Finance,* Insurance and Private Pensions, No. 43, OECD Publishing, Paris,https://doi.org/10.1787/bb2cd70c-en.

81. Da Silva, S., De Faveri, D., Correa, A. and Matsushita, R. (2017) Social Preferences, Financial Literacy and Intertemporal Choice. *Open Access Library Journal* , 4: e3699.

82. Dr. J. Gajendra Naidu(2017). Financial Literacy in India: A Review of Literature, *International Journal of Research in Business Studies and Management*, Volume 4, Issue 6, 2017, pp. 30-32.

83. Harsha Vijay Kumar Jariwala (2017). Predicting Financial Literacy Level in Vuca World/ : A Case of Indian Retail Individual Investors, IOSR journals, Pages 46-57, May.

84. Ali, Husniyati & Omar, Emi Normalina & Abu Nasir, Hanisah & Osman, Muhamad. (2018). Financial Literacy of Entrepreneurs in the Small and Medium Enterprises, *Proceedings of the 2nd Advances in Business Research International Conference* , pp 31-38. 10.1007/978-981-10-6053-3_4.

85. Asandimitra, N. & Kautsar, A. (2017). Financial Self-Efficacy on Women Entrepreneurs Success, *International Journal of Academic Research in Business and Social Sciences*, 7(11), 293-300.

86. Dr. Vijay Rathee, Ritu Yadav (2017) Role of Women Entrepreneurs in Economic Empowerment of Rural Areas, *International Journal of Emerging Research in Management &Technology,* 9359(12), 1–8.

87. Sezgin, H. F. et.al (2017). Impact of Financial Literacy on Personal Savings/ : A Research on Usak, *Journal of Knowledge Management, Economics and Information Technology,* VII(6), 1–19.

88. Ernest, Negou. (2018). The Role of Bookkeeping on the Survival of Very Small Businesses in the Kumba Municipality, *International Journal of Advanced Engineering, Management and Science,* 4. 713-723. 10.22161/ijaems.4.10.1

89. Venkataraman, R., & Venkatesan, T. (2018). Analysis of Factors Determining Financial Literacy using Structural Equation Modelling #, *Sdmimd Journal of management* , 19–29. https://doi.org/10.18311/sdmimd/2018/19998

3

Overview of Financial Literacy and Conceptual Framework

3.1 Introduction

India's former finance minister Shri Arun Jaitley while presenting the economic survey 2013-14 was pointing out that Indians are far below in human development indicators and requested a need for both social and financial inclusion policies to be undertaken. Skill development, women empowerment and development of social infrastructure have to be done at the earliest to come out of the cobweb of poor parameters with respect to human development indicators. One of the main reasons for having poor indicators is the ever increasing population of our country. This population if developed properly could help us improve the position of our country's economic growth and development. Regional imbalances, lack of physical infrastructure, gender disparity and poverty remain a big problem for India and Indians. All these problems could be solved if financial inclusion measures are promoted. Financial services like insurance should be extended to all spheres of the society to protect them from the vulnerabilities associated with their life and livelihood. But large section of the population does not even know how to write even their names in their local language. Human capital available in surplus if turned into a positive aspect can pull India to greater heights.

Development of a nation will be possible only when its citizens develop. Most of the people living in developing and underdeveloped countries have to tackle lot of problems to come into the forefront. Lack of access to education, lack of proper transportation, and lack of skilled manpower, low per capita income, lack of capital availability, lack of banking and credit facilities, poverty and lack of technological knowhow are the very few problems to be encountered by developing countries. World Bank report 1991 classified countries into low income economy, middle income and high income economy. Countries belonging to the low income economy were found to have 320 $ while high income was found to possess 17080 dollars, middle- income had 1930 dollars. These figures illustrate the wide disparity of income between a developed economy and underdeveloped economy. Among the underdeveloped economies, one country will be different from the other country and will have variations based on the social and economic conditions of the countries. But certain features will be common to all the underdeveloped economies. Increasing unemployment of the population, underemployment, and lack of capital, excessive dependence on agriculture, poverty, illiteracy, and non utilization of resources are the common features.

3.2 Entrepreneurship

Odey Francis Acha (2017) evaluated the impact of entrepreneurship in sustainable development and poverty reduction in Nigeria and observed that if constraints are removed for the small scale entrepreneurs, it can alleviate the poverty in Nigeria. Anekwe, Rita. (2018)

in her article, effect of Entrepreneurship Development on Poverty Alleviation in Nigeria mentions Entrepreneurship development as a vital factor for poverty reduction, improving employment opportunities and in achieving economic growth for developing countries. She also suggests entrepreneurship development to be made a part of the school curriculum to develop an attitude for entrepreneurship development right from the roots for the development of human indicators.

Indira Singh in her article, Role of Demographic Variables in the Formation of Entrepreneurial Intention analyzed the various demographic Variables and its influence on the entrepreneurial intention. Business background of the family was identified as a factor that strongly influences the interest of a person in establishing a venture at 5 per cent significance level. Age, parental occupation, income and graduation background are found to positively impact the entrepreneurial traits at 1 per cent significance level. Strobl et.al (2012) aimed to study about the entrepreneurial attitudes and intentions on the basis of gender and opines that male entrepreneurs are exhibiting more positive attitude and enthusiasm than females. Shinnar et.al (2012) confirms the stand of Strobl.

3.3 Gender inequality in India

There is a big gap between the rights enjoyed by a man and those enjoyed by the women. Discrimination and differences against women can be seen in all walks of life right from her childhood. World Economic Forum published Global Gender Gap Index 2018 which measures the Global gender equality which persists in various countries. Progress towards gender parity was evaluated using the Global gender gap index. Improvement on gender equality among 149 countries was evaluated by the world economic forum based on 4 parameters.

Equality in Economic empowerment, political empowerment, educational attainment, health and survival were the 4 parameters used in the study by World Economic Forum. India obtained a rank of 108 among 149 countries in terms of the gender equality. There was no improvement in India's position in gender parity with respect to the rank obtained in 2017. Improvements are required by India in women's participation in economic affairs. More women should come forward to take up roles in professional and senior managerial positions to overcome this situation. Gender equality levels should be improved in areas like health and survival and in education. More avenues should be opened to promote women for establishing business ventures which can result in the holistic development of the countries.

Indian constitution upholds the concept of gender equality through the fundamental rights and duties granted to its citizens. Women have always been appointed as the centre of focus for development. Rather than the welfare of the women, shift has been changed to the development of women. Keeping this in mind,various measures have been taken by the government from reserving seats for women in the local body elections to the fees concessions for women candidates to appear in the exams conducted by the central government.Article 15 of the Indian constitution talks about prohibition of all sorts of discrimination against women and empowers the state to frame special laws to protect the rights of women and children .Many other protective legislations are also there for the safety of women like Sati prevention act 1987, Dowry prohibition Act 1961 and special Marriage Act 1954. Even if legislatures are enacted, if attitude of the society does not change then condition of the ladies won't have a change. A patriarchal society always takes women as a burden and as something inferior to men. Only if women tend to be economically independent they will have the courage to fight against all evils against their existence and welfare. Good education and a good source of income for necessaries will give them the freedom to decide about their life rather than acting as a doll according to the whims and fancies of the male members in the family. Changes in policies of the government giving inheritance of family property to women in the family might bring many changes in the lives of all genders because development of women is expected to bring in development for the family. Lack of property in the name of women keeps many female members away from accessing credit from banks and Financial Institutions. Credit availability is the hurdle which many business people have to overcome when they try to build up a big profit making firm within a short span of time. Rate of growth was found to be low for businesses which had limited commercial credit supplied to them during their necessities for business needs. In addition to the problem of ownership of assets, difficulty to control the assets is a serious challenge for the women entrepreneurs. Our country will be in a position to overcome the problem affecting half of the human population only if women are encouraged to improve their labour market participation and entrepreneurship skills. Investing time, money and efforts on women will give multiplier effect for the economy. Women managed enterprises will be able to generate income for the government, reduce unemployment problems among the local communities in which the business thrives. Above all these things, income generated by the women will be spent for the betterment of families and on education of children which will be a long-term benefit.

3.4 Women Welfare Programmes

For a developed country, opportunities should be available for all the citizens. Men as well as women, irrespective of gender should be provided with opportunities for their development. Increasing the opportunities for women is the only solution to avoid gender inequality. Government is taking every effort for the development of women. Various programmes are designed for the women to support in their progress. The rationale behind the women welfare programmes are:

- To Form women groups for joint learning and collaborating together in achieving productive activities to strengthen their participation in the development process.
- To educate women about their rights, duties and obligations. Various aspects of women related statutes and their implications on the manhood are taught to the ladies.
- To teach the women about areas related to childcare, healthcare, nutrition and family planning for a better life.
- To help women in achieving economic empowerment through literacy measures and other skill development programmes and resources which are specifically designed for women.
- To promote women entrepreneurship for the economic empowerment of ladies and families.

3.5 Women Entrepreneurship

Women entrepreneurs create new openings for work as well as it gives the society with various answers for the problems of Business and Management. Increasing involvement of women in the arena of business in the course of recent decades has changed the statistical attributes of business and financial development of our nation. Female visionaries in business were limited to the small scale sectors which were restricted with limited growth and localized development. Many research studies invite our attention to the fact that the main factor affecting the entry of women or preventing the growth of women established ventures is due to the absence of funds. Usually ladies have very few doors opened before them compared to men in accessing credit due to different reasons including absence of collaterals and negative attitude of the officials against women managed enterprises. Excessive paper works and lack of experience add flavor to the inability of credit purchase. So most ladies generally depend on funds which come generally from near and dear ones, rather than accessing credit from formal financial sources at cheaper rates. This will limit the growth of their enterprise and its survival.

3.6 Government initiatives for promoting women entrepreneurship

Various government initiatives for promoting women entrepreneurship are:

3.6.1 Annapurna Scheme

A scheme designed by government keeping in mind about the upliftment of women who have sustenance of providing food unit. Government with the assistance of MSME department gives a credit up to Rs 50,000 to purchase materials required in running a food supply unit and on physical hard wares like utensils and water channels. The loan is processed taking the assets purchased with the credit amount of 50000 as collateral and it has to be paid back only within 36 installments. An underwriter is required to guarantee the advances taken by the woman entrepreneur.

3.6.2 Bhartiya Mahila Business Bank loan

With the vision of promoting financial empowerment for ladies and to set a way towards the ladies' monetary strengthening, Bhartiya Mahila bank along with SBI has framed a loan for women. It is a loan specifically provided to women entrepreneurs who have a manufacturing firm. This loan is expected to provide funds for meeting the working capital needs of the women entrepreneurs up to 20 cores. Loan can be repaid within a period of 7 years and carries nominal charges only without the requirement for any collateral up to 1 crore.

3.6.3 Cent Kalyani Scheme

Women business owners or Self employed women who are engaged in managing a manufacturing unit or undertaking a service activity in various sectors like agricultural work, handloom, food processing or retail trading are granted funds up to 1 crore by Central Bank of India without any collaterals. Entrepreneurs can utilize this for meeting the working capital needs and the capital requirements of the business. Bank will keep a charge on the stock or the receivables of the entrepreneur as a guarantee for the repayment of the loan amount.

3.6.4 Dena Shakthi Scheme

Dena bank creates a space for providing business finance to the woman entrepreneurs at cheaper rates through this scheme. Those women business visionaries who are connected with Manufacturing, Retail stores, Agriculture, Micro-Credit, and a few more small enterprises, ancillary to these sectors are the beneficiaries of this scheme. They are eligible to get advances up to 20Lakh with a concession of 0.25 per cent interest rate. Loans are given for a tenure of 7 years.

3.6.5 Udyogini Scheme

A scheme which was launched by the Karnataka State Women Development Corporation in Karnataka which focuses on initiating self-employment among women in Karnataka. This is a scheme which helps in the upliftment of women who are poor and particularly illiterate and are living in the backward and rural areas of the nation. Subsidy loans are given to the poor women entrepreneurs for participating in businesses. Interest-free loans will be given to the women entrepreneurs without any sort of bias. Special category women like widows, destitute, or the physically disabled women will not be having any upper limit in their income before granting loans. Otherwise, 1.5 lakhs is the upper limit of annual income for the beneficiaries.

3.6.6 Mahila Udyam Nidhi Scheme

Soft loans are granted under this scheme for the women who are involved in the building up of small scale industries like day care centres, cars, beauty parlors and food processing centres. This was a scheme by Punjab National Bank which aims at promoting the development of women entrepreneurs and indirectly at the economic growth of the country. These soft loans can be repaid back to the bank over a period of 10 years.

3.6.7 Mudra Yojana Scheme For Women

This scheme is designed by the Govt. of India for individuals and groups of women who would like to start new enterprises like tailoring units, beauty parlors and tuition centres. A Mudra card also will be given along with the first installment of the advance to the loanee. This card will function like a credit card. The attractiveness of this loan is that it doesn't require any collateral security. Credit limit of the Mudra card would be 10 per cent of the loan amount granted.

I. Shishu – Businesses which are in its initial stages can avail this loan for a credit up to Rs 50,000.

II. Kishor – Owners having well-established enterprises can avail advances between Rs.50,000 and Rs.5 lakhs.

III. Tarun – Funds will be provided for business expansion purposes. Amount up to Rs.10 lakhs will be granted under this scheme.

3.6.8 Orient Mahila Vikas Yojana

Scheme designed to support those women who have substantive involvement in the decision making of a concern either individually or jointly in at least 51 per cent of the share capital of an establishment. Collaterals are not required for availing loans up to 25 lakhs and loan tenure is for a period of 7 years.

Though plenty of schemes are being framed and developed by governments with women as target groups, researchers like Fletschner and Kenny (2011), is of the opinion that most women business owners interviewed were of the view that restricted financial access was a barrier which they had to face when they initiated their business ventures. ToluiopeBewaji, et al., (2015) observed that majority of the women entrepreneurs found it difficult to access the formal financial system.

3.7 Problems faced by women entrepreneurs

Building an enterprise will be rewarding for an entrepreneur but being an entrepreneur has many responsibilities. Entrepreneurs must keep a watch of the different aspects of the enterprise, from marketing to hiring employees and managing the finances. There are so many complexities involved. Even with all the support from government and other agencies, entrepreneurs in general have many issues. The issues are even more severe for Women entrepreneurs in a patriarchal society. Some of the issues are given below:

3.7.1 Problem of finance

Finance is an integral requirement for all businesses irrespective of its size and nature, whether operating in rural or urban area. Lack of finance will be a problem for all the entrepreneurs. But for women, it is even more difficult in accessing finance due to the lack of property in their names. Banks and formal financial institutions consider it more risky to give loans to the women entrepreneurs. Family and friends or informal sources are the only resort for the women entrepreneurs.

3.7.2 Scarcity of raw materials

Women enterprises are affected by the scarcity of raw material at affordable prices. Inability to purchase the products with maximum discount due to the limitations in mobility is a serious concern. Good quality raw materials at affordable prices will reduce the price of the end product.

3.7.3 Stiff competition

Today's market is a wide one and there is heavy competition everywhere. Women find it difficult to give huge advertisements and publicity to fight in the competition. Lack of finance adds to her difficulty.

3.7.4 Family obligations

Unlike their male counterparts, women are more connected with their family and children. Women tend to remain confined to their families rather than taking up the risky challenges in life, fully devoting their maximum attention to families. When women entrepreneurs are fully devoted to family, it will be difficult for the business in the long run.

3.7.5 Male-Dominated Society

Constitution of India gives maximum support for the progress of women, but male chauvinism is preventing women from taking up leadership roles. They are viewed as inferior to male counterparts and are supposed to be idle at home taking care of the children and family.

3.7.6 Low risk bearing attitude

Unlike men, women have always lived in a protected condition. They are usually not depended upon by the family for income and necessities unless and otherwise in the absence of a male family member. So they are not required to take any risk or financial responsibilities.

3.7.7 Lack of Education

Illiteracy is a problem for vast majority of Indian population irrespective of gender. But statistics say women are lagging far behind man in literacy rates. Lack of education deprives the knowledge about business, finance, technology and about achievement and motivation among the women entrepreneurs. This magnifies the pathetic condition of women.

Sandhu (2012) thinks that bank officials take a decision on the loan applications given by a woman entrepreneur upon the recommendations from a village head or after getting collaterals against the amount advanced. This is done to avoid the situation of bad loans because bankers generally have a feeling that women entrepreneurs have unfavorable conditions for running a business and low risk taking ability compared to males. Difficulty in accessing finance will keep the women entrepreneurs away from the formal financial system which is not good for the country's economy.

3.8 Financial Inclusion

Financial inclusion means the poorest and the most vulnerable sections of the society have access to all available financial products and services which will be of benefit for them. Most important point about financial inclusion is that it should be affordable for the most marginalized one to make the best use of it. Financial inclusion will be useful for the beneficiaries only when there is equality of opportunities to all those who have access to the banking facilities. All sections of the populations should get access to all the formal financial services and products according to their specific needs. Only if the financial providers are able to cater to the needs, then only goals can be met by the poor unbanked population and the governments.

3.9 How Financial Inclusion Helps?

Financial inclusion will help the unbanked category to equip them with enabling more funds to empower themselves and to grow. If citizens get empowered, then that will improve the family conditions of the individuals. When a family improve then the entire community to which the family belongs also improves along with that. Development of the communities would mean development of the country and growth for the country. Through financial inclusion, governments target the lives of the underserved communities who operate mostly in the informal sectors of the economy. A large per cent of the Indians still depend on agriculture for their living. Most of the agrarian farmers have no reliable method to record the payments received from their supplies due to the lack of bank accounts. Banking transactions through an account will ensure that all the receipts and payments transactions are properly recorded for all those who are working in the unorganized sector. If the large masses that belong to the unorganized sector are able to do transactions reliably through a formal regulated segment away from the loan sharks, then their lives will be better soon. Earlier they had to depend on the informal lenders who would charge heavily without any basis.

They might lend money to you on weekly or lighter conditions for borrowal, but most of them charge interest rates weekly or even daily putting the borrower in a difficulty. Interest rates for the borowals from money lenders would be very expensive compared to borowals from banks and formal financial institutions. Money lenders can charge you even 25 times bigger than a normal banker. There will not be any regulations or regulators to control the greedy moneylenders. This condition will loot the poor ones in the unorganized sector and draw out all their savings and money, putting them in a difficult situation. If this exploitation by the loan sharks can be avoided,savings of the marginalized categories will be left with them. If the savings are retained and accumulated then that could be used to enhance the lives of the world's poorest population. Small savings will ensure liquidity for the small account holders. A savings account in a regulated system will be safe from theft or even damages. Poor fellow will be given interest charges for the amount that he has set aside out of his earnings in savings bank account. This will prompt him to save more. Accumulated savings can be invested on a later stage to earn furthermore.

A person's investments will grow by itself making him a rich person in the long run. He will learn to spend wisely and it will give him an order in the way of his spending habits. Having money in the bank will give him peace of mind during contingencies and he will be safe from all forms of exploitations. They will be in a better position to withdraw money to meet emergencies rather than paying exorbitant interest to the money lenders. These savings and investments are not helping the citizens only, but also helping the formal financial channels for their banking business of lending. Banks provide funds which were deposited by the citizens as loans and earns the difference between fixed deposit interest rates and lending rates as income. Compared to the informal sector, banks and formal financial institutions charge only nominal amount for the amount given as loan. Entrepreneurs who need funds for starting a business can approach banks and formal Financial Institutions who will lend to them after conducting a feasibility study on their businesses. Financial requirement can also happen during all stages of the business. When banks are granting loans, feasibility studies will be undertaken before granting of funds to ensure the repayment of loans given. This will make sure that funds saved are not wasted unnecessarily.

Officers are responsible for the periodic monitoring of the business ventures for which loans have been given. Stock statements and fund flow statements are regularly collected and monitored by the banks to ensure proper utilization of finance . Only if enterprises prosper, more and more employment opportunities will open up for the masses. There is no meaning in demanding the government to provide employment for all the citizens. Government by promoting entrepreneurship is laying the path for finding out employment options for the masses by themselves. Along with the women entrepreneurs, their families also develop. When individuals employed in the enterprises established with the loans availed from Financial Institutions prosper, then that will indirectly develop the families of the employees working in the establishments leading to upliftment of the entire society in which the individual employee and the entrepreneur live. Establishment of new enterprises means improvement of the available products and services too. Better products, Technology and Services would ensure better standard of living for the Masses. Thus financial inclusion can pave the blocks for the economic development and growth of our country.

3.10 Current Scenario of financial inclusion in India

Global finder database released by World Bank gives an alarming picture of the position of financial inclusion globally. Though financial inclusion is improving gradually, uneven growth can also be seen across countries as well as within the countries. This unevenness is there with respect to gender too. Men are more likely to have better access to financial services compared to women. According to the data published by World Bank in 2018, 69 per cent of the adult population is found to possess an account either with the bank or with a mobile money provider. This is an improvement from a percentage of 51 per cent in 2011. But the gender disparity gap in access to financial services and products remain unchanged at 9 per cent. The situation should change and women should be provided equal access to financial services and products. Like women, our rural population is also not served by the banks and Financial Institutions. Financial penetration by India is also found to be very low when compared with the other OECD countries and Asian peer group countries. Lack of education is seen as a factor responsible for the poor financial penetration levels.

3.11 Importance of Financial Education

Efforts to improve the literacy rates of the population have always been focused by the government from time and always. This is very important for a developed country, because human capital and economy of a country go in line, particularly in a highly populated country like India. Only if we could convert a weakness into strength, we can develop ourselves in the long run. Population is a problem,so if we convert human resources into skilled and specialized ones increased production and improved economic growth would be the end product. Increased production would mean increased productivity of the physical capital. This is possible only through education. Educating an individual will polish him, train him and teach him to be a better citizen. This includes the skill development and quality enhancement for the citizens. But education for all still remains as a dream to the policy makers because of the gender bias and imbalances that exist in India.

Literacy and levels of education are essential markers of the degree of growth accomplished by the society. Spread of education is considered an important quality for present day improvements like urbanization, modernization, industrialization and business. Education empowers people to fathom their social, cultural and political conditions better and to react for bringing a positive change. Similarly as it was unrealistic to live in an Industrial society without being literate, so today it is imperative for anyone to be financially literate in today's complex financial markets. Literacy on financial matters is poor even among the educated persons which is a serious hardship for the development of a country like India which is lagging far behind many countries when global average on literacy rates are considered.

More trainings and initiatives can bring in progress for the financial and social conditions of the individuals. Women are looked upon as having low status compared to the males who get better facilities. RBI takes every possible effort to spread awareness about financial products and services.

3.12 Financial education and financial inclusion – Mutual dependence

Proficiency in the knowledge of finance is an important compliment for the financial inclusion of an individual. Regardless of the number of bank accounts opened by the individual and the number of boots he has on the ground, if an individual is not aware about the finance related alternatives that are available to him, approaches, plans and monetary instruments, and all his funds may be wasted. An investor or borrower should be aware about the various options before him to consider before making a final choice.

Financial Literacy is the initial move towards accomplishing Financial Inclusion. It is considered very important for promoting awareness about financial products and services, development of customized financial products and services and ultimately leading into financial stability. Entire financial system has been accepted as having prominent significance because the entire monetary markets have turned out to be progressively confusing and the normal man thinks that it is hard to make educated decisions with their level of knowledge. Financial Inclusion without sufficient knowledge about the dealings of financial products and services accompanies potential risks. Recent happenings in the microfinance area has portrayed examples of poor individuals who are unaware about the complications of non-repayment of debt and finally ending up in great trouble with the introduction of financial inclusion. Financial literacy calls our attention at this point as it gives the ability to make educated decisions and to take powerful choices with respect to the utilization and the executives of cash. It is viewed as a significant necessity for living successfully in the current society. It empowers an individual to comprehend the significance of savings. It can give people fundamental apparatuses for planning, helps them to gain the order to spare and consequently, guarantee that they can appreciate a noble life after retirement. In India, the requirement for financial literacy is significantly more noteworthy thinking about the low degrees of education and the enormous size of the population, which still stays out of the formal financial system particularly in the remote regions. Jayasree Raveendran et.al (2017) is of the opinion that socio demographic factors of an individual is responsible for the financial literacy of a person but his financial attitude showed a negative impact.

3.13 Benefits of Financial Education for the Business Owner:

Having knowledge about the working of finance in an organization can contribute to the success of an organization and the success of the women's involvement as an entrepreneur. Success or failure of the enterprise will depend on the options selected by the entrepreneur. Options chosen will have an impact for the finances and well being of the enterprise.

➢ *Guides and track business performance against plans*

Financially knowledgeable person can verify the status of business performance against the plans decided for the business. Corrections for deviations from plans should be treated with utmost vigilance without delay. This will let the entrepreneur know about the growth of the company. Comparison of actual financial position with budgetary plans can be used to improve the growth of the business.

➢ *Access to financial data on hand*

When financial data is easily available in hand, analysis of bills receivable and payable can be done at ease reducing the float. Cash forecasts can also ensure liquidity for the concern and can also keep a vigil on payments without getting overdue. Plans for investing the cash surplus also would be possible for a financially literate person.

➢ *Compliances with Tax rules*

Only a knowledgeable Businessman would be able to do the follow ups and compliances related to the tax structure of the country. Awareness about tax will create a sense of responsibility among the the entrepreneur about the compliances and a fear for non-compliances.

➢ *Transaction monitoring*

Financial knowledge for a person would facilitate transaction monitoring of the business. Transaction monitoring means checking of payments and verifying whether the cheques carry the correct payee name and amount in figures and words. A financially literate person would be able to understand the purpose and nature of each transaction and will be able to judge about whether the funds were spent judiciously.

➢ *Business will be treated as a separate person*

Business entity concept is one of the fundamental concepts of accounting. A person who has knowledge about proper management of finance will not mix up Business Finance with his personal finance. Bookkeeping and accounting will be easier if separate books are maintained for the businesses. Financial statements prepared will give a real image of the business only if accounts are separately maintained.

➢ *Selection of viable investment choices*

When a track of the finances is evaluated on a regular basis, return on investment from specific sectors will be easy to identify and high yielding options can be adopted for future. Those areas which give negative returns or those which are not high yielding businesses can be avoided easily.

➢ *Better payroll management*

Business owners will be able to manage their human resources better if they have adequate knowledge on the payroll compliances. All the financial compliances related to human resources will be met on time without delays and avoiding penalties.

➢ *Better inventory management*

Inventories should not be in surplus or in shortage. Inventories have to be properly managed without keeping excessive stocks leading to unnecessary rents and charges and should avoid shut downs. A proper management of inventory will ensure smooth selling as well as production of goods without wastages. Proper inventory management from a financially knowledgeable person would maintain a trade-off between ordering costs and the holding costs.

➢ *Receivables management*

Knowing the importance of time value of money will help a person to manage the receivables better. When someone owes money to you for a longer period of time, opportunity cost for investing the surplus cash will be lost for the businessman. Creditors to whom you are supposed to pay will not give you the time which you have given to your debtors.

According to Annamaria Lusardi and Olivia S. Mitchell (2013), investing in financial literacy of the human population is highly important considering the impact of economic decisions taken by a financially illiterate person. But having financial knowledge alone will not be enough. There are other dimensions to financial literacy too like financial attitude and financial behaviour.

3.14 Meaning of Financial Literacy

Different researchers have defined financial literacy in different contexts. Most simple definition was given by Norman in 2010, which explains financial literacy as something which gives proper understanding about the usage of money and its importance for the person who has it. But for Lusardi and Mitchell (2007) financial literacy is a person's ability to understand about the various aspects of finance. A person's ability means the skill set possessed and the level of knowledge that guides an individual to take informed decisions which are very effective throughout their practice of finance. Krechovska (2015) thinks financial literacy to mean and includes the capacity to obtain income, ability to handle expenditure decisions, comprehending the pros and cons of personal decisions on current and future prospects of income and job orientations.

Inadequate financial literacy has been quoted in many literatures as a major factor for costly borrowing and mounting debts (Tufano and, Lusardi 2009) inadequate participation in the stock markets (Cole et al., 2008) and insufficient planning to meet the retirement needs (Lusardi and Mitchell, 2006). Totally, this shows the impact of financial illiteracy in the lives of individuals, families and the entire economy. Moreover, it clarifies how financial market effectiveness can be used to achieve the economic growth required for our country.

There are several benefits available for a financially knowledgeable country. These benefits can run from the consumers, the society and to the economy. Benefits for an individual will extend through the society to produce larger benefits for the country's economy and the entire financial system. Financial literacy equip individuals with the necessary skills to enhance and manage their revenue and therefore better life conditions will be available for the individuals like better education and health facilities (Rajat, 2007). Only a financially literate group can better evaluate the financial policies of the governments and activities of the system developed by the policymakers. Presence of vigilant individuals having knowledge on financial matters can bring a huge growth for the economy of the country.

3.14.1 Financial knowledge

Financial arena has become more and more complicated every day with new products and services emerging frequently. It is difficult for a normal individual to understand the complicated financial matters with ease. Financial knowledge means the awareness and conception of the financial concepts and matters related to finance and practical usage of that information to solve the problems related to finance. Understanding financial problems and being pro-active to prevent its recurrence will be possible only for a knowledgeable person. Good financial knowledge will lead a person to take the appropriate decisions that can impact his precious lives otherwise, this will also enable him to have proper discussion with his financial advisor and he will be able to properly communicate the matters to the accountant. If the business owner or individual is not knowledgeable enough to understand the terms, concepts, products and services available, then that may take him to strong choices and decisions.

3.14.2 Financial Attitude

Attitude of a person refers to a particular way of thinking for an individual Cambridge Dictionary defines attitude as a feeling about something or someone. Attitude of a person decides about the choices made by a person as well as the reaction to the challenges that he happens to meet during his choices. Financial attitude is nothing but the way you think about the finances and how you feel about it. Meli Ameliawati et.al (2018) asserts that a person with a good financial attitude will be more responsible about his finances. Yoshihiko Kadoya (2016) examined the relationships between financial literacy and socio economic and demographic factors of a person using financial attitude, financial knowledge and financial behaviour as the three components of financial literacy and came to the conclusion that financial knowledge of males is better than that of females. In the areas of financial attitude and financial behavior, females are better when compared with the male category. Having a positive financial attitude relieves tensions and gives happiness and a world of market opportunities to utilize. Self confidence and prudence are important aspects of financial attitudes. It is expected that knowledge of a person about financial matters will develop a favorable attitude towards financial dealings and will give the person necessary confidence to transact without doubt. Borden et.al (2008) opines that financial attitude is an important predictor for an individual's intention of utilizing various financial products and services like credit cards and savings in a fruitful manner.

Parotta and Johnson (1998) studied about the influence of a person's financial attitude on their financial stability and the practices followed in the management of finance and reached a conclusion that financial attitude influences his financial decision making and financial management practices. Listaini (2011) found that good financial attitude derived through education can impart good personal financial management skills which show that financial attitude is positively related to the financial behavior. Therefore, we can conclude that attitude of a person towards financial products practices, services and dealings are important criteria to determine the financial behaviour of a person.

3.14.3 Financial Behavior

Behavior of someone means the physical actions and observable movements of that particular person according to the stimuli causing the action. Sociological, psychological and biological factors are responsible for the behavior of an individual making it difficult for people to predict the behaviors in advance (Ajzen, 1991: 179). (Heck, 1984: 13) views financial behavior as the planning and management of financial sources and activities by people and families. Level of education, habits, attitudes, morale, experience and even external factors of individual will influence a person's financial decisions. Even income levels of a person can influence the financial attitudes and behaviors of individuals ((Parrotta and Johnson, 1998: 59).

According to Borden et.al (2008: 25-26) college students in America who receive basic financial education are seen to use credit cards in a more responsible manner than their counterparts in other countries. Total debt for such kids from credit card usage is found to be in a deceasing trend. This shows that financial behaviors affect the purchasing decisions of people not only for shorter periods, but for longer periods as well (Ibrahim and Alqaydi, 2013: 126). These studies necessitate a requirement for providing financial education to improve the financial attitude of public.

3.15 Financial Knowledge, Financial Attitude and Financial Behavior

Huston, (2010) is of the opinion that the terms financial knowledge, financial literacy, and financial education seem to be apparently identical in the popular media and in academic literature. But actually financial literacy is not limited to financial knowledge alone. In other words, financial literacy is not the pure knowledge of financial matters in itself but includes financial attitude and financial behaviour also in it in a broader sense. Yadav, M.et.al (2019) asserts that financial attitude, financial behavior and financial knowledge are associated with the financial literacy of an individual from a study conducted among working women in Delhi. Hadiansah I, (2016) opined that financial attitude was the most affecting variable toward financial management behavior; likewise, financial behavior was the most impacting variable in attaining satisfaction about financial matters. Author thinks that giving more attention to financial attitude and financial management behavior is important to achieve financial satisfaction.

3.16 Financial literacy initiatives in India

Financial controllers in India - RBI, SEBI, IRDAI, and PFRDA - have made a cartel called 'National Strategy for Financial Education' itemizing activities taken independently by them and other market players like broking houses, banks, shared assets, stock trades, safety net providers and so forth.

3.16.1 Initiatives by RBI

RBI takes every possible effort to spread awareness about financial products and services. They have published various hand books and pamphlets to be used by banks and other general public on matters related to finance and financial inclusion. Central Bank has uploaded these materials in 13 languages and can be easily downloaded by anyone from RBI website. Financial awareness messages are also sent out by RBI through All India Radio and Dooradarshan to create financial awareness. Financial awareness messages are being sent out on opening a bank account, checking the credit scores, process of filing complaints with banking ombudsman, digital banking, money banking and the basics of Banking. Financial literacy week is organized by RBI during June to spread awareness of financial matters focusing on the farmers to make them also a part of the formal banking system. Financial literacy content has been developed by RBI for the usage of trainers to empower the farmers, small entrepreneurs, self-help groups, school children and senior citizens through the financial literacy programs. Audio visuals have been developed by RBI on the basic financial literacy, going digital and about Unified payment interface to ease the learning of financial matters. Pictorial booklet series of Raju and Money Kumar are also developed by RBI to teach the public about saving habits and functions of RBI.

3.16.2 Initiatives by SEBI

Securities and exchange Board of India is the controller of stock market in India. Active participation of the public in stock markets will give the necessary funds for the development of Companies and indirectly for the nation building. Therefore SEBI is in the forefront to create awareness on financial literacy among the general public. Resource persons having knowledge of financial markets are trained to organize Investor Awareness workshops across the country and classes are being held regularly by the resource persons on savings, investment, income tax return, retirement planning and about money management. Students across the country are invited to SEBI to teach the students about the operations and functions of SEBI. Apart from these, National Institute of securities markets has been established by SEBI to boost the financial skills and knowledge of individuals. An online complaint redressal system SCORES has also been set up to solve the grievances of investors and educate them about financial matters which are unknown to them.

3.16.3 Initiatives by IRDA

Insurance regulatory and Development Authority of India is regulator for the Insurance sector in the country. They are framed to ensure justice to the policyholders and to bring growth for the country through financial inclusion measures. Proper insurance will hedge the risk incidental to the lives of business, crops and even for humans. IRDA has taken a lot of efforts in creating awareness on insurance and insurance products. IRDA has created a documentary film in order to create positive perception in the mindset of the general public about insurance products, role played by IRDA in the welfare and protection of policyholders. Various seminars are being organized and partly sponsored by IRDA to educate the mass on the financial matters related with insurance. Surveys are frequently being conducted on topics related to insurance to know the attitude and thinking of consumers about the services being provided by various insurers. Apart from these, comic strips comic book, animations and Insurance Day celebrations are being conducted to spread the knowledge on insurance. It would be better to carry out singular endeavors less than one large structure to guarantee better results for the betterment of the country rather than doing the work individually.

3.17 Determinants of financial literacy

➢ *Gender*

Gary R. Mottola (2013) is of the opinion that women are observed to have a score lower than men in a survey conducted to evaluate the financial literacy levels. He also pointed out that gender inequalities may negatively influence the financial status of females as lack of financial empowerment is linked to the savings, wealth accumulation and borrowings.

- ***Age***

Lusardi et al. (2010) points out that financial knowledge of a person increases as age increases until a person becomes 65 years and then shows a decline beyond that. But confidence of a person to deal with financial matters increases due to the experiences gained from their lives.

- ***Marital status***

Akshita Arora (2016) conducted a study on working women to study about the influence of marital status and observed that single women are better than married women in the handling of financial matters. They also pointed that even in the absence of proper financial knowledge, financial attitude and behavior of women are seen to be better than that of males.

- ***Educational levels***

Education of a person will influence his attitudes and skills. An illiterate person will be lacking financial skills and knowledge too. Agarwalla (2015) pointed out that age, gender, family income; education level and marital status are found to influence financial literacy.

- ***Parental educational level***

Maria Paula Calamato (2010) evaluated the association between financial literacy of a person and involvement of the parents influence. Higher financial literacy is found in individuals whose parents have given them financial knowledge.

➢ *Income*

Income levels affect a person's conditions in life. Bernheim (1998) performed a survey and found that financial illiteracy may be particularly severe among the poor in America. Poor and the underprivileged people due to their lack of facilities will give little attention in attaining education. Lack of education will make things worse.

➢ *Mobility Issues*

Women have lot of issues in shifting from one place to another for business needs. Scarcity of raw materials, managing the finance and marketing of finished products require the mobility of entrepreneurs for careful monitoring.

3.18 Women Entrepreneurship And Food Processing Industries

It might be an internal desire for the women to utilize aptitudes and gifts in a positive and gainful way. Entrepreneurship is one of the best ways to utilize aptitudes and skills in the best possible manner. Food processing can be considered as an extension of the traditional activities being done at the kitchen.

So the effort required to familiarize with the enterprise can be minimal for a woman entrepreneur. Indian food processing industry is one of the largest industries in our country and it is ranked fifth in terms of consumption, production, export and expected growth accounting for 32 per cent of the nation's total food market supplies. 13 per cent of India's exports, 14 per cent of manufacturing GDP (Gross Domestic Product), and six per cent of total investments in industrial sector is in food processing sector alone. By 2018, it is expected that the Indian food service industry will reach a volume of 78 billion US$. Out of all these, gourmet food market in India is growing at a CAGR (Compound Annual Growth Rate) of 20 per cent.

Healthy citizens are the wealth of every country. Health of an individual happens as a byproduct of good food habits. Earlier, junk foods conquered our markets due to the fast and busy pace of life. Good and tasty food at an affordable cost is an alternative choice for all the junk foods which rule our markets. Women who are unemployed can find their source of income by providing good food at affordable costs, if they start utilizing this opportunity which is increasing everyday. Women entrepreneurship is one such possibility in which skills of the women which lie untapped can be utilized in exploring opportunities which can give end results that are productive. Low capital is an attraction of the food processing industries to welcome more women entrepreneurs.

3.19 Food Processing Industrial Sector

Food processing industry is one of the largest sectors in India in terms of the number of employees and the number of factories involved in the business. The sector gets huge significance because of the less capital investment made in the industry. The food processing industry does not figure anywhere near the top five among the industries with respect to the capital investment required by the industries. But, In spite of the low capital consumed, the yield from the food processing sector isn't undermined and it is the second biggest industry among all the other businesses. Resources in the food processing sector gives job to the biggest number of people when contrasted with other businesses while creating a yield nearly as high as in other businesses. In 2014-15, food processing sector alone gave job to 12.77 per cent of the total employment generated in all the registered factories taken together. A study by CIPHET, Ludhiana on the harvest and post-harvest losses incurred for 46 agricultural produces was conducted in 106 randomly selected districts of the country to find out a solution for the food security issues despite having huge agricultural production. It was observed that 44,143 crores of Indian money per annum at 2009 wholesale prices was lost in the form of harvest and postharvest losses. These losses could be avoided only through processing of the harvests before they get wasted. Reducing the wastages will give attractive prices for the farmer and quality products for the consumer.

3.20 Importance of the Food processing sector

Globally, India stands next to China as the world's second largest producer of food. Food processing industry is one of the biggest industries in India in terms of expected growth in the near future. Growth of production, consumption and export of output from the food processing industry is on a rise. People have developed the culture of spending huge volume of disposable income on food and its ancillary industries. According to Confederation of Indian Industries, food processing sector has the capacity to attract huge investment from foreign countries and therefore could generate employment for about 9 million people. CII estimates around 33 billion US dollars as foreign investment in food processing sector alone. Sophisticated food parks equipped with latest technologies should be developed to facilitate foreign investments in the food processing sector and to uncap the huge potential for employment opportunities with these developments. This is a double edged weapon indeed.

Those people who are connected with the preparation, processing, conversion, preservation and packaging will get income directly from the sector. The farmers who toil day and night to cultivate the harvest necessary for the industry to consume as raw materials also will be benefitted. These jobs are the direct beneficiaries of the sectors while there is plethora of business indirectly connected with the food processing industry.

Transporters, bankers, Supermarket owners, Street vendors are the examples of people who are indirectly connected with the industry. Previously agriculture sector was a supply driven activity. The support provided by the food processing sector to the agricultural sector in converting the agricultural sector to a demand driven one is enormous. Being a supply driven activity reduced the opportunity of agrarians in earning sufficient income for their hard work. Establishment of food processing industries necessitates the continuous supply of raw materials which was the harvest of the farmers. In order to ensure the continuous supply of raw materials, farmer has to be paid well to keep them in being active. As a result, demand for the food materials increased raising the prices for the cultivation.

3.21 Fiscal Incentives For Food Processing Industry

Government has realized the importance of the food processing units and has formulated several plan schemes to provide financial assistance for setting up food processing units in the country. Some of them are given below:

➢ *Section 80-IB of the Income-tax Act 1961:*

This section is for giving deductions for the profits and gains earned from industrial undertakings other than infrastructure development undertakings. Those people engaged in the business of preservation, processing, conversion, preparation and packaging of the food products like meat, hen, veggies, marine, meat products, poultry, dairy products or the integrated commercial establishment of storage, managing and transportation of food materials would qualify for the deduction. 100 per cent of the income and profits derived during the first 5 years would be eligible for the benefit. After 5 years, 25 per cent of the income and profits derived would qualify as deduction.

- According to Section 35-AD of the Income-tax Act, 1961
- Establishment and management of a warehousing arrangement for conserving sugar;
- Construction and working, anywhere in the country, a hotel of two-star or above type as categorized by the Central Government;
- Developing and operating a facility for safekeeping of production from agricultural activities;
- Production of honey, bee-keeping and beeswax
- setting up and operation of a Cold Chain Facility;

"Cold Chain Facility" means a chain of amenities for the safekeeping or translocation of forest and agricultural produce, meat products and meat, marine, poultry and dairy products, horticulture products, apiculture and floriculture and processing of food items under strictly controlled situations including freezing and other arrangements essential for the safeguarding of such production;

Under section 35-AD of the Income Tax Act 1961, Deduction to the extent of 100 per cent or 150 per cent is permitted for expenditure incurred on investment as per the type of business.

➢ ***Concessional Import Tariff rates***

All goods imported for or incidental to the food processing industry are charged at a concessional rate of 5 per cent of the basic customs duty irrespective of the tariffs to which they belong.

➢ *Goods and Services tax*

Majority of the food products are either exempted or are charged at a lower rate of goods and services tax. According to the Ministry of food processing industry, 31.46 per cent of all the food items taken together have been kept out of the purview of GST, i.e., they have been exempted fully (0 per cent)and 34.26 per cent of the items shall have a lower GST rate of 5 per cent. These agricultural produce which are having lower rates will be either consumed directly or will be taken as raw materials for further processing, thereby reducing the per unit cost of the product.

3.22 Chapter Summary

Food processing industry is a promising industry for the future which has linkages with agriculture and women being traditionally connected with the culinary will be able to take care of their family responsibilities while being associated with the business and this will give them handful of money in return if money is properly utilized in the business. Proper utilization of money can happen only if people know where to invest for better returns. Financial literacy is an integral aspect for proper utilization of funds. Various literatures available about financial literacy observes that females are found to have low financial literacy levels compared to their male counterparts in both developed, developing and under developed countries. Survey conducted by OECD says that among women itself, less privileged women like widows, less educated and low income earning ladies are seen to have a lower financial knowledge than other women of their same age. Only if under privileged have access to better facilities, they will be able to perform better in financial and economic parameters. Women have shorter work lives and are able to earn only for a limited period compared to males because of child bearing and family obligations. If they are not careful with their hard earned money, it might be wasted. Lower financial knowledge will keep the under privileged women away from financial opportunities and financial inclusion. Only if women have the required financial literacy, they will be able to be successful in managing their personal, household and business finances. Financial literacy is a composite resultant of financial knowledge, financial attitude and financial behavior. Keeping all these matters in mind, efforts to measure the financial literacy of women entrepreneurs in food processing industries were undertaken.

REFERENCES

1) Heck, R. K. (1984). The Determinants Of Financial Management Behaviors Among College Students: Implicatýons For Consumer Education. *The Journal of Consumer Education*, 2, 12-17.

2) Ajzen, I. (1991). The Theory of Planned Behavior. Organizational Behavior and Human Decision Processes, 50 (2), 179-211.

3) Parrotta, J. M. (1996). The Impact of Financial Attitutes and Knowledge of Financial Management and Satisfaciton. *Thesis of Master*, The University of British Columbia, Canada.

4) Bernheim, B. D. (1998). Financial literacy, education, and retirement saving. In 0. S. Mitchell, & S. J. Schieber (Eds.), *Living with defined contribution pensions*.

5) Parrotta, J. L., & Johnson, P. J. (1998). The Impact of Financial Attitudes and Knowledge on Financial Management and Satisfaction of Recently Married Individuals. *Financial Counseling and Planning*, 9 (2), 59-75.

6) Lusardi, A. and O.S. Mitchell, 2006. Financial literacy and planning: Implications for retirement wellbeing, *MRRC Working Paper, No. 2006-* 144.

7) Borden, L.M., Lee, S. Serido, J. and Collins, D. (2008). Changing College Students' Financial Knowledge, Attitudes, and Behavior through Seminar Participation. Journal of Family and Economic Issues, 29 (1), pp 23-40.

8) Huston, S., 2010. Measuring financial literacy, *Journal of Consumer Affairs,* 44 (Summer): 271-275.

9) Norman, A.S., 2010. Importance of financial education in making informed decision spending, *Journal of Economics and International Finance,* 2 (10): 199-207.

10) Fletschner and Kenny (2011). "Top-management team tenure and organizational outcomes: the moderating role of managerial discretion", *Administrative Science Quarterly,* Vol. 35 No. 3, pp. 484-503.

11) N. Sandhu, J. Hussain and H. Matlay, Barriers to finance experienced by female owner/managers of marginal farms in India, *Journal of Small Business and Enterprise Development,* 19 (4), 2012, 640 – 655.

12) Ramakrishnan, R. (2012). Financial Literacy and Financial Inclusion. http://ssrn.com/abstract=2204173

13) Shinnar, Rachel, O., Giacomin, & Frank, J. (2012). Entrepreneurial Perceptions and Intentions: The Role ofGender and Culture. *Entrepreneurship Theory and Practice,* 36 (3), 465-493.

14) Strobl, A., Christopher, K., & Mike, P. (2012). Entrepreneurial attitudes and intentions: assessing gender specific differences,*International Journal of Entrepreneurship and Small Business,* 15 (4), 452-468. http://dx.doi.org/10.1504/IJESB.2012.046475

15) Damodaran, Akhil 2013. "Financial Inclusion: Issues and Challenges", *AKGEC International Journal of Technology* ,4 4(2): 54-59.

16) Annamaria Lusardi & Olivia S. Mitchell, 2014. "The Economic Importance of Financial Literacy: Theory and Evidence," *Journal of Economic Literature, American Economic Association,* vol. 52 (1), pages 5-44, March.

17) Fletschner, Diana & Kenney, Lisa. (2014). Rural Women's Access to Financial Services: Credit, Savings, and Insurance, *Gender in agriculture*, 187-208. 10. 1007/978-94-017-8616-4_8.

18) Shinnar, Rachel & Hsu, Dan & Powell, Benjamin. (2014). Self-efficacy, entrepreneurial intentions, and gender: Assessing the impact of entrepreneurship education longitudinally, *The International Journal of Management Education*, 12. 10.1016/j.ijme.2014.09.005.

19) Agarwalla S K, Barua S K Jacob J and Varma J R 2015 Financial literacy among working young in urban India World Development 67 101-109.

20) Tolulope Bewaji, Qin Yang, Yunxuan Han. (2015). "Funding accessibility for minority entrepreneurs",*Journal of Small Business and Enterprise Development*, Vol. 22 Iss 4 pp. 716 -733.

21) Unal, S., & Duger, Y. S. (2015). Akademik Personelin Finansal Gonenc Hali ve Finansal Davranis Egilimi Arasindaki Iliskiye Yonelik Ampirik Bir Arastirma. Ekonomik ve Sosyal Arastirmalar Dergisi, 11 (1), 213-226.

22) Yap, R. J., Komalasari, F., & Hadiansah, I. (2016). The Effect of Financial Literacy and Attitude on Financial Management Behavior and Satisfaction, *International Journal of Administrative Science & Organization*, 23 (3), 140-146

23) Eneji Mathias Agri & Dalut Alfred Nanwul & Odey Francis Acha, (2017). "Promoting entrepreneurship for poverty reduction and sustainable development in Nigeria," *E3 Journal of Business Management and Economics.*, E3 Journals, vol. 8 (1), pages 038-046.

24) Mahapatra, M. S., Alok, S., & Raveendran, J. (2017). Financial Literacy of Indian Youth: A Study on the Twin Cities of Hyderabad–Secunderabad, *IIM Kozhikode Society & Management Review*, 6 (2), 132– 147. https://doi.org/10.1177/2277975216667096

25) Anekwe, Rita, Attah Emmanuel Yusuf, Ndubuisi- Okolo Purity, (2018). Effect of Entrepreneurship Development on Poverty Alleviation in Nigeria., *IOSR Journal of Business and Management (IOSR-JBM)* ,Volume 20, Issue 2. Ver. X (February. 2018), PP 80-87

26) Rai, K., Dua, S., & Yadav, M. (2019). Association of Financial Attitude, Financial Behaviour and Financial Knowledge Towards Financial Literacy: A Structural Equation Modeling Approach, *FIIB Business Review*, 8 (1), 51–60. https://doi.org/10.1177/2319714519826651

27) https://economictimes.indiatimes.com/news/economy/finance/financial-inclusion-financial-literacy-role-of-technology/articleshow/47305993.cms?from=mdr

28) https://www.cpapracticeadvisor.com/small-business/news/12340810/the- truth-about-financial-literacy-small-business-owners

29) MSME Report 2017-18

30) https://www.news18.com/news/indiwo/work-and-career-9-schemes-for-women-entrepreneurs-in-india-1522125.html

31) https://www.indiafilings.com/learn/udyogini-scheme/

32) Singh, Charan et al. 2014. " Financial Inclusion in India: Select Issues ", Working Paper, Indian Institute of Management, Bangalore, WP N0. 474.

33) OECD (2005). Improving Financial Literacy: Analysis of Issuesand Policies (e- book, pdf format), ISBN 92-64-01257-5, pp. 21, 178

34) Singh, Anurag, B. and Tandon, Priyanka 2012."Financial Inclusion in India: An Analysis", *International Journal of Marketing, Financial Services and Management Research*, 1(6), ISSN 22773622, Online available at: indianreserarchjournals.com.

35) Rajan, R.G. and Zingales L. 1998. "Financial Dependence and Growth", *American Economic Review*, 88(3):559-586.

36) OECD (2005). Improving Financial Literacy: Analysis of Issues and Policies, ISBN 92-64-01256-7, p. 178

37) OECD (2005). Recommendation on Principles and Good Practices for Financial Education and Awareness, available free on the OECD Web site: www.oecd.org/dataoecd/7/17/35108560.pdf.

4

Analysis of the Study

4.1 Introduction

Finance has a vital part in the lives of both poor and the rich. Fund mobilization and its effective utilization is significant for everyone as it will decide his future. For being able to utilize the available resources in an optimal manner, researchers have pointed out the importance of financial knowledge, attitude and financial behavior for a person.

One of the objectives of the study "Financial Literacy of Women Entrepreneurs in Kerala- With Special Reference To Food Processing Industrial Units" is to study about the association of financial knowledge, financial attitude and financial behavior of a person with the demographic variables of the entrepreneur. Impact of financial knowledge on the credit and investment decision of the women entrepreneurs managing food processing industrial units was also analyzed. Identifying the association of the financial literacy variables with demographics will guide the future financial literacy programs. To understand about the financial literacy level of the women entrepreneurs managing food processing industrial units in Kerala and how they are managing their finances, a survey was conducted by visiting 620 women entrepreneurs randomly taken from Thiruvananthapuram, Kottayam and Wayanad districts and collecting the required information through structured interview schedule. The broader objectives of the study are:-

1. Identify the determinants of financial literacy.
2. Measuring the relationship of financial literacy variables with the demographic profile of women entrepreneurs managing food processing industrial units.
3. Suggesting measures for the improvement of financial literacy of the women entrepreneurs managing food processing industrial units.

4.2 Demographic profile of the women entrepreneurs selected for study

The key demographic profile about the respondents consists of their age, religion, community, marital status, type of family, education, place of living, district, nature of food industry, type of food products related to the industry, type of industry and monthly income of the respondents and is presented in the table given:

Table 4.1 Demographic profile of the respondents

		Frequency	*Per Cent*	*Valid Per cent*	*Cumulative Per cent*
Age	below 25	80	12.9	12.9	12.9
	25-35	120	19.4	19.4	32.3
	36-45	220	35.5	35.5	67.7
	46-55	140	22.6	22.6	90.3
	above 55	60	9.7	9.7	100.0
Religion	Hindu	280	45.2	45.2	45.2
	Christian	120	19.4	19.4	64.5
	Muslim	200	32.3	32.3	96.8
	Others	20	3.2	3.2	100.0

Community	OBC	300	48.4	48.4	48.4
	SC	100	16.1	16.1	64.5
	ST	60	9.7	9.7	74.2
	Others	160	25.8	25.8	100.0
Marital Status	Married	320	51.6	51.6	51.6
	Single	260	41.9	41.9	93.5
	Seperated	40	6.5	6.5	100.0
Education	Primary	80	12.9	12.9	12.9
	Higher Secondary	440	71.0	71.0	83.9
	UG	80	12.9	12.9	96.8
	PG/Professional	20	3.2	3.2	100.0
Place of living	Urban	140	22.6	22.6	22.6
	Rural	400	64.5	64.5	87.1
	Semi Urban	80	12.9	12.9	100.0
District	Thiruvananthapuram	220	35.5	35.5	35.5
	Kottayam	140	22.6	22.6	58.1
	Wayanad	260	41.9	41.9	100.0
Types of food industries	Processing	160	25.8	25.8	25.8
	Conversion	100	16.1	16.1	41.9
	Preparation	200	32.3	32.3	74.2
	Preservation	80	12.9	12.9	87.1
	Packaging	80	12.9	12.9	100.0
	Dairy products	200	32.3	32.3	32.3
Types of food products	Edible Oils	100	16.1	16.1	48.4
	Sea Foods	120	19.4	19.4	67.7
	Spices	100	16.1	16.1	83.9
	Poultry	100	16.1	16.1	100.0
Monthly Income	below 10000	140	22.6	22.6	22.6
	10000-20000	260	41.9	41.9	64.5
	20001-30000	200	32.3	32.3	96.8
	40001-50000	20	3.2	3.2	100.0
Type of industries	Registered	320	51.6	51.6	51.6
	Unregistered	300	48.4	48.4	100.0

Table 4.1 shows that 12.9 per cent of the sample are from the age group below 25, 19.4 per cent between 25-

35, 35.5 per cent between 36-45, 22.26 per cent between 46-55 and 9.7 per cent is above 55. Among the respondents, majority are Hindus (45.2 per cent) followed by Muslims (32.3 per cent). Community wise classification revealed that 48.4 per cent of the respondents are OBC which was followed by 25.8 per cent of the respondents from communities other than OBC, SC and ST. Majority of the respondents in the sample were married (51.6 per cent), 41.9 per cent of the respondents were single and 6.5 per cent were separated. Educational wise classification of women entrepreneurs engaged in food processing industrial units revealed majority of the respondents had higher secondary (71 per cent) education followed by 12.9 per cent of the people having primary level of education and graduation. Only 3.2 per cent had post graduation. 22.6 per cent of the people were living in urban area, 64.5 per cent belong to rural area and 12.9 per cent are staying in semi urban area. 41.9 per cent of the respondents were from Wayanad district followed by Thiruvananthapuram district (35.5 per cent). Classification on the basis of type of industry revealed that 32.3 per cent of the people were doing business related to preparation, 25.8 per cent were involved in processing, 16.1 per cent were involved in conversion followed by 12.9 per cent in packaging and preservation. 54.8 per cent of women entrepreneurs engaged in food processing industrial units of Kerala were from joint families, 38.7 per cent were from nuclear families and 6.5 per cent were from extended families. Majority of the women entrepreneurs engaged in food processing industrial units of Kerala were doing works related to dairy products (32.3 per cent). 41.9 per cent of the women entrepreneurs engaged in food processing industrial units of Kerala were getting an income ranging between 10000-20000, 32.3 per cent were getting income between 20001-30000 and 22.6 per cent were getting a monthly amount below 10000. Registered industries constitute 51.6 per cent of the sample selected whereas unregistered industries account for 48.4 per cent.

4.3 Financial Knowledge

Financial literacy is the ability of a person to take informed and viable choices with all of their finance related matters. For a person to be financially literate, he should have the necessary knowledge of financial products, the knowledge of financial services, the knowledge of financial terms, knowledge of financial concepts along with the appropriate financial attitude towards savings, financial attitude towards borrowings , financial attitude towards investments, financial attitude towards utilization of funds, financial attitude towards spending, financial attitude towards financial planning, financial attitude towards budgeting, financial attitude towards record maintenance, appropriate financial behavior towards savings, financial behavior towards borrowings, financial behavior towards investments, financial behavior towards utilization of funds, financial behavior towards financial planning, financial behavior towards budgeting, financial behavior towards record maintenance and the financial behavior towards spending. On the basis of their nature, financial literacy is broadly organized into

a) Financial knowledge of the respondents

b) Financial attitude of the respondents

c) Financial behaviour of the respondents

In the past, financial literacy and financial knowledge were used interchangeably but it is not one and the same, anymore. financial knowledge refers to the awareness of respondents about various financial products, financial services, financial terms and about the financial concepts. Financial knowledge helps a person to plan his future. Knowledge of the various opportunities available for the public in the form of innovative financial products and financial services will take his business into new heights. Existing literatures reveal that highly educated people with good incomes can be ignorant just like an uneducated low income earning person. So an attempt was undertaken to identify the awareness level of women entrepreneurs engaged in food processing industrial units of Kerala on various financial products, financial services, financial terms and about various financial concepts.

4.3.1 Awareness towards Financial products.

Awareness level of women entrepreneurs of registered and unregistered food processing industrial units towards various financial products available in the financial market was evaluated using multiple discriminant analysis. Output of multiple discriminant analysis is presented in the Table 4.2, 4.3 and 4.4.

Table 4.2 Wilks' Lambda

Test of Function(s)	*Wilks' Lambda*	*Chi-square*	*df*	*Sig.*
1	.780	152.254	11	***0.000***

Source: Primary data

*Significant at 5 per cent level of significance

The Wilks Lambda Matrix (**Table 4.2**) of discriminant analysis gives statistical significance Chi square value **(values of Chi square 152.254 with p=0.00<0.05**) which means that the discriminant function for identifying the financial product which is having the highest awareness level among the women entrepreneurs functioning in food processing industrial units is valid.

Table 4.3 Functions at Group Centroids

Type of industries	*Function*
	1
Registered	-0.514
Unregistered	0.548

Unstandardized canonical discriminant functions evaluated at group means

Source: Primary data

From the function at groups centroids **(Table 4.3)** negative coefficients are found for identifying the financial product which is having the highest awareness level among the registered industries and positive coefficients are found for the identifying the financial product which is having the highest awareness level among women entrepreneurs in unregistered industries.

Table 4.4 Standardized Canonical Discriminant Function Coefficients

	Function
	1
Bank Deposits	2.262
Debit cards	-2.408
Credit cards	0.569
Savings Bank accounts	-1.589
Business Loans	1.147
Pension/PPF	0.774
Overdraft facility	-0.769
Post Office Savings scheme	1.456
NSC/KisanVikas Patra	-1.483
Small Entrepreneur Card	-0.084
Self Employed credit card	0.219

Source: Primary data.

From Standardized Canonical Discriminant Function Coefficient Matrix **(Table 4.4)**, it can be observed that bank deposits (**2.262**) post office savings scheme (**1.456**) and bank loan (**1.147**) have the highest positive coefficient. Similarly debit card **(-2.408)** and savings bank account **(-1.589)** have the highest negative coefficients. Therefore as per the coefficient in groups centroids matrix and Standardized Canonical Discriminant function Coefficient Matrix given in Table 4.4, it can be concluded that bank deposits are the financial product having the highest awareness level among the women entrepreneurs in unregistered industries followed by post office savings scheme and bank loans whereas debit card is the financial product having the highest awareness level among the women entrepreneurs in registered industries followed by savings bank account and NSC /Kisan Vikas Patra.

4.3.2 Awareness Towards Financial Services

Awareness level of women entrepreneurs of registered and unregistered food processing industrial units towards various financial services available in the financial market was evaluated using multiple discriminant analysis. Output of multiple discriminant analysis is presented in the Table 4.5, 4.6 and 4.7.

Table 4.5 Wilks' Lambda

Test of Function(s)	*Wilks' Lambda*	*Chi-square*	*df*	*Sig.*
1	.649	265.099	10	0.000

Source: Primary data ,

*Significant at 5 per cent level of significance

The Wilks' Lambda Matrix **(Table 4.5)** of discriminant analysis gives statistical significance Chi square value **(values of Chi square 265.099 with p=0.00<0.05)** which means that the discriminant function for identifying the financial service which is having the highest awareness level among the women entrepreneurs functioning in food processing industrial units is valid.

Table 4.6 Functions at Group Centroids

Type of industries	*Function*
	1
Registered	.711
Unregistered	-.758
Unstandardized canonical discriminant functions evaluated at group means	

Source: Primary data

From the function at groups centroids **(Table 4.6)** negative coefficients are found for identifying the financial services which is having the highest awareness level among the unregistered industries and positive coefficients are found for the identifying the financial service which is having the highest awareness level among women entrepreneurs in registered industries.

Table 4.7 Standardized Canonical Discriminant Function Coefficients

	Function
	1
Insurance	-.055
Mutual Funds	1.558
Asset management	-1.351
Cash management	.284
Banking Services	-1.775
Letter of Credit	.428
Bills discounting	1.073
Leasing	-.783
Currency Exchange	.599
Fund remittance	.708

Source: Primary data

Therefore from the Standardized Canonical Discriminant Function Coefficient Matrix **(Table 4.7)**, it can be observed that mutual funds **(1.558)**, bills discounting **(1.073)** and fund remittance **(0.708)** have the highest positive coefficients. Similarly banking services **(-1.775)** and asset management **(-1.351)** have the highest negative coefficients. Therefore as per the coefficient in groups centroids matrix and standardized canonical discriminant function coefficient matrix, it can be concluded that mutual fund is the financial service having the highest awareness level among the women entrepreneurs in registered industries followed by bills discounting and fund remittance, whereas banking services is the financial service having the highest awareness level among the women entrepreneurs in unregistered industries followed by asset management and leasing.

4.3.2 Awareness towards Financial terms

Awareness level of women entrepreneurs of registered and unregistered food processing industrial units about various financial terms used in the financial market was evaluated using multiple discriminant analysis. Output of multiple discriminant analysis is presented in the Table 4.8, 4.9 and 4.10.

Table 4.8 Wilks' Lambda

Test of Function(s)	*Wilks' Lambda*	*Chi-square*	*df*	*Sig.*
1	.694	223.640	10	*0.000*

Source: Primary data

*Significant at 5 per cent level

The Wilks Lambda Matrix (Table 4.8) of discriminant analysis explains statistical significance. Here, chi square value (values of chi square 223.640 with $p=0.00<0.05$) means that the discriminant function for identifying the financial term which is having the highest awareness level among the women entrepreneurs functioning in food processing industrial units is valid.

Table 4.9 Functions at Group Centroids

Type of industries	*Function*
	1
Registered	.641
Unregistered	-.684

Unstandardized canonical discriminant functions evaluated at group means

Source: Primary data.

From the function at groups centroids (Table 4.9) negative coefficients are found for identifying the financial term which is having the highest awareness level among the unregistered industries and positive coefficients are found for identifying the financial term which is having the highest awareness level among women entrepreneurs in registered industries.

Table 4.10 Standardized Canonical Discriminant Function Coefficients

	Function
	1
Time Value of Money	.401
Inflation	1.317
Interest rates	-.224
Risk and return trade off	.079
Risk Diversification	-2.807
Net worth	1.138
Capital	-.843
Financial planning	1.961
Working Capital management	.598
Profit Distribution	-1.188

Source: Primary data

Therefore from the Standardized Canonical Discriminant Function Coefficient Matrix **(Table 4.10)**, it can be observed that financial planning **(1.961)**, Inflation **(1.317)** and networth **(1.138)** has the highest positive coefficients. Similarly risk diversification **(-2.807)** and profit distribution **(-1.188)** have the highest negative coefficients. Therefore as per the Coefficient in Groups Centroids matrix and Standardized Canonical Discriminant function Coefficient Matrix, it can be concluded that financial planning is the financial term with the highest level of awareness among the women entrepreneurs in registered industries followed by Inflation and networth, whereas risk diversification is the financial services with the highest level of awareness among the women entrepreneurs in unregistered industries followed by profit distribution and capital.

4.4 Association Between Financial Knowledge and Demographic Variables

Financial knowledge refers to the understanding and awareness about the procedures and concepts connected with finance as well as with the practice of this understanding to resolve the financial problems. A Plethora of products and services is available in this developing financial markets which makes it difficult for the entrepreneurs to make a wise financial decision. Conceptual financial knowledge, Procedural financial knowledge and applied financial knowledge jointly comprise of the term financial knowledge. Appropriate financial knowledge enables personalities to better apportion the resources in a world of ambiguity and imperfections. Financial knowledge level of entrepreneurs is taken as a combination of the

1. Knowledge on financial products,
2. Knowledge on financial services

3. Knowledge on financial terms and the
4. Knowledge on financial concepts.

These variables are closely interconnected and shall be taken together and the differences in the mean score of each of these variables which was later evaluated from the dimensions of age, religion and marital status is presented using the MANOVA model.

MANOVA (Multivariate analysis of variance) can merely be explained as an ANOVA with more number of dependent variables. In short, MANOVA tests for the variance of several vectors of means while ANOVA checks for the variance in means between more groups. MANOVA could be utilized to check this hypothesis. Multivariate F values would be obtained instead of a univariate value for the F, based on the test statistics like Pillai's trace test, Hotelling's Trace , Wilk's Lambda and Roy's largest root test based on a relationship of the error variance or covariance matrix and the effect caused by the covariance matrix. Covariance is included here, because the two values are probably associated and we must consider this association into account while execution of the significance test. Identification of the most important variable out of the several variables will be possible with MANOVA compared to ANOVA. MANOVA basically assess whether the grouping variable which was independent could synchronously explain a notable amount of difference in the dependent variable when measured using statistical techniques.

Results of the MANOVA model is given in Multivariate test table, Estimated marginal means table and Table of Test between subject effect of variables.

Application of MANOVA to study the association between demographic variables and financial knowledge of the respondents

The MANOVA (multivariate analysis of variance) is utilized to analyze data that has more than one dependent variable. MANOVA enables us to test hypotheses about the effect of more independent variables on two or more dependent variables. MANOVA is considered superior to Independent sample 't" test or ANOVA since MANOVA uses multivariate formula with F- Static. It also takes into account about the group means of dependent variables.

H01: There is no significant relationship between demographic variables and financial knowledge of the respondents.

H01-1: There is no significant relationship between age and financial knowledge of the respondents.

Sun, L. et. al (2015) are of the opinion that age is an important demographic variable determining the financial capability of a person. In this investigation , age of the respondent is considered as an Independent Variable while knowledge of financial products, knowledge of financial services, knowledge of financial terms and knowledge of financial concepts were considered as dependent variables.

Table 4.11: MANOVA – Financial Knowledge of Women Entrepreneurs In Food Processing Units and Age

	Effect	*Value*	*F*	*Hypothesis df*	*Error df*	*Sig.*
	Pillai's Trace	0.688	31.696	16	2440	***0.00***
	Wilks' Lambda	0.42	38.014	16	1855.05	***0.00***
Age	Hotelling's Trace	1.133	42.873	16	2422	***0.00***
	Roy's Largest Root	0.888	135.482[c]	4	610	***0.00***

Source: Primary data, *significant at 5 per cent level

On examination of the Table 4.11 , it was found that the four tests of significance were used to measure the impact of age on financial knowledge of the respondents. Pillais trace, Wilk's Lambda, Hotelling's trace, and Roy's Largest root were used to measure the significance. The significance value of all the four tests was observed to be less than .05, pointing to the fact that age is a factor which contributes to the financial knowledge of the respondents. Hence , in this case, further follow up tests were then performed to measure the test of between subject effects between the variables. Since the results of MANOVA was found to be significant, the Univariate results are examined to investigate the significance of age as an independent variable with other dependent variables.

Table 4.12 Tests of Between-Subjects Effects-Financial knowledge of women entrepreneurs and Age

Source	*Dependent Variable*	*Type I Sum of Squares*	*df*	*Mean Square*	*F*	*Sig.*
Age	Knowledge about financial products	39946.49	4	9986.622	105.377	***0.00***
	Knowledge about financial services	17004.8	4	4251.2	26.837	***0.00***
	Knowledge about financial terms	31988.77	4	7997.192	66.577	***0.00***
	Knowledge about financial concepts	3085.276	4	771.319	43.621	***0.00***

Source: Primary data

*Significant at 5 per cent level

Test of between subject effects of the variables were given in Table 4.12. It was observed that there is significant difference between age and financial knowledge of respondents for the knowledge in financial products (F=105.37, p=0.00), knowledge in financial services (F=26.837, p= 0.00), knowledge in financial terms (F=66.57, p= 0.00) and knowledge in financial concepts (F= 43.62, p= 0.00). Hence null hypothesis is rejected and it can be concluded that there is a significant relationship between age of the respondents and the financial knowledge level of the respondents in the study.

Table 4.13 Age Wise Estimated Marginal Means Of Financial Knowledge

Dependent Variable	*Age*	*Mean*	*Std. Error*	*95 per Cent Confidence Interval*	
				Lower Bound	*Upper Bound*
Knowledge About Financial Products	Below 25	**57.314**	1.454	54.458	60.169
	25-35	36.346	1.489	33.422	39.269
	36-45	39.768	1.066	37.674	41.862
	46-55	39.263	1.071	37.160	41.367
	Above 55	29.547	1.448	26.704	32.390
Knowledge About Financial Services	Below 25	**51.983**	1.880	48.292	55.675
	25-35	35.604	1.925	31.824	39.384
	36-45	40.893	1.379	38.186	43.600
	46-55	35.130	1.385	32.410	37.850
	Above 55	40.071	1.872	36.395	43.747
Knowledge About Financial Terms	Below 25	**56.054**	1.637	52.839	59.268
	25-35	32.100	1.676	28.809	35.392
	36-45	46.834	1.200	44.477	49.192
	46-55	39.411	1.206	37.043	41.780
	Above 55	35.054	1.630	31.853	38.255

Knowledge About Financial Concepts	Below 25	17.880	.628	16.646	19.113
	25-35	15.536	.643	14.273	16.799
	36-45	16.192	.461	15.287	17.096
	46-55	**18.451**	.463	17.543	19.360
	Above 55	14.797	.625	13.568	16.025

Source: Primary Data

On evaluation of the descriptive statistics in Table No 4.13, it was seen that knowledge about financial products, knowledge about financial services, and knowledge about financial terms is the highest among those aged below 25. Those aged between 46-55 is found to have better knowledge about financial concepts. Mean value of the knowledge in financial concepts was found to be lesser than knowledge in financial products, knowledge in financial services, and knowledge in financial terms. People aged above 55 had the lowest level of knowledge on financial products. Knowledge in financial services was found to be lowest for people aged between 46-55. It is also clear from the table that knowledge about financial terms is the lowest for people in the age group 25-35. Estimated marginal means of knowledge about financial concepts was found to be lowest among people aged above 55.

H_0 1-2: There is no significant relationship between religion and financial knowledge of the respondents.

In this investigation, religion of the respondent is considered as an independent variable while knowledge of financial products, knowledge of financial services, knowledge of financial terms and knowledge of financial concepts were considered as dependent variables.

Table 4.14 MANOVA – Financial Knowledge of Women Entrepreneurs in Food Processing Units and Religion

	Effect	*Value*	*F*	*Hypothesis df*	*Error df*	*Sig.*
	Pillai's Trace	0.449	26.791	12	1827	*0.00*
	Wilks' Lambda	0.603	28.186	12	1606.26	*0.00*
Religion	Hotelling's Trace	0.575	29.013	12	1817	*0.00*
	Roy's Largest Root	0.392	59.666[c]	4	609	*0.00*

Source: Primary data

*Significant at 5 per cent level

On examination of the Table No. 4.14 , it was found that Pillais trace, Hotelling's trace, Wilk's Lambda, and Roy's Largest root were used to measure the impact of religion on the financial knowledge of the respondents. All the four tests of significance were found to possess a value less than 0.05, indicating that religion is a factor which contributes to the financial knowledge of the respondents. Hence further follow up tests like "test of between subject effects of the variables" were carried down to measure the impact of religion on financial knowledge of the respondents.

Table 4.15 Tests of Between-Subjects Effects- Financial knowledge of women entrepreneurs and Religion

Source	*Dependent Variable*	*Type I Sum of Squares*	*df*	*Mean Square*	*F*	*Sig.*
	Knowledge about financial products	9127.946	3	3042.649	32.105	*0.00*
	Knowledge about financial services	3118.442	3	1039.481	6.562	*0.00*
Religion	Knowledge about financial terms	8828.938	3	2942.979	24.5	*0.00*

Knowledge about financial concepts	2643.426	3	881.142	49.832	*0.00*

Source: Primary data
*Significant at 5 per cent level

Test of between subject effects between the variables under study is given in Table No 4.15. It is clear from the table that there is significant difference between religion and financial knowledge of respondents about the knowledge in financial products (F=32.105, p=0.00), knowledge in financial services (F=6.562, p= 0.00), knowledge in financial terms (F=24.5, p= 0.00) and knowledge in financial concepts (F= 43.62, p= 0.00).

Hence null hypothesis is rejected and it can be concluded that there is a significant relationship between age of the respondents and the financial knowledge level of the respondents in the study.

Table 4.16 Religion Wise Estimated Marginal Means of Financial Knowledge

Dependent Variable	*Religion*	*Mean*	*Std. Error*	*95 per Cent Confidence Interval*	
				Lower Bound	*Upper Bound*
Knowledge About Financial Products	Hindus	**48.796**	1.354	46.136	51.455
	Christian	39.369	1.112	37.184	41.553
	Muslim	38.257	1.446	35.417	41.097
	Others	35.369	2.749	29.970	40.767
Knowledge About Financial Services	Hindus	39.767	1.751	36.328	43.205
	Christian	37.250	1.438	34.425	40.074
	Muslim	33.679	1.870	30.007	37.350
	Others	**52.250**	3.554	45.271	59.229
Knowledge About Financial Terms	Hindus	45.238	1.525	42.244	48.232
	Christian	40.504	1.252	38.045	42.964
	Muslim	31.316	1.628	28.119	34.514
	Others	**50.504**	3.095	44.427	56.582

Knowledge About	Hindus	**19.792**	.585	18.643	20.941
Financial Concepts	Christian	13.428	.481	12.484	14.372
	Muslim	17.636	.625	16.409	18.863
	Others	15.428	1.187	13.096	17.760

Source: Primary data

Table No 4.16 showing Religion wise Estimated Marginal Means of the women entrepreneurs in food processing industries indicate that knowledge about financial products and the knowledge about financial concepts is seen to be the more among Hindus whereas knowledge of financial terms and knowledge of financial services is seen to be more among the religious communities other than Hindus, Christian and Muslims. Thus, it can be arrived at that the financial knowledge of the women entrepreneurs in food processing industries differs according to their religion when taken independently and when they are taken together.

H_0 1-3: There is no significant relationship between marital status and financial knowledge of the respondents.

In this investigation, marital status of the respondent is considered as an independent variable while knowledge of financial products, knowledge of financial services, knowledge of financial terms and knowledge of financial concepts were considered as dependent variables.

Table 4.17 MANOVA – Financial Knowledge of Women Entrepreneurs in Food Processing Units and Marital Status

	Effect	*Value*	*F*	*Hypothesis df*	*Error df*	*Sig.*
Marital status	Pillai's Trace	0.155	12.802	8	1216	***0.00***
	Wilks' Lambda	0.847	13.146[b]	8	1214	***0.00***
	Hotelling's Trace	0.178	13.489	8	1212	***0.00***
	Roy's Largest Root	0.161	24.537[c]	4	608	***0.00***

Source: Primary data

*Significant at 5 per cent level

On examination of the Table No 4.17 , it was found that Hotelling's trace, Pillais trace, Roy's Largest root, and Wilk's Lambda were used to measure the impact of marital status on financial knowledge of the respondents. Test statistic gave a value which was found to be statistically significant for all the variables ***(p=0.000< 0.05)*** at 5 per cent level. Hence, null hypothesis is rejected and it can be concluded that marital status is a factor which contributes to the financial knowledge of the respondents. Hence follow up tests like "test of between subject effects of the variables" were further carried down to measure the impact of marital status on financial knowledge of the respondents.

Table 4.18 Test of between subject effects – Financial Knowledge of Women Entrepreneurs in Food Processing Units and Marital Status

Source	*Dependent Variable*	*Type I Sum of Squares*	*df*	*Mean Square*	*F*	*Sig.*
Marital status	Knowledge about financial products	5266.51	2	2633.26	27.786	***0.00***
	Knowledge about financial services	1582.76	2	791.381	4.996	***0.007***
	Knowledge about financial terms	7018.89	2	3509.44	29.216	***0.00***
	Knowledge about financial concepts	2.624	2	1.312	0.074	0.928

Source: Primary data

**Significant at 5 per cent level*

Table No 4.18 reveals that when the variables of financial knowledge were taken independently, variation is found to be statistically very significant for all variables in the test of between subjects effects except in the case of knowledge of financial concepts(**p=0.928>0.05**). Knowledge of financial concepts was found to be insignificant because p value was found to be more than 0.05. It is clear from the table, that that there is significant difference between marital status of respondents and the financial knowledge of respondents in the respondent's knowledge on financial products (F=27.786, p=0.00), knowledge in financial services(F=4.996, p= 0.007), and knowledge in financial terms (F=29.216, p= 0.00).

Table 4.19 Marital Status Wise Estimated Marginal Means of Financial Knowledge

Dependent Variable	*Marital Status*	*Mean*	*Std. Error*	*95 per Cent Confidence Interval*	
				Lower Bound	*Upper Bound*
Knowledge About Financial Products	Married	**44.544**	1.064	42.455	46.632
	Single	36.536	1.29	34.003	39.069
	Separated	40.263	2.397	35.556	44.97
Knowledge About Financial Services	Married	**44.394**	1.375	41.693	47.094
	Single	41.722	1.667	38.448	44.997
	Separated	36.093	3.099	30.007	42.179
Knowledge About Financial Terms	Married	**48.317**	1.197	45.965	50.668
	Single	40.49	1.452	37.639	43.341
	Separated	36.866	2.699	31.566	42.166
Knowledge About Financial Concepts	Married	**16.73**	0.459	15.828	17.632
	Single	16.72	0.557	15.626	17.814
	Separated	16.263	1.035	14.229	18.296

Source: Primary data

It was seen in the table 4.15 that knowledge about financial products was found to be more among married people (Mean = **44.544)** followed by separated (Mean = **40.263)** and single (Mean = **36.54)** respectively. Knowledge about financial services was found to be more among married people (Mean = **44.394)** followed by single (Mean = **41.722)** and separated (Mean = **36.09)** respectively.

Knowledge about financial terms was found to be more among married people (Mean = **48.317)** followed by single (Mean = **40.49)** and separated (Mean = **36.86)** respectively. Knowledge about financial concepts was found to be more among married people (Mean = **16.73)** followed by single (Mean = **16.72)** and separated (Mean = **16.263)** respectively. In short, Table No 4.19 which depicts about marital status wise estimated marginal means of the women entrepreneurs in food processing industries indicates that married respondents are found to exhibit higher mean scores of interconnection with financial knowledge.

4.5 Association of Financial Attitude And Demographic Variables

Financial attitude refers to the individual characteristics of the respondents which lead him to a particular course of action. It is an important aspect which determines a person's financial literacy levels. Proper attitude about the financial matters is very important for an entrepreneur as it has the capacity to build the success or failure of the enterprise.

a) Financial attitude towards savings
b) Financial attitude towards borrowings
c) Financial attitude towards investments
d) Financial attitude towards utilization of funds
e) Financial attitude towards spending
f) Financial attitude towards financial planning
g) Financial attitude towards budgeting
h) Financial attitude towards record maintenance

These 8 variables are interconnected and so may be taken collectively as the financial attitude of the women entrepreneurs in food processing industries and the differences in the mean figures of the variables calculated based on age, religion and marital status are evaluated using MANOVA model. Multivariate test table, Estimated Marginal Means table and Table of Test between subject effect of variables were used to present the results of MANOVA test.

Application of MANOVA to study the association between demographic variables and financial attitude of the respondents

In this investigation, age of the respondent is considered as an Independent Variable while financial attitude towards savings, financial attitude towards borrowings, financial attitude towards investments, financial attitude towards utilization of funds, financial attitude towards spending, financial attitude towards financial planning, financial attitude towards budgeting, and financial attitude towards record maintenance were considered as dependent variables.

H_0 2: There is no significant relationship between demographic variables and financial attitude of the respondents.

H_0 2-1: There is no significant relationship between age and financial attitude of the respondents.

Table 4.20 MANOVA- Financial Attitude of Women Entrepreneurs In Food Processing Units with Age

	Effect	*Value*	*F*	*Hypothesis df*	*Error df*	*Sig.*
	Pillai's Trace	1.583	49.626	32	2424	***0.00***
Age	Wilks' Lambda	0.093	63.046	32	2225.35	***0.00***
	Hotelling's Trace	3.99	75.006	32	2406	***0.00***
	Roy's Largest Root	2.421	183.417[c]	8	606	***0.00***

Source: Primary data

**Significant at 5 per cent level*

On examination of the Table No 4.20, the test statistics adopted to measure the impact of age on financial attitude of the respondents was given. All the four tests gave value less than .05, indicating that there is an association between the variables. Hence, in this case, further follow up tests were then performed to measure the test of between subject effects of the variables.

Table 4.21 Tests of Between-Subjects Effects – Financial Attitude of Women Entrepreneurs in food processing units and Age

Source	*Dependent Variable*	*Type I Sum of Squares*	*df*	*Mean Square*	*F*	*Sig.*
	Financial Attitude Towards Budgeting	1706.72	4	426.68	7.357	***0.00***
	Financial Attitude Towards Investment	12470.9	4	3117.74	25.447	***0.00***
	Financial Attitude Towards Financial Planning	20533.5	4	5133.39	42.132	***0.00***
	Financial Attitude Towards Record Maintenance	5576.26	4	1394.07	56.074	***0.00***
	Financial Attitude Towards Savings	10471.7	4	2617.93	68.637	***0.00***
Age	Financial Attitude Towards Borrowings	6652.65	4	1663.16	63.923	***0.00***
	Financial Attitude	7073.7	4	1768.43	26.723	***0.00***
	Towards Utilization of Funds					
	Financial Attitude Towards Spendings	23123.3	4	5780.82	88.725	***0.00***

Source: Primary data, * Significant at 5 per cent level

Table No 4.21 shows financial attitude towards savings(F=68.637, p=0.00), financial attitude towards borrowings(F=63.923, p=0.00), financial attitude towards investments(F=25.447, p=0.00), financial attitude towards utilization of funds (F=26.72, p=0.00), financial attitude towards spending (F=88.725, p=0.00), financial attitude towards financial planning (F=42.132, p=0.00), financial attitude towards budgeting (F=7.357, p=0.00), and financial attitude towards record maintenance (F=56.074, p=0.00) showed significant difference when tested with age of the respondent (***All p values were less than 0.05***). Hence, null hypothesis is rejected and it can be concluded that there is a significant relationship between age and financial attitude levels of the respondents.

Table 4.22 Age Wise Estimated Marginal Means of Financial Attitude

Dependent Variable	*Age*	*Mean*	*Std. Error*	*95 per Cent Confidence Interval*	
				Lower Bound	*Upper Bound*
	below 25	**23.084**	1.137	20.85	25.317
	25-35	24.059	1.165	21.772	26.347
Financial Attitude	36-45	22.552	0.834	20.914	24.191
Towards Budgeting	46-55	18.239	0.838	16.594	19.885
	above 55	19.599	1.133	17.375	21.823
	•below 25	**43.937**	1.653	40.69	47.183
Financial Attitude	25-35	35.583	1.693	32.259	38.907
Towards Investment	36-45	37.283	1.212	34.902	39.664
	46-55	35.045	1.218	32.653	37.437
	above 55	42.396	1.646	39.164	45.629
	below 25	**55.788**	1.649	52.551	59.026
Financial Attitude	25-35	46.162	1.688	42.847	49.477
Towards Financial	36-45	39.128	1.209	36.753	41.502
Planning	46-55	37.782	1.215	35.397	40.167
	above 55	51.656	1.642	48.432	54.88

	below 25	**27.907**	0.745	26.445	29.369
Financial Attitude	25-35	19.595	0.763	18.098	21.093
Towards Record	36-45	17.927	0.546	16.855	19
Maintenance	46-55	20.604	0.549	19.527	21.682
	above 55	23.471	0.742	22.014	24.927
	below 25	**47.21**	0.922	45.399	49.022
Financial Attitude	25-35	28.832	0.944	26.977	30.686
Towards Savings	36-45	36.75	0.676	35.422	38.079
	46-55	32.495	0.68	31.161	33.83
	above 55	32.043	0.918	30.239	33.847
	below 25	25.478	0.762	23.982	26.974
Financial Attitude	25-35	21.318	0.78	19.786	22.849
Towards Borrowings	36-45	20.444	0.559	19.346	21.541
	46-55	17.952	0.561	16.849	19.054
	above 55	**27.322**	0.759	25.832	28.812
	below 25	**36.8**	1.215	34.414	39.186
Financial Attitude	25-35	31.108	1.244	28.664	33.551
Towards Utilization of	36-45	30.812	0.891	29.063	32.562
Funds	46-55	30.794	0.895	29.036	32.552
	above 55	34.476	1.21	32.1	36.852
	below 25	**44.347**	1.206	41.98	46.714
Financial Attitude	25-35	35.677	1.234	33.253	38.102
Towards Spendings	36-45	30.991	0.884	29.255	32.727
	46-55	33.448	0.888	31.704	35.192
	above 55	43.882	1.2	41.524	46.239

Source: Primary Data

Table No 4.22 showing Age wise Estimated Marginal Means of the women entrepreneurs in food processing industries indicate that financial attitude of women entrepreneurs in food processing industries was the most favourable for the age group below 25 except in their attitude towards borrowings. Attitude towards borrowings was the most favourable among the age group above

55. We can thus arrive at a conclusion that, the financial attitude of the women entrepreneurs in food processing industries differ with the age of the entrepreneur.

H_0 2-2: There is no significant relationship between religion and financial attitude of the respondents.

In this investigation, religion of the respondent is considered as an independent variable while financial attitude towards borrowings, financial attitude towards savings, financial attitude towards investments, financial attitude towards spendings, financial attitude towards utilization of funds, financial attitude towards financial planning, financial attitude towards budgeting, and financial attitude towards record maintenance were considered as dependent variables.

Table 4.23 MANOVA- Financial Attitude of Women Entrepreneurs In Food Processing Units

	Effect	*Value*	*F*	*Hypothesis df*	*Error df*	*Sig.*
	Pillai's Trace	0.75	25.187	24	1815	***0.00***
	Wilks' Lambda	0.413	25.995	24	1749.49	***0.00***
Religion	Hotelling's Trace	1.059	26.551	24	1805	***0.00***
	Roy's Largest Root	0.57	43.129[c]	8	605	***0.00***

Source: Primary data

*Significant at 5 per cent level of significance

Wilk's Lambda, Pillais trace, Hotelling's trace, and Roy's Largest root were utilized in measuring the impact of religion on the financial attitude of the respondents. Table No. 4.23 reveals that all the test statistics gave a value which was found to be statistically significant ***(p=0.000< 0.05)*** at 5 per cent level of significance.

Since all the test statistics in MANOVA were found to be significant, tests were further carried out to know if variation is found to be statistically very significant when the variables are taken independently.

Table 4.24 Tests of Between-Subjects Effects – Financial Attitude of Women Entrepreneurs in food processing units

Source	*Dependent Variable*	*Type I Sum of Squares*	*df*	*Mean Square*	*F*	*Sig.*
	Financial Attitude Towards Budgeting	3605.15	3	1201.72	20.722	***0.00***
	Financial Attitude Towards Investment	10175.3	3	3391.77	27.684	***0.00***
	Financial Attitude	5310.81	3	1770.27	14.529	***0.00***
	Towards Financial Planning					
Religion	Financial Attitude Towards Record Maintenance	571.794	3	190.598	7.666	***0.00***
	Financial Attitude Towards Savings	828.236	3	276.079	7.238	***0.00***
	Financial Attitude Towards Borrowings	1684.85	3	561.617	21.586	***0.00***
	Financial Attitude Towards Utilization of Funds	5799.57	3	1933.19	29.213	***0.00***
	Financial Attitude Towards Spendings	4475.67	3	1491.89	22.898	***0.00***

Source: Primary data

*Significant at 5 per cent level of significance

When the variables of financial attitude were taken independently, in the test of between subject effects in Table No 4.24, variation was found to be statistically very significant for all the variables since all p values were found to be lesser than 0.05. Hence, null hypothesis is rejected and it can be concluded that there is a significant relationship between religion and the financial attitude levels of the respondents.

Table No 4.25 Religion Wise Estimated Marginal Means of Financial Attitude

Dependent Variable	*Religion*	*Mean*	*Std. Error*	*95 per Cent Confidence Interval*	
				Lower Bound	*Upper Bound*
Financial Attitude Towards Budgeting	Hindus	23.759	1.059	21.679	25.84
	Christian	16.895	0.87	15.186	18.604
	Muslim	18.477	1.131	16.255	20.698
	Others	**26.895**	2.15	22.673	31.118
Financial Attitude Towards Investment	Hindus	**45.252**	1.54	42.228	48.276
	Christian	38.48	1.265	35.996	40.964
	Muslim	34.184	1.644	30.955	37.413
	Others	37.48	3.125	31.342	43.617
Financial Attitude Towards Financial Planning	Hindus	47.943	1.535	44.927	50.958
	Christian	37.944	1.261	35.466	40.421
	Muslim	42.582	1.64	39.362	45.802
	Others	**55.944**	3.117	49.823	62.064
Financial Attitude Towards Record Maintenance	Hindus	19.202	0.694	17.839	20.564
	Christian	19.323	0.57	18.204	20.442
	Muslim	17.756	0.741	16.301	19.21
	Others	**31.323**	1.408	28.558	34.088
Financial Attitude Towards Savings	Hindus	32.563	0.859	30.876	34.25
	Christian	35.79	0.706	34.404	37.176
	Muslim	27.723	0.917	25.921	29.524
	Others	**45.79**	1.744	42.365	49.214
Financial Attitude Towards Borrowings	Hindus	23.63	0.71	22.237	25.023
	Christian	22.277	0.583	21.133	23.422
	Muslim	18.826	0.758	17.338	20.314
	Others	**25.277**	1.44	22.449	28.106

Financial Attitude Towards Utilization of Funds	Hindus	32.97	1.132	30.748	35.192
	Christian	28.609	0.93	26.784	30.435
	Muslim	25.004	1.208	22.631	27.377
	Others	**44.609**	2.297	40.098	49.12
Financial Attitude Towards Spending	Hindus	38.659	1.123	36.454	40.864
	Christian	35.041	0.922	33.23	36.853
	Muslim	28.935	1.199	26.58	31.29
	Others	**48.041**	2.279	43.565	52.517

Source: Primary data

Table no 4.25 showing Religion wise Estimated Marginal Means of the women entrepreneurs in food processing industries indicate that financial attitude of women entrepreneurs in food processing industries was the most favourable for communities other than Hindus, Christian and Muslims except in their attitude towards investments. Hindus community shows better attitude about investments.

H_0 2-3: There is no significant relationship between marital status and financial attitude of the respondents.

In this investigation marital status of the respondent is considered as an Independent Variable while financial attitude towards borrowings, financial attitude towards savings, financial attitude towards investments, financial attitude towards spending, financial attitude towards utilization of funds, financial attitude towards financial planning, financial attitude towards budgeting, and financial attitude towards record maintenance were considered as dependent variables.

Table 4.28 Marital Status Wise Estimated Marginal Means of Financial Attitude

Dependent Variable	*Marital Status*	*Mean*	*Std. Error*	*95 per Cent Confidence Interval*	
				Lower Bound	*Upper Bound*
Financial Attitude Towards Budgeting	Married	**23.471**	.832	21.837	25.105
	Single	21.170	1.009	19.189	23.152
	Separated	19.879	1.875	16.196	23.561
Financial Attitude Towards Investment	Married	**40.614**	1.209	38.239	42.989
	Single	38.759	1.466	35.880	41.639
	Separated	37.173	2.725	31.820	42.525
Financial Attitude Towards Financial Planning	Married	**49.353**	1.206	46.985	51.722
	Single	43.475	1.462	40.603	46.347
	Separated	45.481	2.718	40.143	50.818
Financial Attitude Toward Record Maintenance	Married	**25.885**	.545	24.815	26.955
	Single	21.943	.661	20.646	23.240
	Separated	17.874	1.228	15.463	20.285
Financial Attitude Towards Savings	Married	**41.842**	.675	40.517	43.167
	Single	35.909	.818	34.302	37.516
	Separated	28.647	1.521	25.661	31.634
Financial Attitude Towards Borrowing	Married	22.584	.557	21.490	23.679
	Single	22.147	.676	20.820	23.474
	Separated	**22.776**	1.256	20.310	25.243
Financial Attitude Towards Utilization of Funds	Married	**35.625**	.889	33.880	37.371
	Single	33.576	1.078	31.460	35.692
	Separated	29.193	2.003	25.259	33.127
Financial Attitude Towards Spending	Married	**42.576**	.882	40.844	44.308
	Single	36.582	1.069	34.482	38.682
	Separated	33.849	1.987	29.946	37.752

Source: Primary data

Table No 4.28 showing marital status wise estimated marginal means of the women entrepreneurs in food processing industries indicate that married respondents are found to exhibit higher mean scores of interconnection with financial attitude of the respondents except in the case of financial attitude towards borrowings. People living separated are found to have higher mean scores for the financial attitude towards borrowings. Thus we can say that, financial attitude of the respondents differ according to their marital status when they are taken collectively and when they are taken independently.

4.6 Association of Financial Behavior and Demographic Variables

Financial behaviour refers to the practices and decisions taken by a person about financial matters. It is vital for every business unit to take apt decisions related to financial management for retaining its going concern status. Financial behavior can be summed up with the following variables:

a) Financial behavior towards savings
b) Financial behavior towards borrowings
c) Financial behavior towards investments
d) Financial behavior towards utilization of funds
e) Financial behavior towards spending
f) Financial behavior towards financial planning
g) Financial behavior towards budgeting
h) Financial behavior towards record maintenance

These 8 variables are interconnected and so may be taken collectively as the financial behaviour of the women entrepreneurs in food processing industries and the differences in the mean figures of the variables calculated based on age, religion and marital status are evaluated using MANOVA model. Multivariate test table, Estimated Marginal Means table and Table of Test between subject effect of variables were used to present the results of MANOVA test.

Application of MANOVA to study the association between demographic variables and financial behaviour of the respondents

H_0 3: There is no significant relationship between demographic variables and financial behaviour of the respondents.

H_0 3-1: There is no significant relationship between age and financial behaviour of the respondents.

In this investigation age of the respondents is considered as an independent variable while financial behaviour towards borrowings, financial behaviour towards savings, financial behaviour towards investments, financial behaviour towards spending, financial behaviour towards utilization of funds, financial behaviour towards financial planning, financial behaviour towards budgeting, and financial behaviour towards record maintenance were considered as dependent variables.

Table 4.29 MANOVA- Financial Behaviour of Women Entrepreneurs in food processing units

	Effect	*Value*	*F*	*Hypothesis df*	*Error df*	*Sig.*
	Pillai's Trace	1.384	40.07	32	2424	***0.00***
	Wilks' Lambda	0.116	55.179	32	2225.35	***0.00***
Age	Hotelling's Trace	3.724	70	32	2406	***0.00***
	Roy's Largest Root	2.24	169.678[c]	8	606	***0.00***

Source: Primary data

*Significant at 5 per cent level of significance

Impact of age on the financial behaviour of the respondents was examined using Hotelling's trace, Wilk's Lambda, Pillais trace, & Roy's Largest root. Table No 4.29 reveals that all the test statistics had value lesser than 0.05 which point towards the fact that all the variables are statistically significant ***(p=0.000< 0.05)*** at 5 per cent level of significance. Hence, null hypothesis is rejected and it can be concluded that there is a significant relationship between age and financial behaviour levels of the respondents.

Table 4.30 Tests of Between-Subjects Effects Financial Behaviour of Women Entrepreneurs In Food Processing Units and Age

Source	*Dependent Variable*	*Type I Sum of Squares*	*df*	*Mean Square*	*F*	*Sig.*
	Financial Behaviour Towards Budgeting	6581.8	4	1645.45	63.998	***0.00***
	Financial Behaviour Towards Investments	6246.58	4	1561.65	42.305	***0.00***
	Financial Behaviour Towards Financial Planning	10188.5	4	2547.12	23.715	***0.00***
Age	Financial Behaviour Towards Record Maintenance	1166.22	4	291.556	13.32	***0.00***
	Financial Behaviour Towards Savings	13709	4	3427.25	27.281	***0.00***
	Financial Behaviour Towards Borrowals	6328.07	4	1582.02	33.344	***0.00***
	Financial Behaviour Towards Utilization of Funds	4346.95	4	1086.74	31.831	***0.00***
	Financial Behaviour Towards Spendings	11706.8	4	2926.69	100.331	***0.00***

Source: Primary data

*Significant at 5 per cent level of significance

Test of between subject effects is a measure of the analysis of variance between the variables independently. Test of between subject effects shows separate ANOVA for each of the dependent variable. Results similar to normal ANOVA will be obtained if separate regression tests were used for variables rather than combining variables together. Table No 4.30 shows that Financial behaviour towards savings (F= 27.281, p=0.00),financial behaviour towards borrowings (F= 33.34, p=0.00),financial behaviour towards investments (F= 42.305, p=0.00), financial behaviour towards utilization of funds (F=31.831, p=0.00), financial behaviour towards spending (F=100.33, p=0.00), financial behaviour towards financial planning (F= 23.715, p=0.00), financial behaviour towards budgeting (F=63.998, p=0.00), and financial behaviour towards record maintenance (F=13.32, p=0.00) showed significant difference when tested with age of the respondent.(***All p values were less than 0.05***). Hence, null hypothesis is rejected and it can be concluded that there is a significant relationship between age and variables of financial behaviour when taken independently also.

Table 4.31 Age Wise Estimated Marginal Means of Financial Behaviour

Dependent Variable	*Age*	*Mean*	*Std. Error*	*95 per Cent Confidence Interval*	
				Lower Bound	*Upper Bound*
	below 25	**24.911**	0.757	23.423	26.398
Financial Behaviour	25-35	18.278	0.775	16.755	19.801
Towards Budgeting	36-45	19.616	0.555	18.525	20.706
	46-55	21.23	0.558	20.135	22.326
	above 55	20.075	0.754	18.594	21.556
	below 25	**30.913**	0.907	29.131	32.695
Financial Behaviour	25-35	27.846	0.929	26.022	29.671
Towards Investments	36-45	23.83	0.665	22.523	25.137
	46-55	22.267	0.669	20.954	23.58
	above 55	27.242	0.904	25.468	29.017

Financial Behaviour Towards Financial Planning	below 25	48.729	1.548	45.689	51.768
	25-35	41.158	1.585	38.045	44.27
	36-45	41.424	1.135	39.194	43.653
	46-55	36.128	1.14	33.888	38.368
	above 55	**49.82**	1.541	46.793	52.846
Financial Behaviour Towards Record Maintenance	below 25	17.595	0.699	16.223	18.967
	25-35	15.818	0.715	14.413	17.224
	36-45	17.017	0.512	16.011	18.024
	46-55	14.217	0.515	13.206	15.228
	above 55	**20.488**	0.696	19.121	21.854
Financial Behaviour Towards Savings	below 25	**54.607**	1.674	51.32	57.895
	25-35	45.01	1.714	41.644	48.377
	36-45	41.352	1.228	38.941	43.763
	46-55	35.592	1.233	33.17	38.014
	above 55	50.423	1.667	47.149	53.697
Financial Behaviour Towards Borrowals	below 25	**33.685**	1.029	31.665	35.706
	25-35	28.619	1.053	26.55	30.688
	36-45	24.973	0.754	23.491	26.455
	46-55	19.901	0.758	18.413	21.39
	above 55	31.27	1.024	29.259	33.282
Financial Behaviour Towards Utilization of Funds	below 25	**29.478**	0.873	27.764	31.192
	25-35	23.568	0.894	21.813	25.322
	36-45	23.194	0.64	21.937	24.451
	46-55	16.702	0.643	15.439	17.964
	above 55	27.072	0.869	25.366	28.779
Behaviour Towards Spending	below 25	**39.408**	0.807	37.824	40.992
	25-35	32.598	0.826	30.976	34.22
	36-45	31.087	0.592	29.925	32.248
	46-55	26.898	0.594	25.731	28.066
	above 55	37.772	0.803	36.194	39.349

Source: Primary data

Table No 4.31 shows that Age wise Estimated Marginal Means of the women entrepreneurs in food processing industries indicate that financial behaviour of women entrepreneurs in food processing industries is found to exhibit higher mean scores of relationship for the age group below 25 except in their behaviour towards financial planning **(Mean=49.820)** and the behavior towards record maintenance **(Mean=20.488)** for which respondents of the age above 55 had better scores. We can thus arrive at a conclusion that, the financial behaviour of the women entrepreneurs in food processing industries differ with the age of the entrepreneur taken independently and collectively.

H_0 3-2: There is no significant relationship between religion and financial behaviour of the respondents.

In this study, religion of the entrepreneur is considered as an Independent Variable while financial behaviour towards savings, financial behaviour towards budgeting, financial behaviour towards borrowings, financial behaviour towards spending, financial behaviour towards investments, financial behaviour towards utilization of funds, financial behaviour towards financial planning, and financial behaviour towards record maintenance were considered as dependent variables.

Table 4.32 MANOVA- Financial Behaviour of Women Entrepreneurs in food processing units

	Effect	*Value*	*F*	*Hypothesis df*	*Error df*	*Sig.*
	Pillai's Trace	0.871	30.936	24	1815	***0.00***
	Wilks' Lambda	0.342	32.603	24	1749.49	***0.00***
Religion	Hotelling's Trace	1.353	33.93	24	1805	***0.00***
	Roy's Largest Root	0.793	59.952[c]	8	605	***0.00***

Source: Primary data

*Significant at 5 per cent level

Influence of religion on the financial behaviour of the women entrepreneurs in food processing industrial units was studied using Hotelling' s trace, Pillai's trace, Wilk's Lambda & Roy's Largest root. Table No 4.32 indicates that the test results had value lesser than 0.05 indicating to the fact that all the variables are statistically significant ***(p=0.000< 0.05)*** at 5 per cent level of significance. Hence, null hypothesis is rejected and it can be concluded that there is a significant association between religion and financial behaviour of the respondents. Since the MANOVA test gave result which was found to be significant for all the tests, further follow up trials like test of between subject effects was carried out to measure the association of each of the dependent variables with religion.

Table 4.33 Tests of Between-Subjects Effects Financial Behaviour of Women Entrepreneurs in Food Processing Units and Religion

Source	*Dependent Variable*	*Type I Sum of Squares*	*df*	*Mean Square*	*F*	*Sig.*
	Financial Behaviour Towards Budgeting	3236.39	3	1078.8	41.959	***0.00***
	Financial Behaviour Towards Investments	1358.04	3	452.678	12.263	***0.00***
	Financial Behaviour Towards Financial Planning	3860.67	3	1286.89	11.981	***0.00***
	Financial Behaviour Towards Record Maintenance	1062.55	3	354.182	16.181	***0.00***
Religion	Financial Behaviour Towards Savings	5558.12	3	1852.71	14.748	***0.00***
	Financial Behaviour Towards Borrowals	1180.97	3	393.658	8.297	***0.00***
	Financial Behaviour Towards Utilization of Funds	1868.9	3	622.967	18.247	***0.00***
	Financial Behaviour Towards Spending	5102.68	3	1700.9	58.309	***0.00***

Source: Primary Data

* Significant at 5 per cent level

Table 4.33 shows the results of test of between subject effects of religion with financial behaviour of the women entrepreneurs in food processing industrial units.

When the variables of financial behaviour were taken independently, variation is found to be statistically very significant for all the variables in the test ofbetween subject effects. ***P values are found to be lesser than 0.05*** for the financial behaviour towards budgeting (F= 42.305, p=0.00),financial behaviour towards savings (F= 42.305, p=0.00), financial behaviour towards spending (F= 42.305, p=0.00), financial behaviour towards borrowings (F= 42.305, p=0.00), financial behaviour towards investments (F= 42.305, p=0.00), financial behaviour towards fund utilization (F= 42.305, p=0.00), financial behaviour towards financial planning (F= 42.305, p=0.00), & financial behaviour towards record maintenance (F= 42.305, p=0.00). Hence, it can be concluded that there is a significant relationship between religion and variables of financial behaviour when taken independently also.

Table 4.34 Religion Wise Estimated Marginal Means of Financial Behaviour

Dependent Variable	*Religion*	*Mean*	*Std. Error*	*95 per Cent Confidence Interval*	
				Lower Bound	*Upper Bound*
Financial Behaviour Towards Budgeting	HINDUS	18.609	0.705	17.224	19.994
	CHRISTIAN	22.938	0.579	21.8	24.075
	MUSLIM	12.804	0.753	11.324	14.283
	OTHERS	**28.938**	1.432	26.126	31.749
Financial Behaviour Towards Investments	HINDUS	27.378	0.845	25.718	29.037
	CHRISTIAN	26.539	0.694	25.175	27.902
	MUSLIM	21.224	0.903	19.451	22.996
	OTHERS	**30.539**	1.716	27.17	33.908

Financial Behaviour Towards Financial planning	HINDUS	42.633	1.442	39.802	45.464
	CHRISTIAN	39.577	1.184	37.251	41.903
	MUSLIM	39.019	1.539	35.996	42.042
	OTHERS	**52.577**	2.926	46.83	58.324
Financial Behaviour Towards Record Maintenance	HINDUS	15.893	0.651	14.615	17.172
	CHRISTIAN	15.668	0.535	14.618	16.718
	MUSLIM	14.88	0.695	13.515	16.244
	OTHERS	**21.668**	1.321	19.073	24.262
Financial Behaviour Towards Savings	HINDUS	41.342	1.559	38.28	44.404
	CHRISTIAN	43.142	1.281	40.626	45.657
	MUSLIM	40.963	1.665	37.694	44.233
	OTHERS	**56.142**	3.165	49.926	62.357
Financial Behaviour Towards Borrowals	HINDUS	28.581	0.958	26.7	30.463
	CHRISTIAN	24.999	0.787	23.453	26.545
	MUSLIM	25.18	1.023	23.17	27.189
	OTHERS	**31.999**	1.945	28.179	35.818
Financial Behaviour Towards Utilization of Funds	HINDUS	25.38	0.813	23.784	26.976
	CHRISTIAN	20.027	0.668	18.716	21.339
	MUSLIM	20.576	0.868	18.871	22.28
	OTHERS	**30.027**	1.65	26.787	33.267
Financial Behaviour Towards Spendings	HINDUS	35.96	0.751	34.485	37.436
	CHRISTIAN	31.875	0.617	30.662	33.087
	MUSLIM	27.5	0.802	25.925	29.076
	OTHERS	**38.875**	1.525	35.88	41.869

Source: Primary Data

Table 4.34 exhibits Religion wise Estimated Marginal Means of the women entrepreneurs in food processing industries indicating that financial behaviour is seen to be more strategic among the religious communities other than Hindus, Christian and Muslims. Thus, it can be arrived at a conclusion that the financial behaviour of the women entrepreneurs in food processing industries differ according to their religion when taken independently and when they are taken together.

H_0 3-3: There is no significant relationship between marital status and financial behaviour of the respondents.

During this investigation marital status of the women entrepreneur is considered as an Independent Variable while financial behaviour towards borrowings, financial behaviour towards savings, financial behaviour towards investments, financial behaviour towards spendings, financial behaviour towards utilization of funds, financial behaviour towards financial planning, financial behaviour towards budgeting, and financial behaviour towards record maintenance were considered as dependent variables.

Table 4.35 MANOVA- Financial Behaviour of Women Entrepreneurs in food processing units

	Effect	*Value*	*F*	*Hypothesis df*	*Error df*	*Sig.*
Marital status	Pillai's Trace	0.621	33.978	16	1208	***0.00***
	Wilks' Lambda	0.43	39.614[b]	16	1206	***0.00***
	Hotelling's Trace	1.21	45.526	16	1204	***0.00***
	Roy's Largest Root	1.104	83.329[c]	8	604	***0.00***

Source: Primary data

*Significant at 5 per cent level

MANOVA was used to test the impact of marital status on the financial behaviour of the women respondents using Hotelling's trace test, Wilk's Lambda test , Pillais trace test, & Roy's Largest root . Table No 4.35 elucidates that P values of all the test statistics had value lesser than 0.05 which indicates to the fact that all the variables are statistically noteworthy ***(p=0.000< 0.05)*** at 5 per cent level of significance. Hence, null hypothesis is rejected and it can be concluded that there is a significant association between marital status and financial behaviour of the respondents. Subsequently,

Table 4.36 indicates the result of test of between subject effects which was carried out to measure the association of marital status on the financial behaviour variables of the women entrepreneurs engaged in food processing industrial units.

Table 4.36 Tests of Between-Subjects Effects Financial Behaviour of Women Entrepreneurs In Food Processing Units

Source	*Dependent Variable*	*Type I Sum of Squares*	*df*	*Mean Square*	*F*	*Sig.*
Marital Status	Financial Behaviour Towards Budgeting	713.642	2	356.821	13.878	***0.00***
	Financial Behaviour Towards Investments	2014.65	2	1007.33	27.288	***0.00***
	Financial Behaviour Towards Financial Planning	72.579	2	36.29	0.338	0.713
	Financial Behaviour Towards Record Maintenance	47.192	2	23.596	1.078	0.341
	Financial Behaviour Towards Savings	618.197	2	309.099	2.46	0.086
	Financial Behaviour Towards Borrowals	1353.06	2	676.532	14.259	***0.00***
	Financial Behaviour Towards Utilization of Funds	2067.76	2	1033.88	30.283	***0.00***
	Financial Behaviour Towards Spendings	426.346	2	213.173	7.308	***0.001***

Source: Primary data

*Significant at 5 per cent level

Table 4.37 depicts that Financial behaviour towards budgeting (F= 13.878, p=0.00), financial behaviour towards spending (F= 7.308, p=0.001), financial behaviour towardsborrowing (F= 14.259, p=0.000),financial behaviour towards investments (F= 27.288, p=0.00), and financial behaviour towards fund utilization (F= 30.283, p=0.00) were found to possess significant relationship with marital status of the women entrepreneurs involved in food processing industrial units at 5 per cent level of significance since, p value was found to be less than 0.05. Financial behaviour towards financial planning, financial behaviour towards record maintenance & financial behaviour towards savings were found not to have a significant relationship with marital status of the respondent.

Table 4.37 Marital Status Wise Estimated Marginal Means of Financial Behaviour

Dependent Variable	*Religion*	*Mean*	*Std. Error*	*95 per Cent Confidence Interval*	
				Lower Bound	*Upper Bound*
Financial Behaviour Towards Budgeting	Married	**23.365**	0.554	22.278	24.453
	Single	23.624	0.672	22.305	24.943
	Separated	15.476	1.249	13.024	17.928
Financial Behaviour Towards Investments	Married	**29.426**	0.664	28.122	30.729
	Single	24.799	0.805	23.219	26.38
	Separated	25.034	1.496	22.096	27.972
Financial Behaviour Towards Financial Planning	Married	42.865	1.132	40.641	45.089
	Single	42.292	1.373	39.595	44.988
	Separated	**45.198**	2.552	40.187	50.209
Financial Behaviour Towards Record Maintenance	Married	16.346	0.511	15.342	17.35
	Single	16.566	0.62	15.349	17.783
	Separated	**18.169**	1.152	15.907	20.432
Financial Behaviour Towards Savings	Married	45.536	1.225	43.131	47.941
	Single	42.595	1.485	39.679	45.511
	Separated	**48.06**	2.76	42.64	53.48

Financial Behaviour Towards Borrowals	Married	27.977	0.753	26.499	29.455
	Single	23.613	0.912	21.821	25.405
	Separated	**31.479**	1.696	28.149	34.81
Financial Behaviour Towards Utilization of Funds	Married	25.084	0.638	23.831	26.338
	Single	19.647	0.774	18.127	21.167
	Separated	**27.276**	1.439	24.451	30.102
Financial Behaviour Towards Spendings	Married	33.338	0.59	32.179	34.497
	Single	30.987	0.715	29.582	32.392
	Separated	**36.332**	1.33	33.72	38.943

Source: Primary data

Table 4.37 reveals about marital status wise estimated marginal means of the respondents which indicates that respondents who live separated are found to exhibit higher mean scores of interconnection with financial behaviour except in the case of married respondents who exhibit higher mean scores in the case of financial behaviour towards budgeting **(Mean=23.365)** and financial behaviour towards investments **(Mean=29.426)**. Thus we can say that, financial behaviour of the respondents differ according to their marital status when they are taken collectively and when they are taken independently.

4.7 Effect of Financial Knowledge On Borrowing Decisions

H_0 5. There is no significant effect of financial knowledge on borrowing decisions of women entrepreneurs managing food processing industrial units.

Table 4.38 Model Summary

Model	*R*	*R Square*	*Adjusted R Square*	*Std. Error of the Estimate*
1	.291[a]	.085	.083	7.48322

a. Predictors: (Constant), Knowledge About Financial Concepts

Source: Primary data

Table 4.38 shows the Model summary for impact of financial knowledge on borrowing decisions of women entrepreneurs managing food processing industrial units. R-square is 0.085 demonstrating that 8.5 per cent of the difference is accounted to the combined linear impact of the variables which were independent. Adjusted square value is 0.083, inferring that the model has 8.3 per cent of the fluctuation of the criterion variable.

Table 4.39 ANOVA[a]

Model		Sum of Squares	Df	Mean Square	F	Sig.
	Regression	3196.705	1	3196.705	57.085	*.000[b]*
1	Residual	34607.166	618	55.999		
	Total	37803.871	619			

a. Dependent Variable: Financial Behaviour Towards Borrowals

b. Predictors: (Constant), Knowledge About Financial Concepts

Source: Primary data

*Significant at 5 per cent level

The above table 4.39 shows the ANOVA of financial knowledge on borrowing decisions. The significant value for the above test was found to be less than 0.05. Hence, the null hypothesis is rejected and it is concluded that there is a significant effect of financial knowledge on borrowing decisions.

Table 4.40 Coefficients[a]

Model		Unstandardized Coefficients		Standardized Coefficients	t	Sig.
		B	Std. Error	Beta		
	(Constant)		16.271	1.087	14.973	*0.00*
1	Knowledge About Financial Concepts	0.44	0.058	0.291	7.555	*0.00*

a. Dependent Variable: Financial Behaviour Towards Borrowals

Source: Primary data, *Significant at 5 per cent level

From the Table 4.38, it can be seen that the regression showed 8.5 per cent explanation is given by the differences in financial knowledge and that this explanation of the regression is statistically valid, as the associated value (**57.085**) is statistically significant as it can be seen in Table 4.39. Table 4.40 shows that the coefficient of Knowledge about Financial Concepts is found to be significant, as the t values of the beta coefficient is significant (**observed p<0.05**). Therefore, we can say that financial knowledge of women entrepreneurs managing food processing industrial units influence the borrowing decisions of the entrepreneur.

4.8 Impact of Financial Knowledge on Investment Decisions

H_0 4. There is no significant effect of financial knowledge on investment decisions of women entrepreneurs managing food processing industrial units.

Surplus funds earned from the business has to be invested properly. If investment decisions are not wise, then that will affect the prosperity of the business. Investment will create wealth and value to the organization. To evaluate the effect of financial knowledge on the investment decisions of an entrepreneur, Regression model was used. Results of the regression analysis is given through the tables below:

Table 4.41 Model Summary

Model	*R*	*R Square*	*Adjusted R Square*	*Std. Error of the Estimate*
1	.180[a]	.032	.031	7.09337

a. Predictors: (Constant), Knowledge About Financial Concepts
Source: Primary data

Table 4.41 shows the Model summary for impact of financial knowledge on investment decisions of women entrepreneurs managing food processing industrial units. R=0.180 indicates that there is a weak relationship. R-square is 0.032 indicating that 3.2 per cent of the variation is accounted to the combined linear impact of the independent variables. Adjusted square value is 0.031 implying that the model has 3.1 per cent of the variance in the criterion variable.

Table 4.42 ANOVA[a]

Model		*Sum of Squares*	*df*	*Mean Square*	*F*	*Sig.*
	Regression	1041.553	1	1041.553	20.700	*.000*[b]
1	Residual	31095.221	618	50.316		
	Total	32136.774	619			

A. Dependent Variable: Financial Behaviour Towards Investments

B. Predictors: (Constant), Knowledge About Financial Concepts

Source: Primary data

*Significant at 5 per cent level

The above table 4.42 shows the ANOVA of financial knowledge on investment decisions. The significant value for the above test was found to be less than 0.05. Hence, the null hypothesis is rejected and it is concluded that there is a significant effect of financial knowledge on investment decisions.

Table 4.43 Coefficients[a]

Model		*Unstandardized Coefficients*		*Standardized Coefficients*	*t*	*Sig.*
		B	*Std. Error*	*Beta*		
	(Constant)	20.690	1.030		20.085	*.000*
1	Knowledge About Financial Concepts	.251	.055	.180	4.550	*.000*

a. Dependent Variable: Financial Behaviour Towards Investments
Source: Primary data
*Significant at 5 per cent level

From the Table 4.41, it can be seen that the regression

showed 3.2 per cent explanation of the differences in financial knowledge and that this explanation of the regression is statistically valid, as the associated value (**20.700**) is statistically significant as it is seen in Table 4.42. It can be observed in Table 4.43 that the beta coefficient of Knowledge About Financial Concepts is found to be significant, as the t values of the beta coefficient is significant (**observed p<0.05**). Therefore, we can say that financial knowledge of women entrepreneurs managing food processing industrial units influence the investment decisions of the entrepreneur.

4.9 Fund utilization

$H_0$6. There is no significant difference in the utilization of funds among women entrepreneurs according to the nature of activities undertaken in the food processing industrial units.

Appropriate use and timely utilization of assets facilitates operational proficiency of the business concern. When the use of funds and timely utilization of assets are in order, wealth of the business will increase and cost related to management of the firm will come down. Hence, fund utilization in the organization was analyzed to know if funds are utilized properly.

Table 4.44 Ranks – Fund Utilization

	Mean Rank
Purchase of fixed asset	4.29
Invested in current assets	5.00
Business Expansion	4.58
Business modernization	4.39
Paying off the expenses	4.74
Paying off the liabilities	4.50
Dividend payment	**4.13**
Maintained as reserves	4.37

Source : Primary data

Table 4.44 provides the mean ranks obtained for the fund utilization by women entrepreneurs engaged in food processing industrial units of Kerala. Lower the mean ranks, higher will be the preference. Therefore, rank one should have the lowest mean. Thus from the table, it is evident that "dividend payment" is the most utilized financial activity in a business. **(Mean rank 4.13)** followed by "purchase of fixed assets" and "maintained as reserves" with mean ranks of **4.29** and **4.37** respectively. Also the least preferred activity for fund utilization is "investment in current assets".

Table 4.45 Test Statistics[a]

N	620
Chi-Square	54.376
Df	7
Asymp. Sig.	*.000*

a. Friedman Test

Source: Primary data

*Significant at 5 per cent level

Table 4.45 shows that the Chi-square statistic had the value of **54.376** which is significant at 5 per cent level ***($p < 0.05$)*** . Hence, null hypothesis is rejected and it may be concluded that there is significant difference in utilizing funds among the women entrepreneurs engaged in food processing industrial units in Kerala.

4.9.1 Relationship of dividend payment with type of industry

Table 4.46 Ranks

	Type of industries	*N*	*Mean Rank*	*Sum of Ranks*
Dividend payment	Registered	320	345.50	110560.00
	Unregistered	300	**273.17**	81950.00
	Total	620		

Source : Primary data

Lowest mean values denote highest preference for Mann Whitney U test. Table 4.46 indicate that the food industries engaged in food processing industrial units which are unregistered (**Mean rank 273.17)** are utilizing finance mostly for dividend payment when compared to registered food processing industrial units (**Mean rank 345.50)** .

Table 4.47 Test Statistics[a]

	Dividend payment
Mann-Whitney U	36800.000
Wilcoxon W	81950.000
Z	-5.314
Asymp. Sig. (2-tailed)	***.000***

a. Grouping Variable: Type of industries

Source: Primary data

*Significant at 5 per cent level

Table 4.47 reveals that **P** value was found to be less than **0.05** per cent indicating that there is significant difference in fund utilization according to the type of industry.

4.9.2 Relationship of dividend payment with nature of activities undertaken.

Table 4.48 Ranks

	Types of food industries	*N*	*Mean Rank*
	Processing	160	271.75
	Conversion	100	368.50
Dividend	Preparation	200	308.50
payment	Preservation	80	208.00
	Packaging	80	423.00
	Total	620	

Source: Primary data

*Significant at 5 per cent level

Lowest mean values denotes highest preference for Kruskal Wallis test. Table 4.48 indicates that the food industries engaged in preservation activities (**Mean rank 208.00**) are utilizing finance mostly for "**dividend payment**" followed by food industrial units engaged in "processing" (**Mean rank 271.75**) .

Table 4.49 Test Statistics[a,b]

	Dividend payment
Chi-Square	84.710
Df	4
Asymp. Sig.	*.000*

a. Kruskal Wallis Test

b. Grouping Variable: Types of food industries

Source: Primary data

*Significant at 5 per cent level

It can be seen in Table 4.49 that Chi square value obtained is **84.710** with 4 degrees of freedom, and was seen to be significant at 5 per cent level **(observed $p<0.05$)**. This shows that there is significant difference in the preference of fund utilization according to the nature of activities being undertaken in food processing industrial units.

4.10 Problems in managing the finance

Table 4.50 Friedman test

	Mean Rank
Managing cash flows of the organization	2.71
Maintaining bank accounts	3.39
Documentation of expenses and incomes	3.87
Unable to record financial transactions properly	4.58
Accessing the sources of funds	5.13
Lack of financial knowledge	5.48
Difficulty in reconciling bank and cash statements	6.19
Pressure from spouse and children	6.71
Financial insecurity	6.94

Source : Primary data

Mean rank values of the problems in managing finance of the organization was depicted in Table 4.50. It provides the mean ranks obtained for the problems in managing the finances by women entrepreneurs in food processing industrial units. Lower the mean ranks, higher will be the preference. Therefore, rank one should have the lowest mean.

Thus from the table, it is evident that "**managing cash flows of the organization**" is the most important problem in managing the finances. **(Mean rank 2.71)** followed by "Maintaining bank accounts" and "Documentation of expenses and incomes" with mean ranks of **3.39** and **3.87** respectively. Also the least important problem in managing finances is " **financial insecurity**".

Table 4.51 Test Statistics[a]

N	620
Chi-Square	**1458.409**
Df	7
Asymp. Sig.	***.000***

a. Friedman Test

Source: Primary data

*Significant at 5 per cent level

It is seen In Table 4.51 that Chi-square statistic had the value of **1458.409** which is significant at 5 per cent level **(observed p< 0.05)** . It may be concluded that there is significant difference among the women entrepreneurs with respect to the problems in managing finances.

4.10.1 Relationship of managing cash flow of the organization with type of industry

Table 4.52 Mean Ranks

	Type of industries	*N*	*Mean Rank*	*Sum of Ranks*
Managing cash flows of the organization	Registered	320	314.88	100760.00
	Unregistered	300	305.83	91750.00
	Total	620		

Source : Primary data

Managing cash flows can determine the success of a firm. If cash is not properly managed, it can be detrimental for the firm within a short span of time.

Lowest mean values denote highest preference for Mann Whitney U test. Table 4.52 indicates that food processing industrial units which are unregistered (**Mean rank 305.83)** are facing the highest difficulty in managing cash flows followed by food industrial units which are registered (**Mean rank 314.88)** .

Table 4.53 Test Statistics[a]

	managing cash flows of the organization
Mann-Whitney U	46600.000
Wilcoxon W	91750.000
Z	-.788
Asymp. Sig. (2-tailed)	***.431***

a. Grouping Variable: Type of industries
Source: Primary data
*Significant at 5 per cent level

Table 4.53 shows that ***P value was found to be more than 0.05 per cent*** indicating that there is no significant difference in managing the cash flows according to the nature of activities being undertaken in food processing industrial units.

4.10.2 Relationship of Managing Cash Flow of The Organization With Nature of Activities Undertaken

Table 4.54 Kruskal Wallis Test Mean Ranks

	Types of food industries	*N*	*Mean Rank*
	Processing	160	291.75
	Conversion	100	356.50
Managing cash flows of the organization	Preparation	200	**246.50**
	Preservation	80	390.50
	Packaging	80	370.50
	Total	620	

Source : Primary data

Lowest mean value denotes highest preference for Kruskal Wallis test. Table 4.54 point out that the food industries engaged in Preparation activities (**Mean rank 246.50**) are facing the highest difficulty in managing cash flows followed by food industrial units engaged in "processing" (**Mean rank 291.75**) .

Table 4.55 Test Statistics[a,b]

	Managing Cash Flows of the Organization
Chi-Square	92.617
Df	4
Asymp. Sig.	*.000*

a. Kruskal Wallis Test

b. Grouping Variable: Types of food industries

Source: Primary data

*Significant at 5 per cent level

Table 4.55 reveals that the Chi square value obtained is **92.617** with 4 degrees of freedom, and was seen to be significant at 5 per cent level **(p value is less than 0.05).** This shows that there is significant difference in the problems according to the nature of activities being undertaken in food processing industrial units.

4.11 Relationship Between Financial Knowledge and Nature of Food Processing Activity Undertaken

Financial knowledge is an important determinant of the financial literacy of a person. An attempt was made to know whether financial knowledge of women entrepreneurs managing food industries is seen to vary with the nature of food processing activities carried down by them.

4.11.1 Knowledge about Financial Products

Knowledge about Financial Products is an important factor which decides the choice of the most suitable product by the entrepreneur according to the needs of the business. Relation between Knowledge of financial products and nature of food processing activity was evaluated using Kruskal Wallis test.

Table 4.56 Kruskal Wallis test – Mean ranks

	Types of food industries	*N*	*Mean Rank*
Knowledge About Financial Products	Processing	160	326.75
	Conversion	100	404.50
	Preparation	200	**197.50**
	Preservation	80	368.00
	Packaging	80	385.50
	Total	620	

Source: Primary data

Table 4.56 depicts that the women entrepreneurs managing food industries involved in preparation activities **(Mean rank 197.50)** is having the highest knowledge level about financial products followed by women entrepreneurs managing food industries involved in processing activities **(Mean rank 326.75)** .

Table No. 4.57 Test Statistics

	Knowledge about Financial Products
Chi-Square	131.226
Df	4
Asymp. Sig.	***.000***

a. Kruskal Wallis Test

b.b. Grouping Variable: Types of food industries

Source: Primary data

*Significant at 5 per cent level

Table No. 4.57 shows that Chi square value obtained for Knowledge about Financial Products is **131.226** with 4 degrees of freedom, and was seen to be significant at 5 per cent level **(p value is less than 0.05)** . This shows that there is significant difference in the knowledge level of financial products according to the nature of activities being undertaken in food processing industrial units.

4.11.2 Knowledge about Financial Services

Knowledge about Financial Services is an important factor which decides the choice of the most suitable financial service according to the needs of the business. Relationship of knowledge about financial service and nature of food processing activity was evaluated using Kruskal Wallis test.

Table 4.58 Kruskal Wallis test – Mean ranks

	Types of food industries	*N*	*Mean Rank*
Knowledge About Financial Services	Processing	160	281.75
	Conversion	100	364.50
	Preparation	200	299.50
	Preservation	80	350.50
	Packaging	80	288.00
	Total	620	

Source: Primary data

Table 4.58 shows that Knowledge level about financial services is the highest for women entrepreneurs managing food industries involved in processing activities (**Mean rank 281.75**) followed by women entrepreneurs managing food industries involved in packaging **(Mean rank 288.00)**.

Table 4.59 Test Statistics

	Knowledge about Financial Services
Chi-Square	19.256
Df	4
Asymp. Sig.	*.001*

c. Kruskal Wallis Test

d. b. Grouping Variable: Types of food industries

Source: Primary data

*Significant at 5 per cent level

Table 4.59 depicts Chi square value obtained for Knowledge about Financial Services is **19.256** with 4 degrees of freedom, and was seen to be significant at 5 per cent level **(p value is less than 0.05).** This shows that there is significant difference in the knowledge level of financial services according to the nature of activities being undertaken in food processing industrial units.

4.11.3 Knowledge About Financial Terms

A person who has knowledge about the terms commonly used in business will be able to identify and keep a track of the happenings related to the business.

Table 4.60 Kruskal Wallis test – Mean ranks

	Types of food industries	*N*	*Mean Rank*
	Processing	160	353.00
	Conversion	100	384.50
Knowledge About	Preparation	200	243.50
Financial Terms	Preservation	80	275.50
	Packaging	80	335.50
	Total	620	

Source: Primary data

*Significant at 5 per cent level

Table 4.60 reveals Knowledge level about financial terms is the highest for women entrepreneurs managing food industries involved in preparation activities (**Mean rank 243.50)** followed by women entrepreneurs managing food industries involved in preservation (**Mean rank 275.50)** .

Table 4.61 Test statisctics

	Knowledge About Financial Terms
Chi-Square	58.908
Df	4
Asymp. Sig.	***.000***

e. Kruskal Wallis Test

f. b. Grouping Variable: Types of food industries

Source: Primary data

*Significant at 5 per cent level

Table 4.61 shows that Chi square value obtained for Knowledge about Financial terms is **58.908** with 4 degrees of freedom, and was seen to be significant at 5 per cent level **(p value is less than 0.05).** This shows that there is significant difference in the knowledge level of financial terms according to the nature of activities being undertaken in food processing industrial unit.

4.11.4 Knowledge About Financial Concepts

Managing a business has to be carried out according to the general principles being followed globally. General principles to be followed in business is termed as financial concepts.

Table No. 4.62 Kruskal Wallis test – Mean ranks

	Types of food industries	*N*	*Mean Rank*
	Processing	160	316.75
Knowledge About	Conversion	100	356.50
Financial Concepts	Preparation	200	255.50
	Preservation	80	368.00
	Packaging	80	320.50
	Total	620	

Source: Primary data
*Significant at 5 per cent level

Table 4.62 reveals that Knowledge level about financial concepts is the highest for women entrepreneurs managing food industries involved in preparation activities **(Mean rank 255.50)** followed by women entrepreneurs managing food industries involved in processing **(Mean rank 316.75)** .

Table 4.63 Test statistics

	Knowledge About Financial Concepts
Chi-Square	34.431
Df	4
Asymp. Sig.	***.000***

g. Kruskal Wallis Test
h. b. Grouping Variable: Types of food industries
Source: Primary data
*Significant at 5 per cent level

Table 4.63 reveals the value obtained for Knowledge about Financial Concepts is **34.431** with 4 df, and was seen to be significant at 5 per cent level **(p value is less than 0.05)** . This shows that there is significant difference in the knowledge level of financial concepts according to the nature of activities being undertaken in food processing industrial units.

4.12 Relationship Between Financial Attitude and Nature of Food Processing Activity Undertaken

4.12.1 Financial Attitude Towards Budgeting and Nature of Food Processing Activity

Table 4.64 Kruskal Wallis Test - Mean Ranks

	Types of food industries	*N*	*Mean Rank*
	Processing	160	271.75
Financial	Conversion	100	386.50
Attitude	Preparation	200	250.50
Towards	Preservation	80	375.50
Budgeting	Packaging	80	378.00
	Total	620	

Source: Primary data

Lowest mean values denotes highest preference according to Kruskal Wallis test. It can be seen in table No. 4.64 that the women entrepreneurs managing food industries involved in Preparation activities (**Mean rank 250.50)** are having the most favourable attitude towards budgeting followed by women entrepreneurs managing food industries involved in processing activities (**Mean rank 271.75**)

Table 4.65 Test statistics

	Attitude towards Budgeting
Chi-Square	70.195
Df	4
Asymp. Sig.	***.000***

i. Kruskal Wallis Test

j. b. Grouping Variable: Types of food industries

Source: Primary data

*Significant at 5 per cent level

Table 4.65 reveals that the Chi square value obtained for the attitude towards budgeting is **70.195** with 4 degrees of freedom, and was seen to be significant at 5 per cent level **(p value is less than 0.05).** This shows that there is significant difference in the attitude of women entrepreneurs managing food industries in Kerala towards budgeting according to the nature of activities being undertaken in food processing industrial units.

4.12.2 Financial Attitude Towards Investment and Nature of Food Processing Activity

Investments ensures long-term financial security now and for the future. The money produced from investments is the reason for the financial security and income. Attempt was made to check whether financial attitude towards budgeting and nature of food processing activity has a connection.

Table 4.66 Kruskal Wallis Test - Mean Ranks

	Types of food industries	*N*	*Mean Rank*
	Processing	160	295.50
Financial Attitude	Conversion	100	408.50
Towards Investment	Preparation	200	**263.50**
	Preservation	80	288.00
	Packaging	80	358.00
	Total	620	

Source: Primary data

Table 4.66 indicates that the attitude towards investment is the most favouarable for women entrepreneurs managing food industries involved in Preparation activities (**Mean rank 263.50**) followed by women entrepreneurs managing food industries involved in preservation (**Mean rank 288.00**)

Table 4.67 Test statistics

	Attitude towards Investments
Chi-Square	51.850
Df	4
Asymp. Sig.	*.000*

k. Kruskal Wallis Test

l. b. Grouping Variable: Types of food industries

Source: Primary data

*Significant at 5 per cent level

Table 4.67 elucidates that the Chi square value obtained for attitude towards investment is **51.850** with 4 degrees of freedom, and was seen to be significant at 5 per cent level **(p value is less than 0.05)**.This shows that there is significant difference in the attitude towards investment among the women entrepreneurs managing food industries in Kerala according to the nature of activities being undertaken in food processing industrial units.

4.12.3 Financial Attitude Towards Financial Planning and Nature of Food Processing Activity

In order to achieve financial well being in the long run, entrepreneurs have to plan their actions well on time to avoid wastages and to increase the savings. Attempt was made to check whether Financial Attitude Towards Financial Planning and nature of food processing activity has a connection.

Table 4.68 Kruskal Wallis Test - Mean Ranks

	Nature of food industries	*N*	*Mean Rank*
	Processing	160	340.50
Financial Attitude	Conversion	100	356.50
Towards	Preparation	200	**239.50**
Financial Planning	Preservation	80	380.50
	Packaging	80	300.50
	Total	620	

Source: Primary data

According to Table 4.68 , Attitude towards financial planning is the most favourable for women entrepreneurs managing food industries involved in Preparation activities (**Mean rank 239.50**) followed by women entrepreneurs managing food industries involved in preservation (**Mean rank 300.50**) .

Table 4.69 Test statistics

	Attitude towards financial planning
Chi-Square	55.174
Df	4
Asymp. Sig.	***.000***

m. Kruskal Wallis Test

n. b. Grouping Variable: Types of food industries

*Significant at 5 per cent level

Table 4.69 depicts the Chi square value obtained for attitude towards financial planning is **55.174** with 4 degrees of freedom, and was seen to be significant at 5 per cent level **(p value is less than 0.05).** This shows that there is significant difference in the attitude towards financial planning among the women entrepreneurs managing food industries in Kerala according to the nature of activities being undertaken in food processing industrial units.

4.12.4 Financial Attitude Towards Record Maintenance And Nature of Food Processing Activity

Proper financial documentation is required for smooth management of the business. Mismanagement of funds could be traced with evidence from your organization's income and expenses.

Table 4.70 Kruskal Wallis Test - Mean Ranks

	Types of food industries	*N*	*Mean Rank*
	Processing	160	343.00
Financial Attitude	Conversion	100	364.50
Towards Record	Preparation	200	235.50
Maintenance	Preservation	80	358.00
	Packaging	80	318.00
	Total	620	

Source: Primary data

As per Table 4.70, attitude towards financial record maintenance is the most favourable for women entrepreneurs managing food industries involved in Preparation activities (**Mean rank 235.50**) followed by women entrepreneurs managing food industries involved in preservation (**Mean rank 318.00**).

Table 4.71 Test statistics

	Attitude towards record maintenance
Chi-Square	**55.174**
Df	4
Asymp. Sig.	***.000***

o. Kruskal Wallis Test b. Grouping Variable: Types of food industries

Source: Primay data, *Significant at 5 per cent level

Table 4.71 gives Chi square value obtained for attitude towards financial record maintenance is **55.174** with 4 degrees of freedom, and was seen to be significant at 5 per cent level **(P value is less than 0.05).** This shows that there is significant difference in the Attitude towards financial record maintenance among the women entrepreneurs managing food industries in Kerala according to the nature of activities being undertaken in food processing units.

4.12.5 Financial Attitude Towards Savings and Nature of Food Processing Activity

Savings are a necessity for replacing the assets of the business and can help save the money of the business owner in the long term. It can give the funds to meet the emergencies in case of financial crunches. Proper attitude of the entrepreneur can help save funds for the business.

Table 4.72 Kruskal Wallis Test - Mean Ranks

	Types of food industries	*N*	*Mean Rank*
	Processing	160	354.25
	Conversion	100	346.50
Financial Attitude	Preparation	200	266.50
Towards Savings	Preservation	80	275.50
	Packaging	80	323.00
	Total	620	

Source: Primary data

Table 4.72 shows that attitude towards financial savings is the most suitable for women entrepreneurs managing food industries involved in Preparation activities (**Mean rank 266.50**) followed by women entrepreneurs managing food industries involved in preservation (**Mean rank 275.50**) .

Table 4.73 Test statistics

	Attitude Towards Financial Savings
Chi-Square	29.209
Df	4
Asymp. Sig.	*.000*

p. Kruskal Wallis Test
q. b. Grouping Variable: Types of food industries
Source: Primary data
*Significant at 5 per cent level

Table 4.73 indicates that the Chi square value for the attitude towards financial savings is **29.209** with 4 degrees of freedom, and was seen to be significant at 5 per cent level **(p value is less than 0.05).** This shows that there is significant difference in the attitude towards financial savings among the women entrepreneurs managing food industries in Kerala according to the nature of activities being undertaken in food processing industrial units.

4.12.6 Financial Attitude Towards Borrowings and Nature of Food Processing Activity

Proper flow of money into and out of the business will promote or slow down the business. Borrowings will ensure adequate fund flow into the business without liquidity crunch.

Table 4.74 Kruskal Wallis Test - Mean Ranks

	Types of food industries	*N*	*Mean Rank*
	Processing	160	354.25
Financial Attitude	Conversion	100	346.50
Towards Savings	Preparation	200	**266.50**
	Preservation	80	275.50
	Packaging	80	323.00
	Total	620	

Source: Primary data

According to Table 4.74, Attitude towards financial borrowings is the most favourable for women entrepreneurs managing food industries involved in preservation activities (**Mean rank 290.50**) followed by women entrepreneurs managing food industries involved in packaging (**Mean rank 293.00**) .

Table 4.75 Test statistics

	Attitude towards borrowings
Chi-Square	5.761
Df	4
Asymp. Sig.	*.000*

r. Kruskal Wallis Test

s. b. Grouping Variable: Types of food industries

Source: Primary data

*Significant at 5 per cent level

Table 4.75 gives Chi square value for attitude towards financial borrowings as **5.761** at 4 degrees of freedom **(p=0.218)** and was seen to be insignificant at 5 per cent level **(P value is more than 0.05)** . This shows that there is no significant difference in the attitude towards financial borrowings among the women entrepreneurs managing food industries in Kerala according to the nature of activities being undertaken in food processing industrial units.

4. 12.7 Financial Attitude Towards Utilization of Funds and Nature of Food Processing Activity

Prudent decisions related to funding strategies and cash flow should be managed to ensure that Funds are utilized in an optimal manner

Table 4.76 Kruskal Wallis Test - Mean Ranks

	Types of food industries	*N*	*Mean Rank*
	Processing	160	330.25
Financial Attitude	Conversion	100	318.20
Towards Utilization	Preparation	200	291.85
of Funds	Preservation	80	**268.00**
	Packaging	80	350.50
	Total	620	

Source: Primary data

According to Table 4.76, Attitude towards utilization of funds is the most favourable for women entrepreneurs managing food industries involved in preservation activities (**Mean rank 268.00**) followed by women entrepreneurs managing food industries involved in Preparation (**Mean rank 291.85**).

Table 4.77 Test statistics

	Attitude towards utilization of funds
.Chi-Square	12.867
Df	4
Asymp. Sig.	***.000***

t. Kruskal Wallis Test

u. b. Grouping Variable: Types of food industries

Source: Primary data

*Significant at 5 per cent level

As per Table 4.77, Chi square value for attitude towards utilization of funds is **12.867** with 4 degrees of freedom **(p=0.012)** and was seen to be significant at 5 per cent level **(P value is less than 0.05)**. This shows that there is significant difference in the attitude towards utilization of funds among the women entrepreneurs managing food industries in Kerala according to the nature of activities being undertaken in food processing industrial units.

4.12.8 Financial Attitude Towards Spendings and Nature of Food Processing Activity

Spendings by the business owner takes out fund for meeting the expenditures of the business. If sufficient care is not taken with regard to the expenditures, it will wash off the liquidity from the business.

Table 4.78 Kruskal Wallis Test - Mean Ranks

	Types of food industries	*N*	*Mean Rank*
	Processing	160	313.00
	Conversion	100	366.50
Financial Attitude	Preparation	200	296.50
Towards Spendings	Preservation	80	363.00
	Packaging	80	**218.00**
	Total	620	

Source: Primary data

Table 4.78 shows attitude towards spendings as the most favourable for women entrepreneurs managing food industries involved in packaging activities (**Mean rank 218.00**) followed by women entrepreneurs managing food industries involved in Preparation (**Mean rank 296.50**).

Table 4.79 Test statistics

	Attitude towards Spendings
Chi-Square	39.489
Df	4
Asymp. Sig.	***.000***

v. Kruskal Wallis Test

w. b. Grouping Variable: Types of food industries

Source: Primary data

*Significant at 5 per cent level

Table 4.79 gives Chi-square value for attitude towards spending of funds is **39.489** with 4 degrees of freedom **(p=0.000)** and was seen to be significant at 5 per cent level **(p value is less than 0.05).** This shows that there is significant difference in the attitude towards spending of funds among the women entrepreneurs managing food industries in Kerala according to the nature of activities being undertaken in food processing industrial units.

4.13 Relationship Between Financial Behaviour and Nature of Food Processing Activity Undertaken

Financial behavior can be said as any type of human behavior that is related to money management. Good financial behavior can lead to the success of a household, an individual , society, nation and the world at large. Therefore, an attempt was made to study about the relationship between financial behaviour and nature of food processing activity being undertaken through Kruskal Wallis test.

4.13.1 Financial Behaviour Towards Budgeting and Nature of Food Processing Activity

Budgeting is an activity which helps to balance the expenses with income of a business. Attempt was made to check whether financial behaviour towards budgeting and nature of food processing activity has a relation.

Table 4.80 Kruskal Wallis Test - Mean Ranks

	Types of food industries	*N*	*Mean Rank*
	Processing	160	306.75
	Conversion	100	394.50
Financial Behaviour	Preparation	200	300.50
Towards Budgeting	Preservation	80	298.00
	Packaging	80	**250.50**
	Total	620	

Source: Primary data

Lowest mean values denotes highest preference according to Kruskal Wallis test. From Table 4.80, it can be understood that the women entrepreneurs managing food industries involved in packaging activities **(Mean rank 250.50)** are having the most favourable behaviour towards budgeting followed by women entrepreneurs managing food industries involved in preservation activities **(Mean rank 298.00)** .

Table 4.81 Test statistics Behaviour towards Budgeting

Chi-Square	32.437
Df	4
Asymp. Sig.	*.000*

x. Kruskal Wallis Test

y. b. Grouping Variable: Types of food industries

Source: Primary data

*Significant at 5 per cent level

Table 4.81 indicates that the Chi square value obtained for the behaviour towards budgeting is **32.437** with 4 degrees of freedom **(p=0.000)**, and was seen to be significant at 5 per cent level **(P value is less than 0.05)**. This shows that there is significant difference in the behaviour of women entrepreneurs managing food industries in Kerala towards budgeting according to the nature of activities being undertaken in food processing industrial units.

4.13.2 Financial Behaviour Towards Investment and Nature of Food Processing Activity

Ways and means of proper investing of funds decide the growth of funds invested. Proper behaviour of investing at the right place can be decisive about the success of the establishment. An attempt was made to evaluate about the relationship between the behaviour towards investment and nature of food processing activity using Kruskal Wallis method.

Table 4.82 Kruskal Wallis Test - Mean Ranks

	Types of food industries	*N*	*Mean Rank*
Financial Behaviour Towards Investments	Processing	160	300.50
	Conversion	100	302.50
	Preparation	200	294.50
	Preservation	80	353.00
	Packaging	80	338.00
	Total	620	

Source: Primary data

According to Table 4.82, Most suitable behavior towards investment was found among women entrepreneurs managing food industries involved in Preparation activities (**Mean rank 294.50**) followed by women entrepreneurs managing food industries involved in processing (**Mean rank 300.50**) .

Table 4.83 Test statistics

	Behaviour towards Investment
Chi-Square	8.743
Df	4
Asymp. Sig.	*.000*

z. Kruskal Wallis Test

aa. b. Grouping Variable: Types of food industries

Source: Primary data

*Significant at 5 per cent level

Table 4.83 gives Chi square value for behaviour towards investment as **8.743** with 4 degrees of freedom **(p=0.068)** and was seen to be insignificant at 5 per cent level **(P value is more than 0.05).** This shows that there is no significant difference in the behaviour towards investment among the women entrepreneurs managing food industries in Kerala according to the nature of activities being undertaken in food processing industrial units.

4.13.3 Financial Behaviour Towards Financial Planning and Nature of Food Processing Activity

Financial planning helps an entrepreneur to determine the short term and long- term financial aims of the business and he will ensure that a balanced plan is devised to meet those goals. Prudent spending, proper tax planning, and careful budgeting are the end results of financial planning. Having a balanced plan to meet the goals of every business can give positive numbers in the financial statements.

Table 4.84 Kruskal Wallis Test - Mean Ranks

	Types of food industries	*N*	*Mean Rank*
Financial Behaviour Towards Financial Planning	Processing	160	299.25
	Conversion	100	316.50
	Preparation	200	262.50
	Preservation	80	423.00
	Packaging	80	333.00
	Total	620	

Source: Primary data

According to Table 4.84, Most suitable behavior towards financial planning was found among women entrepreneurs managing food industries involved in Preparation activities (**Mean rank 262.50**) followed by women entrepreneurs managing food industries involved in processing (**Mean rank 299.25**) .

Table 4.85 Test statistics

	Behavior towards financial planning
Chi-Square	48.178
Df	4
Asymp. Sig.	*.000*

bb. Kruskal Wallis Test

cc. b. Grouping Variable: Types of food industries

Source: Primary data

*Significant at 5 per cent level

Table 4.85 gives Chi square value for behaviour towards financial planning as **48.178** with 4 degrees of freedom **(p=0.000)** and was seen to be significant at 5 per cent level **(P value is less than 0.05)** . This shows that there is significant difference in the behaviour towards financial planning among the women entrepreneurs managing food industries in Kerala according to the nature of activities being undertaken in food processing industrial units.

4.12.4 Financial Behaviour Towards Record Maintenance and Nature of Food Processing Activity

Table 4.86 Kruskal Wallis Test - Mean Ranks

	Types of food industries	*N*	*Mean Rank*
	Processing	160	276.75
	Conversion	100	278.50
Financial Behaviour	Preparation	200	289.50
Towards Record	Preservation	80	410.50
Maintenance	Packaging	80	370.50
	Total	620	

Source: Primary data

According to Table 4.86, Most suitable behavior towards financial record maintenance was found among women entrepreneurs managing food industries involved in processing activities (**Mean rank 276.75**) followed by women entrepreneurs managing food industries involved in conversion (**Mean rank 278.50**).

Table 4.87 Test statistics

	Behavior towards record maintenance
Chi-Square	47.488
Df	4
Asymp. Sig.	*.000*

dd. Kruskal Wallis Test

ee. b. Grouping Variable: Types of food industries

Source: Primary data

*Significant at 5 per cent level

Table 4.87 gives Chi-square value for behaviour towards financial record maintenance as **47.488** with 4 degrees of freedom **(p=0.000)** and was seen to be significant at 5 per cent level **(P value is less than 0.05)** . This shows that there is significant difference in the behaviour towards financial record maintenance among the women entrepreneurs managing food industries in Kerala according to the nature of activities being undertaken in food processing industrial units.

4.13.4 Financial Behaviour Towards Savings and Nature of Food Processing Activity

Table 4.88 Kruskal Wallis Test - Mean Ranks

	Types of food industries	*N*	*Mean Rank*
Financial Behaviour Towards Savings	Processing	160	286.75
	Conversion	100	256.50
	Preparation	200	291.50
	Preservation	80	398.00
	Packaging	80	385.50
	Total	620	

Source: Primary data

Most suitable behavior towards financial savings was found among women entrepreneurs managing food industries involved in conversion activities (**Mean rank 256.50**) followed by women entrepreneurs managing food industries involved in processing (**Mean rank 286.75**).

Table 4.89 Test statistics

	Behavior towards financial savings
Chi-Square	47.488
Df	4
Asymp. Sig.	***.000***

ff. Kruskal Wallis Test

gg. b. Grouping Variable: Types of food industries

Source: Primary data

*Significant at 5 per cent level

Table 4.89 gives, Chi square value for behaviour towards financial savings as **47.488** with 4 degrees of freedom **(p=0.000),** and was seen to be significant at 5 per cent level **(P value is less than 0.05)**. This shows that there is significant difference in the behaviour towards financial savings among the women entrepreneurs managing food industries in Kerala according to the nature of activities being undertaken in food processing industrial units.

4.13.5 Financial behaviour towards borrowings and nature of food processing activity

Table 4.90 Kruskal Wallis Test - Mean Ranks

	Types of food industries	*N*	*Mean Rank*
	Processing	160	281.75
	Conversion	100	290.50
Financial Behaviour	Preparation	200	310.50
Towards Borrowals	Preservation	80	338.00
	Packaging	80	365.50
	Total	620	

Source: Primary data

According to Table 4.90, Most suitable behavior towards financial borrowings was found among women entrepreneurs managing food industries involved in processing activities (**Mean rank 281.75**) followed by women entrepreneurs managing food industries involved in conversion (**Mean rank 290.50**).

Table 4.91 Test statistics

	Behavior towards financial borrowings
Chi-Square	14.866
Df 4	
Asymp. Sig.	***.000***

hh. Kruskal Wallis Test

ii. b. Grouping Variable: Types of food industries

Source: Primary data

*Significant at 5 per cent level

Table 4.91 mentions Chi square value obtained for behaviour towards financial borrowings as **14.866** with 4 degrees of freedom **(p=0.005)** and was seen to be significant at 5 per cent level **(P value is less than 0.05)**. This shows that there is significant difference in the behaviour towards financial borrowings among the women entrepreneurs managing food industries in Kerala according to the nature of activities being undertaken in food processing industrial units.

4.13.6 Financial Behaviour Towards Utilization of Funds and Nature of Food Processing Activity

Table 4.92 Kruskal Wallis Test - Mean Ranks

	Types of food industries	*N*	*Mean Rank*
Financial Behaviour Towards Utilization of Funds	Processing	160	394.25
	Conversion	100	282.50
	Preparation	200	277.50
	Preservation	80	305.50
	Packaging	80	265.50
	Total	620	

Source: Primary data

Table 4.92 indicates that the Most suitable behavior towards towards utilization of funds was found among women entrepreneurs managing food industries involved in packaging activities (**Mean rank 265.50**) followed by women entrepreneurs managing food industries involved in Preparation (**Mean rank 277.50**).

Table 4.93 Test statistics

	Behavior towards utilization of funds
Chi-Square	49.875
Df	4
Asymp. Sig.	*.000*

jj. Kruskal Wallis Test

kk. b. Grouping Variable: Types of food industries

Source: Primary data

*Significant at 5 per cent level

As per Table 4.93, Chi square value for behaviour towards utilization of funds is **49.875** with 4 degrees of freedom **(p=0.000)** and was seen to be significant at 5 per cent level **(P value is less than 0.05)**. This shows that there is significant difference in the behaviour towards utilization of funds among the women entrepreneurs managing food industries in Kerala according to the nature of activities being undertaken in food processing industrial units.

4.13.7 Financial Behaviour Towards Spending and Nature of Food Processing Activity

Table 4.94 Kruskal Wallis Test - Mean Ranks

	Types of food industries	*N*	*Mean Rank*
	Processing	160	330.50
	Conversion	100	364.50
Financial Behaviour	Preparation	200	279.50
Towards Spendings	Preservation	80	293.00
	Packaging	80	298.00
	Total	620	

Source: Primary data

Table 4.94 indicates that the most suitable behavior towards spending was found among women entrepreneurs managing food industries involved in Preparation activities (**Mean rank 279.50**) followed by women entrepreneurs managing food industries involved in preservation (**Mean rank 293.00**).

Table 4.95 Test statistics

	Behavior towards spending
Chi-Square	18.409
Df	4
Asymp. Sig.	***.000***

ll. Kruskal Wallis Test

mm. b. Grouping Variable: Types of food industries

Source: Primary data

*Significant at 5 per cent level

Table 4.95 reveals Chi square for behaviour towards spending of funds as **18.409** with 4 degrees of freedom **(p=0.001)** and was seen to be significant at 5 per cent level **(p value is less than 0.05)**. This shows that there is significant difference in the behaviour towards spending of funds among the women entrepreneurs managing food industries in Kerala according to the nature of activities being undertaken in food processing industrial units.

4.14 Relationship Between Financial Knowledge and Type of Food Industry

4.14.1 Knowledge about Financial Products and type of food industry

Differences in the knowledge levels about financial products between registered and unregistered units were evaluated using Mann Whitney U test.

Table 4.96 Mean Ranks

	Type of industries	*N*	*Mean Rank*	*Sum of Ranks*
Knowledge About	Registered	320	316.75	101360.00
Financial Products	Unregistered	300	303.83	91150.00
	Total	620		

Source: Primary data

Table No.4.96 indicate that the women entrepreneurs of unregistered food industries **(Mean rank 303.83)** have better knowledge level about the various financial products when compared to women entrepreneurs belonging to registered food processing industrial units **(Mean rank 316.75)**.

Table 4.97 Test Statistics

	Knowledge about Financial Products
Mann-Whitney U	46000.000
Wilcoxon W	91150.000
Z	-.899
Asymp. Sig. (2-tailed)	***.369***

a. Grouping Variable: Type of industries

Source: Primary data

*Significant at 5 per cent level

At 5 per cent level of significance, it was found in Table 4.97 that the ***p value was found to be more than 0.05 per cent*** indicating that there is no significant difference in the knowledge of financial products among the women entrepreneurs of food industry according to the type of industry.

4.14.2 Knowledge about Financial Services and type of food industry

Differences in the knowledge levels about financial services between registered and unregistered units were evaluated using Mann Whitney U test.

Table 4.98 Mean Ranks

	Type of industries	*N*	*Mean Rank*	*Sum of Ranks*
Knowledge About Financial Services	Registered	320	353.00	112960.00
	Unregistered	300	265.17	79550.00
	Total	620		

Source: Primary data

Table No.4.98 indicate that the women entrepreneurs of unregistered food industries **(Mean rank 265.17)** have better knowledge level about the various financial services when compared to women entrepreneurs belonging to registered food processing industrial units **(Mean rank 353.00)** .

Table 4.99 Test Statistics

	Knowledge about Financial Products
Mann-Whitney U	34400.000
Wilcoxon W	79550.000
Z	-6.108
Asymp. Sig. (2-tailed)	***.000***

a. Grouping Variable: Type of industries

Source: Primary data

*Significant at 5 per cent level

At 5 per cent level of significance, it was found in Table 4.99 that the ***p value was found to be less than 0.05 per cent*** indicating that there is significant difference in the knowledge of financial services among the women entrepreneurs of food industry according to the type of industry.

4.14.3 Knowledge About Financial Terms and type of food industry

Differences in the knowledge levels about financial terms between registered and unregistered units was evaluated using Mann Whitney U test.

Table 4.100 Mean Ranks

	Type of industries	*N*	*Mean Rank*	*Sum of Ranks*
Knowledge About	Registered	320	333.63	106760.00
Financial Terms	Unregistered	300	**285.83**	85750.00
	Total	620		

Source: Primary data

Table No 4.100 indicate that the women entrepreneurs of unregistered food industries **(Mean rank 285.83)** has better knowledge level about the various financial terms when compared to women entrepreneurs belonging to registered food processing industrial units **(Mean rank 333.63)**.

Table 4.101 Test Statistics

	Knowledge About Financial Terms
Mann-Whitney U	40600.000
Wilcoxon W	85750.000
Z	-3.327
Asymp. Sig. (2-tailed)	***.001***

a. Grouping Variable: Type of industries

Source: Primary data

*Significant at 5 per cent level

In Table 4.101, it was observed that at 5 per cent level of significance, the ***p value was found to be less than 0.05 per cent*** indicating that there is significant difference in the knowledge of financial terms among the women entrepreneurs of food industry according to the type of industry.

4.14.4 Knowledge About Financial Concepts and type of food industry

Differences in the knowledge levels about financial concepts between registered and unregistered units were evaluated using Mann Whitney U test.

Table 4.102 Mean Ranks

	Type of industries	*N*	*Mean Rank*	*Sum of Ranks*
Knowledge About	Registered	320	310.50	99360.00
Financial Concepts	Unregistered	300	310.50	93150.00
	Total		620	

Source: Primary data

Table No.4.102 indicates that the women entrepreneurs of food industries differ according to the type of industry to which they belong. It was understood from the figures in the table that being registered and unregistered did not make any change in their Knowledge About Financial Concepts since mean scores obtained did not differ between registered and unregistered.

Table 4.103 Test Statistics

	Knowledge About Financial Concepts
Mann-Whitney U	48000.000
Wilcoxon W	93150.000
Z	.000
Asymp. Sig. (2-tailed)	***1.000***

a. Grouping Variable: Type of industries
Source: Primary data
*Significant at 5 per cent level

From Table No. 4.103, we can see that at 5 per cent level of significance, it was found that the ***p value was found to be more than 0.05 per cent*** indicating that there is no significant difference in the knowledge of financial concepts among the women entrepreneurs of food processing units according to the type of industry.

4.15 Relationship Between Financial Attitude and Type of Food Industry

Financial attitudes are believed to be the predictors of financial behaviour according to the previous literatures. Hence vital for the study of financial literacy.

4.15.1 Financial attitude towards budgeting and type of food industry

Table 4.104 Mean Ranks

	Type of industries	*N*	*Mean Rank*	*Sum of Ranks*
Financial Attitude Towards Budgeting	Registered	320	**293.00**	93760.00
	Unregistered	300	329.17	98750.00
	Total	620		

Source: Primary data

Mean values obtained for registered and unregistered food processing industrial units were compared using Man Whitney U test to identify the type of industry which is having women entrepreneurs with better financial attitudes. In this study, it was seen in Table 4.104 that registered food processing industrial units **(Mean rank = 293.00)** managed by women entrepreneurs showed more favourable financial attitude towards budgeting compared to unregistered food processing industrial units **(Mean rank = 329.17).**

Table 4.105 Test Statistics

	Financial Attitude Towards Budgeting
Mann-Whitney U	42400.000
Wilcoxon W	93760.000
Z	-2.519
Asymp. Sig. (2-tailed)	***.012***

a. Grouping Variable: Type of industries

*Significant at 5 per cent level

Table No.4.105 shows that at 5 per cent level of significance, ***p value has a value 0.012***, which is less than **0.05** indicating significant difference between the two categories under study.

4.15.2 Financial Attitude Towards Investment and type of food industry

Table 4.106 Mean Ranks

	Type of industries	*N*	*Mean Rank*	*Sum of Ranks*
Financial Attitude	Registered	320	318.00	101760.00
Towards Investment	Unregistered	300	**302.50**	90750.00
	Total		620	

Source : Primary data

Difference in attitude towards investment among registered and unregistered industries was then evaluated using Mann Whitney U test. It was learned from the Table 4.106, that unregistered food processing industrial units **(Mean rank = 302.50)** managed by women entrepreneurs showed more favourable Financial Attitude Towards Investments when compared to registered food processing industrial units **(Mean rank = 318.00)**.

Table 4.107 Test Statistics

	Finacial Attitude Towards Investment
Mann-Whitney U	42400.000
Wilcoxon W	93760.000
Z	-2.519
Asymp. Sig. (2-tailed)	***.012***

a. Grouping Variable: Type of industries

Source: Primary data

*Significant at 5 per cent level

Table 4.107 shows that at 5 per cent level of significance, ***p has a value 0.281, which is more than 0.05*** indicating insignificant difference between registered and unregistered industries.

4.15.3 Financial Attitude Towards Financial Planning and type of food industry

Financial planning sets the goals and strategies for the businesses. Without goals, none of the business units can survive in the long run, attitude of women entrepreneurs in food processing industrial units towards financial planning among registered and unregistered food processing units was done using Mann Whitney U test.

Table 4.108 Mean Ranks

	Type of industries	*N*	*Mean Rank*	*Sum of Ranks*
Financial Attitude Towards Financial Planning	Registered	320	326.75	104560.00
	Unregistered	300	**293.17**	87950.00
	Total	620		

Source: Primary data

It was observed from the Table No.4.108 that unregistered food processing industrial units **(Mean rank = 293.17)** managed by women entrepreneurs showed more favourable Financial Attitude Towards Financial Planning when compared to registered food processing industrial units **(Mean rank = 326.75).**

Table 4.109 Test Statistics

	Financial Attitude Towards Financial Planning
Mann-Whitney U	42800.000
Wilcoxon W	87950.000
Z	-2.337
Asymp. Sig. (2-tailed)	***.019***

a. Grouping Variable: Type of industries

Source: Primary data

*Significant at 5 per cent level

Table 4.109 shows that at 5 per cent level of significance, ***p has a value 0.019, which is less than 0.05*** indicating significant difference between registered and unregistered industries in the attitude towards financial planning among the women entrepreneurs of food processing industrial units.

4.15.4 Financial Attitude Towards Record Maintenance and type of food industry

Record maintenance was vital for every business to keep evidence and provides a track of the financial happenings in the business. Attitude of women entrepreneurs in food processing industrial units towards record maintenance among registered and unregistered food processing industrial units was measured using Mann Whitney U test.

Table 4.110 Mean Ranks

	Type of industries	*N*	*Mean Rank*	*Sum of Ranks*
Financial Attitude Towards Record Maintenance	Registered	320	**291.13**	93160.00
	Unregistered	300	331.17	99350.00
	Total		620	

Source: Primary data

It was seen in Table No.4.110, that registered food processing industrial units **(Mean rank = 291.13)** exhibit better Financial Attitude Towards Record Maintenance than unregistered food processing industrial units **(Mean rank = 331.17).**

Table 4.111 Test Statistics

	Financial Attitude Towards Record maintenance
Mann-Whitney U	41800.000
Wilcoxon W	93160.000
Z	-2.795
Asymp. Sig. (2-tailed)	***.005***

a. Grouping Variable: Type of industries

Source: Primary data

*Significant at 5 per cent level

Table No.4.111 depicts that at 5 per cent level of significance, ***p has a value 0.005, which is less than 0.05*** pointing towards significant difference between registered and unregistered industries in the attitude towards Record maintenance in the women entrepreneurs of food processing industrial units.

4.15.5 Financial Attitude Towards Savings and type of food industry

Savings for a person show his pro activeness towards financial contingencies. Attitude of women entrepreneurs in food processing industrial units towards savings among registered and unregistered food processing industrial units was measured using Mann Whitney U test.

Table 4.112 Mean Ranks

	Type of industries	*N*	*Mean Rank*	*Sum of Ranks*
Financial Attitude	Registered	320	**278.00**	88960.00
Towards Savings	Unregistered	300	345.17	103550.00
	Total	620		

Source: Primary data

It was seen in Table 4.112, that registered food processing industrial units **(Mean rank = 278.00)** exhibit more favourable financial attitude towards savings than unregistered food processing industrial units **(Mean rank = 345.17).**

Table 4.113 Test Statistics

	Financial Attitude Towards Savings
Mann-Whitney U	37600.000
Wilcoxon W	88960.000
Z	-4.675
Asymp. Sig. (2-tailed)	***.000***

a. Grouping Variable: Type of industries

Source: Primary data

*Significant at 5 per cent level

Table 4.113 indicates that at 5 per cent level of significance, ***p* has a value 0.000, which is less than 0.05** pointing towards significant difference between registered and unregistered industries in the attitude towards savings in the women entrepreneurs of food processing industrial units.

4.15.6 Financial attitude towards borrowing and type of food industry

Borrowals by an entrepreneur can give the funds for the advancement and maintenance of his business. Borrowings can be from internal and external sources. Attitude of women entrepreneurs in food processing industrial units towards borrowings among registered and unregistered food processing industrial units was measured using Mann Whitney U test.

Table 4.114 Mean Ranks

	Type of industries	*N*	*Mean Rank*	*Sum of Ranks*
FinancialAttitude	Registered	320	361.75	115760.00
Towards Borrowings	Unregistered	300	**255.83**	76750.00
	Total	620		

Source: Primary data

It was observed in Table 4.114, that unregistered food processing industrial units **(Mean rank = 255.83)** exhibit more favourable financial attitude towards borrowings than registered food processing industrial units **(Mean rank = 361.75).**

Table 4.115 Test Statistics

	Financial Attitude Towards Borrowings
Mann-Whitney U	31600.000
Wilcoxon W	76750.000
Z	-7.389
Asymp. Sig. (2-tailed)	***.000***

a. Grouping Variable: Type of industries

Source: Primary data

*Significant at 5 per cent level

Table 4.115 indicates that at 5 per cent level of significance, ***p value has a value 0.000, which is less than 0.05*** pointing towards significant difference between registered and unregistered industries in the attitude towards borrowings among the women entrepreneurs of food processing industrial units.

4.15.7 Financial Attitude Towards Utilization of Funds and type of food industry

Funds if not properly utilized will lead to the fall of the business. If entrepreneurs are not cautious about fund utilization, it will create issues. Attitude of women entrepreneurs in food processing industrial units towards utilization of funds among registered and unregistered food processing industrial units was measured using Mann Whitney U test.

Table 4.116 Mean Ranks

	Type of industries	*N*	*Mean Rank*	*Sum of Ranks*
Financial Attitude Towards Utilization of Funds	Registered	320	328.94	105260.00
	Unregistered	300	**290.83**	87250.00
	Total	620		

Source: Primary data

It was seen in the Table No. 4.116 that unregistered food processing industrial units **(Mean rank = 290.83)** exhibit more favourable financial attitude towards utilization of funds than registered food processing industrial units **(Mean rank = 328.94).**

Table 4.117 Test Statistics

	Financial Attitude Towards Utilization of Funds
Mann-Whitney U	42100.000
Wilcoxon W	87250.000
Z	-2.655
Asymp. Sig. (2-tailed)	***.008***

a. Grouping Variable: Type of industries
Source: Primary data
****Significant at 5 per cent level***

Table 4.117 shows that at 5 per cent level of significance, ***p value has a value 0.008, which is less than 0.05*** pointing towards significant difference between registered and unregistered industries in the attitude towards utilization of funds in the women entrepreneurs of food processing industrial units.

4.15.8 Financial Attitude Towards Spending and Type of Food Industry

Judicious spending is a necessity for every business. If funds are not utilized well, funds will get depleted very quickly. So careful use of finance should be the policy of the business. Attitude of women entrepreneurs in food processing industrial units towards spending among registered and unregistered food processing industrial units was measured using Mann Whitney U test.

Table 4.118 Mean Ranks

	Type of industries	*N*	*Mean Rank*	*Sum of Ranks*
Financial Attitude	Registered	320	339.88	108760.00
Towards Spendings	Unregistered	300	**279.17**	83750.00
	Total	620		

Source: Primary data

It was seen in Table No.4.118 that unregistered food processing industrial units **(Mean rank = 279.17)** exhibit more favourable reviews on the financial attitude towards spendings than registered food processing industrial units **(Mean rank = 339.88).**

Table 4.119 Test Statistics

	Financial Attitude Towards Spendings
Mann-Whitney U	38600.000
Wilcoxon W	83750.000
Z	-4.231
Asymp. Sig. (2-tailed)	***.000***

a. Grouping Variable: Type of industries
Source: Primary data
Significant at 5 per cent level

Table 4.119 reveals that ***p has a value 0.000, which is less than 0.05*** pointing towards significant difference between registered and unregistered industries in the attitude towards spending among the women entrepreneurs of food processing industrial units.

4.16 Relationship Between Financial Behaviour and Type of Food Industry

Positive financial behaviours are believed to be the predictors of success for business units according to the previous literatures.

4.16.1 Financial behaviour towards budgeting and type of food industry

Mean values obtained for registered and unregistered food processing industrial units were compared using Man Whitney U test to identify the type of industry which is having women entrepreneurs with better financial behaviours.

Table 4.120 Mean Ranks

	Type of industries	*N*	*Mean Rank*	*Sum of Ranks*
Financial Behaviour	Registered	320	325.50	104160.00
Towards Budgeting	Unregistered	300	**294.50**	88350.00
	Total	620		

Source: Primary data

It was seen in Table 4.120, that unregistered food processing industrial units **(Mean rank=294.50)** managed by women entrepreneurs showed more favourable financial behaviour towards budgeting compared to registered food processing industrial units **(Mean rank** = 325.50).

Table 4.121 Test Statistics

	Financial Behavior Towards Budgeting
Mann-Whitney U	43200.000
Wilcoxon W	88350.000
Z	-2.166
Asymp. Sig. (2-tailed)	***.030***

a. Grouping Variable: Type of industries

Source: Primary data

****Significant at 5 per cent level***

Table 4.121 shows that at 5 per cent level of significance, ***less than 0.05*** indicating the presence of significant categories under study, ***p has a value 0.030, which is*** difference between the two.

4.16.2 Financial Behaviour Towards Investments and type of food industry

Difference in the Behaviour towards investment among registered and unregistered food processing industrial units was then evaluated using Mann Whitney U test.

Table 4.122 Mean Ranks

	Type of industries	*N*	*Mean Rank*	*Sum of Ranks*
Financial Behaviour Towards Investments	Registered	320	347.38	111160.00
	Unregistered	300	**271.17**	81350.00
	Total	620		

Source: Primary data

It was learned from Table 4.122 that unregistered food processing industrial units **(Mean rank = 271.17)** managed by women entrepreneurs showed more favourable financial behaviour towards investments when compared to registered food processing industrial units **(Mean rank = 347.38)**.

Table 4.123 Test Statistics

	Financial Behaviour Towards Investments
Mann-Whitney U	36200.000
Wilcoxon W	81350.000
Z	-5.312
Asymp. Sig. (2-tailed)	***0.000***

a. Grouping Variable: Type of industries

Source: Primary data

*Significant at 5 per cent level

Table 4.123 indicates that at 5 per cent level of significance, ***p has a value 0.000, which is less than***

0.05 indicating that there is significant difference between the behaviour of women entrepreneurs towards investment among registered and unregistered food processing units

4.16.3 Financial Behaviour Towards Financial Planning and type of food industry

Financial planning sets the strategies for the businesses. Without goals, none of the business units can survive in the long run, behaviour of women entrepreneurs in food processing industrial units towards financial planning among registered and unregistered food processing units was done using Mann Whitney U test. Difference in the Behaviour towards financial planning among registered and unregistered food processing industrial units was then evaluated using Mann Whitney U test.

Table 4.124 Mean Ranks

	Type of industries	*N*	*Mean Rank*	*Sum of Ranks*
Financial Behaviour Towards Financial Planning	Registered	320	361.13	115560.00
	Unregistered	300	**256.50**	76950.00
	Total	620		

Source:Primary data

It was noticed in table 4.124 that unregistered food processing industrial units **(Mean rank = 256.50)** managed by women entrepreneurs showed more favourable financial behaviour towards financial planning when compared to registered food processing industrial units **(Mean rank = 361.13)**.

Table 4.125 Test Statistics

	Financial Behaviour Towards Financial planning
Mann-Whitney U	31800.000
Wilcoxon W	76950.000
Z	-7.287
Asymp. Sig. (2-tailed)	***.000***

a. Grouping Variable: Type of industries
Source: Primary data
*Significant at 5 per cent level

According to Table 4.125, at 5 per cent level of significance, **P has a value 0.000, which is less than 0.05** indicating significant difference between registered and unregistered industries in the behaviour towards financial planning in the women entrepreneurs of food processing industrial units.

4.16.4 Financial Behaviour Towards Record maintenance and type of food industry

Record maintenance was vital for every business to keep evidence and provides a track of the financial happenings in the business. Difference in the Behaviour towards record maintenance among registered and unregistered food processing industrial units was then evaluated using Mann Whitney U test.

Table 4.126 Mean Ranks

	Type of industries	*N*	*Mean Rank*	*Sum of Ranks*
Financial Behaviour Towards Record Maintenance	Registered	320	361.13	115560.00
	Unregistered	300	**256.50**	76950.00
	Total	620		

Source: Primary data

Behaviour of women entrepreneurs in food processing industrial units towards record maintenance among registered and unregistered food processing industrial units was measured using Mann Whitney U test. It was seen in Table 4.126 that registered food processing industrial units **(Mean rank = 361.13)** exhibit better financial behaviour towards record maintenance than unregistered food processing industrial units (**Mean rank = 256.50**).

Table 4.127 Test Statistics

	Financial ehaviour Towards Record Maintenance
Mann-Whitney U	31800.000
Wilcoxon W	76950.000
Z	-7.287
Asymp. Sig. (2-tailed)	***.000***

a. Grouping Variable: Type of industries

Source: Primary data

*Significant at 5 per cent level

According to Table 4.127, at 5 per cent level of significance, p has a value 0.005, which is less than 0.05 pointing towards significant difference between registered and unregistered industries in the behaviour towards Record maintenance among the women entrepreneurs of food processing industrial units.

4.16.5 Financial Behaviour Towards Savings and Type of Food Industry

Savings for a person shows his outlook towards financial contingencies. Behaviour of women entrepreneurs in food processing industrial units towards savings among registered and unregistered food processing industrial units was measured using Mann Whitney U test.

Table 4.128 Mean Ranks

	Type of industries	*N*	*Mean Rank*	*Sum of Ranks*
Financial Behaviour Towards Savings	Registered	320	348.00	111360.00
	Unregistered	300	**270.50**	81150.00
	Total	620		

Source: Primary data

It was observed in Table 4.128 that unregistered food processing industrial units **(Mean rank = 270.50)** exhibit more favourable financial behaviour towards Savings than registered food processing industrial units **(Mean rank = 348.00).**

Table 4.129 Test Statistics

	Financial Behaviour Towards Savings
Mann-Whitney U	31800.000
Wilcoxon W	76950.000
Z	-7.287
Asymp. Sig. (2-tailed)	*.000*

a. Grouping Variable: Type of industries

Source: Primary data

*Significant at 5 per cent level

Table 4.129 depicts that at 5 per cent level of significance, ***P has a value 0.000, which is less than 0.05*** pointing towards significant difference between registered and unregistered industries in the behaviour towards Savings in the women entrepreneurs of food processing industrial units.

4.16.6 Financial Behaviour Towards Borrowings and type of food industry

Borrowals by an entrepreneur can give the funds

for the advancement and maintenance of his business. Borrowings can be from internal and external sources. Behaviour of women entrepreneurs in food processing industrial units towards borrowings among registered and unregistered food processing industrial units was measured using Mann Whitney U test.

Table 4.130 Mean Ranks

	Type of industries	*N*	*Mean Rank*	*Sum of Ranks*
Financial Behaviour	Registered	320	374.88	119960.00
Towards Borrowals	Unregistered	300	**241.83**	72550.00
	Total	620		

Source: Primary data

It was seen in Table 4.130 that unregistered food processing industrial units **(Mean rank =241.83)** exhibit more favourable financial behaviour towards borrowings than registered food processing industrial units **(Mean rank = 374.88).**

Table 4.131 Test Statistics

	Financial Behaviour Towards Borrowings
Mann-Whitney U	27400.000
Wilcoxon W	72550.000
Z	-9.264
Asymp. Sig. (2-tailed)	***.000***

a. Grouping Variable: Type of industries

Source: Primary data

Significant at 5 per cent level

Table 4.131 elucidates that at 5 per cent level of significance, *p has a value 0.000, which is less than*

0.05 pointing towards significant difference between registered and unregistered industries in the behaviour towards borrowings in the women entrepreneurs of food processing industrial units.

4.16.7 Financial Behaviour Towards utilization of funds and type of food industry

Funds if not properly utilized will lead to the fall of the business. If entrepreneurs are not cautious about fund utilization, it will create issues. Behaviour of women entrepreneurs in food processing industrial units towards utilization of funds among registered and unregistered food processing industrial units was measured using Mann Whitney U test.

Table 4.132 Mean Ranks

	Type of industries	*N*	*Mean Rank*	*Sum of Ranks*
FinancialBehaviour Towards Utilization of Funds	Registered	320	352.38	112760.00
	Unregistered	300	**265.83**	79750.00
	Total	620		

Source: Primary data

It was seen in Table 4.132, that unregistered food processing industrial units **(Mean rank = 265.83)** exhibit more favourable financial behaviour towards utilization of funds than registered food processing industrial units **(Mean rank = 352.38).**

Table 4.133 Test Statistics

	Financial Behaviour Towards Utilization of Funds
Mann-Whitney U	27400.000
Wilcoxon W	72550.000

Z	-9.264
Asymp. Sig. (2-tailed)	***.000***

a. Grouping Variable: Type of industries

Source: Primary data,

*Significant at 5 per cent level

Table 4.133 reveals that at 5 per cent level of significance, ***p has a value 0.000, which is less than 0.05*** pointing towards significant difference between registered and unregistered industries in the behaviour towards utilization of funds in the women entrepreneurs of food processing industrial units.

4.16.8 Financial Behaviour Towards spending and type of food industry

Judicious spending are a necessity for every business. If funds are not utilized well, funds will get depleted very quickly. So careful use of finance should be the policy of the business. Behaviour of women entrepreneurs in food processing industrial units towards spending among registered and unregistered food processing industrial units was measured using Mann Whitney U test.

Table 4.134 Mean Ranks

	Type of industries	*N*	*Mean Rank*	*Sum of Ranks*
Financial Behaviour Towards Utilization of Funds	Registered	320	352.38	112760.00
	Unregistered	300	**265.83**	79750.00
	Total	620		

Source: Primary data

It was observed in table 4.134 that unregistered food processing industrial units **(Mean rank = 250.50)** exhibit more favourable reviews on the financial behaviour towards spending than registered food processing industrial units **(Mean rank = 366.75).**

Table 4.135 Test Statistics

	Financial Behaviour Towards spending
Mann-Whitney U	30000.000
Wilcoxon W	75150.000
Z	-8.116
Asymp. Sig. (2-tailed)	***.000***

a. Grouping Variable: Type of industries

Source: Primary data

*Significant at 5 per cent level

Table 4.135 shows that at 5 per cent level of significance, ***P has a value 0.000, which is less than 0.05*** pointing towards significant difference between registered and unregistered industries in the behaviour towards spending in the women entrepreneurs of food processing industrial units.

4.17 Influence of Financial Attitude on Financial Behaviour

4.17.1 Budgeting

$H_0$7: There is no significant effect of financial attitude on financial behaviour of the respondents

$H_0$7-1: There is no significant effect of financial attitude towards budgeting on the financial behaviour towards budgeting of the respondents

Budgets are tools used by the owners to prepare the strategies and goals for the organization. Budgets should be properly designed and utilized according to the plans of the organization. Influence of financial attitude in deciding the behaviour of women entrepreneurs towards budgeting was studied using regression with financial attitude towards budgeting as a predictor variable and financial behaviour towards budgeting as the dependent variable.

Table 4.136 Model Summary

Model	*R*	*R Square*	*Adjusted R Square*	*Std. Error of the Estimate*
1	.505[a]	.255	.254	5.62063

a. Predictors: (Constant), Financial Attitude Towards Budgeting
Source : Primary data

Table 4.136 shows model summary for the impact of financial attitude towards budgeting on financial behaviour towards budgeting among the women entrepreneurs managing food processing industrial units. R-square is 0.255 indicating that 25.5 per cent of the variation is accounted to the combined linear impact of the independent variables. Adjusted R square value is 0.254, implying that the model has 25.4 per cent of the variance in the criterion variable.

Table 4.137 ANOVA[a]

Model		*Sum of Squares*	*df*	*Mean Square*	*F*	*Sig.*
1	Regression	6691.963	1	6691.963	211.828	*.000*[b]
	Residual	19523.521	618	31.591		
	Total	26215.484	619			

A. Dependent variable: financial behaviour towards budgeting

B. Predictors: (constant) , Finacial Attitude Towards Budgeting

Source: Primary data

*Significant at 5 per cent level

Table 4.137 shows the ANOVA of financial attitude towards budgeting on financial behaviour towards budgeting. It can be seen that the associated F value **(211.828)** is statistically significant **($p < 0.05$)**. Hence, the null hypothesis is rejected and it is concluded that there is a significant effect of financial attitude towards budgeting on financial behaviour towards budgeting.

Table 4.138 Coefficients[a]

Model		*Unstandardized Coefficients*		*Standardized Coefficients*	*T*	*Sig.*
		B	*Std. Error*	*Beta*		
1	(Constant)	10.928	.642		17.017	*.000*
	Finacial Attitude Towards Budgeting	.402	.028	.505	14.554	*.000*

a. Dependent Variable: Financial Behaviour Towards Budgeting

Source: Primary data

*Significant at 5 per cent level

Table 4.138 indicates that the Beta coefficients are significant as the associated t-values are significant **(observed $p < 0.05$).** Positive value of the Beta coefficients indicates that with every increase in financial attitude towards budgeting, there is a similar increase in the independent variable "financial behaviour towards budgeting". Therefore, it means that the financial behaviour towards budgeting is influenced by the financial attitude towards budgeting among the women entrepreneurs engaged in food processing units.

$H_0$7 - 2: There is no significant effect of financial attitude towards investments on the financial behaviour towards investments of the respondents

Investments have undergone a sea change from what it was in the past. It is very important to make prudent decisions with regard to the investments to create wealth and value to the firm. Influence of financial attitude in deciding the behaviour of women entrepreneurs towards investments was studied using regression with financial attitude towards investments as a predictor variable and financial behaviour towards investments as the dependent variable.

Table 4.139 Model Summary

Model	*R*	*R Square*	*Adjusted R Square*	*Std. Error of the Estimate*
1	.496[a]	.246	.245	6.26265

a. Predictors: (Constant) , Financial Attitude Towards Investment

Source: Primary data

Table 4.139 shows model summary for the impact of financial attitude towards Investment on financial behaviour towards Investment among the women entrepreneurs managing food processing industrial units. R=.496 indicates that there is a relationship. R-square is 0.246 indicating that 24.6 per cent of the variation is accounted to the combined linear impact of the independent variables. Adjusted R square value is 0.245, implying that the model has 24.5 per cent of the variance in the criterion variable.

Table 4.140 Anova[a]

Model		*Sum of Squares*	*df*	*Mean Square*	*F*	*Sig.*
1	Regression	7898.340	1	7898.340	201.382	*.000*[b]
	Residual	24238.435	618	39.221		
	Total	32136.774	619			

A. Dependent Variable: Financial Behaviour towards Investments

B. Predictors: (Constant) , Financial Attitude Towards Investment

Source: Primary data

*Significant at 5 per cent level

Table 4.140 shows the ANOVA of financial attitude towards investments on financial behaviour towards investments. It can be seen in the table that the associated F value **(201.382)** is found to be statistically significant **($p < 0.05$)**. Hence, the null hypothesis is rejected and it is concluded that there is a significant effect of financial attitude towards investments on financial behaviour towards investments.

Table 4.141 coefficients[a]

Model		*Unstandardized Coefficients*		*Standardized Coefficients*	*T*	*Sig.*
		B	*Std. Error*	*Beta*		
1	(Constant)	13.875	.836		16.590	*.000*
	Financial Attitude Towards Investment	.284	.020	.496	14.191	*.000*

A. Dependent Variable: Financial Behaviour Towards Investments
Source: Primary data

*Significant at 5 per cent level

Tables 4.139 and 4.140 point out that the regression has the required qualities explaining **24.60** per cent of the variation in financial attitude towards investment among women entrepreneurs in food processing industrial units and that this explanation is statistically valid, as the associated F value **(201.382)** is statistically significant **($p < 0.05$)**. Table 4.141 indicates that the Beta coefficients are significant as the associated t-values of the regression equation is significant at 5 per cent level of significance **(observed $p < 0.05$)**. Positive value of the Beta coefficients indicates that with every increase in financial attitude towards investment, there is a similar increase in the independent variable "financial behaviour towards investment". Therefore, it means that the financial attitude towards investment influences the financial behaviour towards investment among the women entrepreneurs engaged in food processing units.

4.17.3 Financial planning

Business should have definite plans for achieving the strategies. It is important to have financial plans to avoid road blocks which might result in losses for the firm. Influence of financial attitude in deciding the behaviour of women entrepreneurs towards financial planning was studied using regression with Financial Attitude Towards Financial Planning as a predictor variable and financial behaviour towards financial planning as the dependent variable.

$H_0$7 - 3: There is no significant effect of financial attitude towards financial planning on the financial behaviour towards financial planning of the respondents

Table 4.142 Model Summary

Model	*R*	*R Square*	*Adjusted R Square*	*Std. Error of the Estimate*
1	.549[a]	.302	.301	9.48582

a. Predictors: (Constant) , Financial Attitude Towards Financial Planning

Source data : Primary data

Table 4.142 shows model summary for the impact of financial attitude towards financial planning on financial behaviour towards financial planning among the women entrepreneurs managing food processing industrial units. R= .549 indicates that there is a relationship between the variables. R-square is 0.302 indicating that 30.2 per cent of the variation is accounted to the combined linear impact of the independent variables. Adjusted R square value is 0.301, implying that the model has 30.1 per cent of the variance in the criterion variable.

Table 4.143 ANOVA[a]

Model		*Sum of Squares*	*df*	*Mean Square*	*F*	*Sig.*
1	Regression	24031.928	1	24031.928	267.079	***.000[b]***
	Residual	55608.072		618	89.981	
	Total	79640.000		619		

a. Dependent Variable: financial behaviour towards financial planning
b. Predictors: (Constant) , Financial Attitude Towards Financial Planning

Source: Primary Data, * Significant at 5 per cent level

Table 4.143 shows the ANOVA of financial attitude towards financial planning on financial behaviour towards financial planning. It can be seen in the table that the associated F value **(267.079)** is found to be statistically significant **($p < 0.05$)**. Hence, the null hypothesis is rejected and it is concluded that there is a significant effect of financial attitude towards financial planning on financial behaviour towards financial planning.

Table 4.144 Coefficients

Model		*Unstandardized Coefficients*		*Standardized Coefficients*	*T*	*Sig.*
		B	*Std. Error*	*Beta*		
1	(Constant)	18.475	1.312		14.077	***.000***
	Financial Attitude Towards Financial Planning	.483	.030	.549	16.343	***.000***

a. Dependent Variable: Financial Behaviour Towards Financial Planning
Source: Primary data

*Significant at 5 per cent level

Table 4.144 describes that the Beta coefficients are significant as the associated t-values of the regression equation is significant at 5 per cent level of significance **(observed $p < 0.05$).** Positive value of the Beta coefficients indicates that with every increase in financial attitude towards financial planning, there is a similar increase in the independent variable " financial behaviour towards financial planning". Therefore, it means that the financial behaviour towards financial planning is influenced by the financial attitude towards financial planning among the women entrepreneurs engaged in food processing units.

4.17.4 Record maintenance

Maintaining records can be an evidence as well as a tool of control for the management. Influence of financial attitude in deciding the behaviour of women entrepreneurs towards record maintenance was studied using regression with financial attitude towards record maintenance as a predictor variable and financial behaviour towards record maintenance as the dependent variable.

$H_0$7 - 4: There is no significant effect of financial attitude towards record maintenance on the financial behaviour towards record maintenance of the respondents

Table 4.145 Model Summary

Model	*R*	*R Square*	*Adjusted R Square*	*Std. Error of the Estimate*
1	.415[a]	.172	.171	4.57520

a. Predictors: (Constant), Financial Attitude Towards Record Maintenance

Source: Primary data

Table 4.145 shows model summary for the impact of financial attitude towards record maintenance on financial behaviour towards record maintenance among the women entrepreneurs managing food processing industrial units. R=0.415 indicates that there is a relationship between the variables. R-square is 0.172 indicating that 17.2 per cent of the variation is accounted to the combined linear impact of the independent variables. Adjusted R square value is 0.171, implying that the model has 17.1 per cent of the variance in the criterion variable.

Table 4.146 ANOVA[a]

Model		*Sum of Squares*	*df*	*Mean Square*	*F*	*Sig.*
1	Regression	2692.136	1	2692.136	128.611	*.000*[b]
	Residual	12936.252	618	20.932		
	Total	15628.387	619			

a. Dependent Variable: Financial Behaviour Towards Record Maintenance
b. Predictors: (Constant), Financial Attitude Towards Record Maintenance

Source: Primary data

*Significant at 5 per cent level

Table 4.146 shows the ANOVA of financial attitude towards record maintenance on financial behaviour towards record maintenance. It can be seen in the table that the associated F value **(128.611)** is found to be statistically significant **($p < 0.05$)**. Hence, the null hypothesis is rejected and it is concluded that there is a significant effect of financial attitude towards record maintenance on financial behaviour towards record maintenance.

Table 4.147 Coefficients[a]

Model		*Unstandardized Coefficients*		*Standardized Coefficients*	*T*	*Sig.*
		B	*Std. Error*	*Beta*		
	(Constant)	8.101	.616		13.140	*.000*
1	Financial Attitude				.415	
	Towards Record	.338	.030		11.341	*.000*
	Maintenance					

a. Dependent Variable: Financial Behaviour Towards Record Maintenance

Source: Primary data

*Significant at 5 per cent level

It is visible in the tables 4..145 and 4.146 that **17.20** per cent of the variation in financial attitude towards record maintenance among women entrepreneurs in food processing industrial units is explained by the regression equation and that this explanation is statistically valid, as the associated F value **(128.611)** is statistically significant **($p < 0.05$)**. Table 4.147 indicates that the Beta coefficients are significant as the associated t-values of the regression equation is significant at 5 per cent level of significance **(observed $p < 0.05$)**. Positive value of the Beta coefficients indicate that with every increase in financial attitude towards record maintenance, there is a similar increase in the independent variable "financial behaviour towards record maintenance". Therefore, it means that the financial behaviour towards record maintenance is influenced by the financial attitude towards record maintenance among the women entrepreneurs engaged in food processing units.

4.17.5 Savings

Finance is very important for business. Correct amount of savings can save the business from emergencies and liquidity issues. Influence of financial attitude in deciding the behaviour of women entrepreneurs towards savings was explained using regression with financial attitude towards savings as a predictor variable and financial behaviour towards savings as the dependent variable

$H_0$7 - 5: There is no significant effect of financial attitude towards savings on the financial behaviour towards savings of the respondents

Table 4.148 Summary

Model	*R*	*R Square*	*Adjusted R Square*	*Std. Error of the Estimate*
1	.292[a]	.085	.084	11.95304

a. Predictors: (Constant), Financial Attitude Towards Savings
Source: Primary data

Table 4.148 shows model summary for the impact of financial attitude towards savings on financial behaviour towards savings among the women entrepreneurs managing food processing industrial units. R= .292 indicates that there is a relationship between the variables. R-square is .085 indicating that 8.5 per cent of the variation is accounted to the combined linear impact of the independent variables. Adjusted R square value is 0.084, implying that the model has 8.4 per cent of the variance in the criterion variable.

Table 4.149 ANOVA[a]

Model		*Sum of Squares*	*df*	*Mean Square*	*F*	*Sig.*
	Regression	8220.630	1	8220.630	57.537	*.000[b]*
1	Residual	88296.790	618	142.875		
	Total	96517.419	619			

A. Dependent variable: financial behaviour towards savings
B. Predictors: (constant), Financial Attitude Towards Savings
Source: Primary data
*Significant at 5 per cent level

Table 4.149 shows the ANOVA of financial attitude towards savings on financial behaviour towards savings. It can be seen in the table that the associated F value **(57.537)** is found to be statistically significant **($p < 0.05$)**. Hence, the null hypothesis is rejected and it is concluded that there is a significant effect of financial attitude towards savings on financial behaviour towards savings among the respondents.

Table 4.150 Coefficients[a]

Model		Unstandardized Coefficients		Standardized Coefficients	T	Sig.
		B	Std. Error	Beta		
	(Constant)	23.313	2.131		10.939	**.000**
1	Financial Attitude Towards Savings	.453	.060	.292	7.585	**.000**

a. Dependent Variable: financial behaviour towards savings

Source: Primary data

*Significant at 5 per cent level

Table 4.150 reveals that the Beta coefficients are significant as the associated t-values are significant **(observed $p < 0.05$).** Positive value of the Beta coefficients indicate that with every increase in Financial Attitude Towards Savings, there is a similar increase in the independent variable "financial behaviour towards savings". Therefore, it means that the financial behaviour towards savings is influenced by the financial behaviour towards savings among the women entrepreneurs engaged in food processing units.

4.17.6 Borrowings

Borrowals can provide the required funds for the business. Loans are available at varying rates for the women entrepreneur. But the decision whether to borrow or not lies with the entrepreneur. Influence of financial attitude in deciding the behaviour of women entrepreneurs towards borrowings was explained using regression with financial attitude towards borrowings as a predictor variable and financial behaviour towards borrowings as the dependent variable.

$H_0$7 - 6: There is no significant effect of financial attitude towards borrowings on the financial behaviour towards borrowings of the respondents

Table 4.151 Model Summary

Model	*R*	*R Square*	*Adjusted R Square*	*Std. Error of the Estimate*
1	.509[a]	.260	.258	6.73024

a. Predictors: (Constant), Financial Attitude Towards Borrowing

Source: Primary data

Table 4.151 shows model summary for the impact of financial attitude towards borrowings on financial behaviour towards borrowings among the women entrepreneurs managing food processing industrial units. R= 0.509 indicates that there is a relationship between the variables. R-square is 0.260 indicating that 26.0 per cent of the variation is accounted to the combined linear impact of the independent variables. Adjusted R square value is 0.258, implying that the model has 25.8 per cent of the variance in the criterion variable.

Table 4.152 ANOVA[a]

Model		*Sum of Squares*	*df*	*Mean Square*	*F*	*Sig.*
	Regression	9810.824	1	9810.824	216.593	*.000*[b]
1	Residual	27993.047		618	45.296	
	Total	37803.871		619		

A. Dependent Variable: Financial Behaviour Towards Borrowals

B. Predictors: (Constant), Financial Attitude Towards Borrowing

Source: Primary data

*Significant at 5 per cent level

Table 4.152 shows the ANOVA of financial attitude towards borrowings on financial behaviour towards borrowings. It can be seen in the table that the associated F value **(216.593)** is found to be statistically significant

($p < 0.05$). Hence, the null hypothesis is rejected and it is concluded that there is a significant effect of financial attitude towards borrowings on financial behaviour towards borrowings among the respondents.

Table 4.153 Coefficients[a]

Model		*Unstandardized Coefficients*		*Standardized Coefficients*	*T*	*Sig.*
		B	*Std. Error*	*Beta*		
	(Constant)	11.022	.933		11.816	***.000***
1	Financial Attitude Towards Borrowing	.636	.043	.509	14.717	***.000***

A. Dependent Variable: Financial Behaviour Towards Borrowals

Source: Primary data

*Significant at 5 per cent level

Table 4.153 shows that the Beta coefficients are significant as the associated t-values of the regression equation is significant at 5 per cent level of significance **(observed $p < 0.05$).** Positive value of the Beta coefficients indicate that with every increase in financial attitude towards borrowings, there is a similar increase in the independent variable "financial behaviour towards borrowings". Therefore, it means that the financial behaviour towards borrowings is influenced by the financial attitude towards borrowings among the women entrepreneurs engaged in food processing units.

4.15.7 Utilization of funds

Finance is a resource which is very limited. Expenses and incomes of the organization should be handled very carefully. Proper utilization of financial resources will ensure the going concern status of the organization. Influence of financial attitude in deciding the behaviour of women entrepreneurs towards utilization of funds was explained using regression with financial attitude towards utilization of funds as a predictor variable and financial behaviour towards utilization of funds as the dependent variable.

$H_0$7 - 7: There is no significant effect of financial attitude towards fund utilization on the financial behaviour towards fund utilization among the respondents

Table 4.154 Model Summary

Model	*R*	*R Square*	*Adjusted R Square*	*Std. Error of the Estimate*
1	.340[a]	.116	.114	6.45459

a. Predictors: (Constant), Financial Attitude Towards Utilization of Funds

Source: Primary data

Table 4.154 shows model summary for the impact of financial attitude towards borrowings on financial behaviour towards borrowings among the women entrepreneurs managing food processing industrial units. R= .340 indicates that there is a relationship between the variables. R-square is .116 indicating that 11.6 per cent of the variation is accounted to the combined linear impact of the independent variables. Adjusted R square value is 0.114, implying that the model has 11.4 per cent of the variance in the criterion variable.

Table 4.155 ANOVA[a]

Model		*Sum of Squares*	*df*	*Mean Square*	*F*	*Sig.*
	Regression	3362.757	1	3362.757	80.716	*.000*[b]
1	Residual	25746.920	618	41.662		
	Total	29109.677	619			

A. Dependent Variable: Financial Behaviour Towards Utilization Of Funds

B. Predictors: (Constant), Financial Attitude Towards Utilization Of Funds

Source: Primary data

*Significant at 5 per cent level

Table 4.155 shows the ANOVA of financial attitude towards fund utilization on financial behaviour towards fund utilization. It can be seen in the table that the associated F value **(216.593)** is found to be statistically significant **($p < 0.05$)**.Hence, the null hypothesis is rejected and it is concluded that there is a significant effect of financial attitude towards fund utilization on financial behaviour towards fund utilization among the respondents.

Table 4.156 Coefficients[a]

Model		*Unstandardized Coefficients*		*Standardized Coefficients*	*T*	*Sig.*
		B	*Std. Error*	*Beta*		
	(Constant)	13.228	.889		14.874	***.000***
1	Financial Attitude Towards Utilization Of Funds	.249	.028	.340	8.984	***.000***

a. Dependent Variable: financial behaviour towards utilization of funds

Source: Primary data

*Significant at 5 per cent level

Tables 4.156 indicate that the Beta coefficients are significant as the associated t-values of the regression equation is significant at 5 per cent level of significance **(observed $p < 0.05$)**. Positive value of the Beta coefficients indicate that with every increase in financial attitude towards borrowings, there is a similar increase in the independent variable "financial behaviour towards borrowings". Presence of **11.60** per cent of the variation in financial attitude towards fund utilization among women entrepreneurs in food processing industrial units is explained by the regression equation and that this explanation is statistically valid, as the associated F value

(80.716) is statistically significant **($p < 0.05$).** Therefore, it means that the financial behaviour towards fund utilization is influenced by the financial attitude towards fund utilization among the women entrepreneurs engaged in food processing units.

4.17.8 Spendings

Monitoring and controlling of the business expenditures should be done on time to achieve profits for the business. If spending are not watched, it might end in the failure of the organization. Influence of financial attitude in deciding the behaviour of women entrepreneurs towards spendings was explained using regression with financial attitude towards spendings as a predictor variable and financial behaviour towards spendings as the dependent variable.

$H_0$7 - 8: There is no significant effect of financial attitude towards spendings on the financial behaviour towards spendings among the respondents.

Table 4.157 Model Summary

Model	*R*	*R Square*	*Adjusted R Square*	*Std. Error of the Estimate*
1	.650[a]	.422	.421	5.72329

a. Predictors: (Constant), Financial Attitude Towards Spendings
Source: Primary data

Table 4.157 shows model summary for the impact of financial attitude towards spendings on financial behaviour towards spendings among the women entrepreneurs managing food processing industrial units. R= .650 indicates that there is a strong relationship between the variables. R-square is .422 indicating that 42.2 per cent of the variation is accounted to the combined linear impact of the independent variables. Adjusted R square value is 0.421, implying that the model has 42.1 per cent of the variance in the criterion variable.

Table 4.158 ANOVA[a]

Model		Sum of Squares	df	Mean Square	F	Sig.
	Regression	14786.467	1	14786.467	451.412	**.000[b]**
1	Residual	20243.210	618	32.756		
	Total	35029.677	619			

A. Dependent Variable: Financial Behaviour Towards Spendings

B. Predictors: (Constant) , Financial Attitude Towards Spendings

Source: Primary data

Table 4.158 shows the ANOVA of financial attitude towards spendings on financial behaviour towards spendings. It can be seen in the table that the associated F value **(216.593)** is found to be statistically significant **($p < 0.05$)**. Hence, the null hypothesis is rejected and it is concluded that there is a significant effect of financial attitude towards spendings on financial behaviour towards spendings among the respondents

Table 4.159 Coefficients[a]

Model		Unstandardized Coefficients		Standardized Coefficients	T	Sig.
		B	Std. Error	Beta		
	(Constant)	14.339	.778		18.432	**.000**
1	Financial Attitude Towards Spendings	.455	.021	.650	21.246	**.000**

a. Dependent Variable: Financial Behaviour Towards Spendings

Source: Primary data

Table 4.159 indicates that the Beta coefficients are significant as the associated t-values of the regression equation is significant at 5 per cent level of significance **(observed $p < 0.05$)**. Positive value of the Beta coefficients indicate that with every increase in financial attitude towards spendings, there is a similar increase in the independent variable "financial behaviour towards spendings".

4.18 Chapter Summary

This chapter has been embarked on to analyze the financial literacy of women entrepreneurs managing food processing industrial units located in Kerala. Financial awareness of women entrepreneurs towards various financial products, financial services and financial terms and concepts was analyzed. Attempt has been made also to know whether financial attitude of the women entrepreneur has a role in influencing their financial behavior.

REFERENCES

1. Darren, G & Paul M.(2011). *SPSS for Windows Step by Step* (10th Edition). New DELHI: Pearson
2. Kothari C. R(2015). *Research Methodology: Methods and Techniques:* New Delhi: New Age International Publishers, 25-100
3. Lawrence Newman.(2008). *Social Research Methods: Quantitative and Qualitative Approaches* (6th Edition) New Delhi : Pearson Education Inc, 110-146

5

Summary of Findings, Recommendations and Conclusion

5.1 Introduction

Financial literacy is one of the most important factors determining the success of business considering the complexities and innovations happening everyday with regard to the financial markets and financial system. More and more financial products and services are introduced into the financial markets daily making the situation worse for the ordinary man doing business. Existing literatures available in the area of financial literacy levels among the general public revealed that the situation of the public with regard to the awareness of financial products and services is very low . Researches which studied about gender differences found that gender is an important differentiating factor which influences the literacy levels of an individual because of a patriarchal society and poor living conditions for the women across the globe. Women are considered as people to be bound within the four walls of the house and were not given education and other facilities in the past for their development thinking the cost involved in providing education to women as an extravaganza. For many of the poor income earning households, lack of proper financial knowledge on financial matters is deepening their poverty levels due to improper management of funds. Even many of the educated ones are unaware about the basic interest rates, inflation, procedures in opening a bank account, taking a loan and about risk minimization techniques in financial management. Basic understanding of financial products, financial services, financial terms and financial concepts is important for an entrepreneur for the growth and development of his business, so much as it is in his private limit as a customer.

An entrepreneur is required to have the knowledge on financial matters to get an understanding of the financial statements analysis, inventory management, working capital management, capital budgeting, forex management, banking operations, debt management, receivables management, managing the float, and for record maintenance and book keeping. Without proper understanding of these factors, management of a business will be a Herculean task for an entrepreneur. Situation becomes even worse for the lady entrepreneurs who are in shortage of time due to responsibilities related to family and children. Progress report prepared by OECD on financial education for MSMEs and potential entrepreneurs states that financial education if provided can solve the financial management issues of the entrepreneur and can guide him through innovation to be successful in the business development. Hence a study on the financial literacy among women entrepreneurs engaged in food processing industrial units was carried down and this chapter gives a brief description about the findings of the study.

5.2 Major Findings of the Study

The major findings of the study are presented below.

5.2.1 Demographic Profile of women entrepreneurs Selected for the Study

Religion, age, marital status, community, type of family, education, place of living, district, nature of food industry, type of food products related to the industry, type of industry and monthly income of the respondents is presented as demographic profile of the respondents.

1. Among the 620 women entrepreneurs chosen for the purpose of this study, 12.9 per cent of the sample are from the age group below 25, 19.4 per cent between 25-35, 35.5 per cent between 36-45, 22.26 per cent between 46-55 and 9.7 per cent is above 55.
2. When religion of the women entrepreneurs involved in food processing industries were considered, majority of them were Hindus (45.2 per cent) followed by Muslims (32.3 per cent) and Christians respectively
3. With regard to the Community of the women entrepreneurs involved in food processing industries, it was observed that 48.4 per cent of the respondents are OBC which was followed by 25.8 per cent of the respondents from communities other than OBC, SC and ST.
4. As many as 51.6 per cent of the women entrepreneurs involved in food processing industries were married, 41.9 per cent of the respondents were single and 6.5 per cent were separated.
5. When education of women entrepreneurs engaged in food processing industrial units was considered, it was revealed that majority of the respondents had higher secondary (71 per cent) education followed by 12.9 per cent of the people having

primary and graduation. Only 3.2 per cent had post graduation.

6. Among the 620 women entrepreneurs chosen for the study, 22.6 per cent of the people were living in urban area, 64.5 belong to rural area and 12.9 are staying in semi urban area.
7. 41.9 per cent of the respondents were from Wayanad district followed by 35.50 per cent from Thiruvananthapuram district and 22.60 per cent from Kottayam district.
8. Among the respondents, 32.3 per cent of the people were doing business related to preparation of food, 25.8 per cent were involved in processing of food, 16.1 per cent were involved in conversion of food followed by 12.9 per cent in packaging of food and preservation of food.
9. Out of 620 women entrepreneurs engaged in food processing industrial units, 54.8 per cent of women entrepreneurs were from joint families, 38.7 per cent were from nuclear families and 6.5 per cent were from extended families.
10. When type of food products related to the food processing industrial units of the women entrepreneurs were enquired, majority of the women entrepreneurs were dealing with dairy products (32.3 per cent), 16.1 per cent was dealing with edible oils, 19.4 per cent was dealing with sea foods, and 16.1 per cent each for poultryandspices.
11. Among the women entrepreneurs engaged in food processing industrial units in Kerala, 41.9 per cent were getting an income ranging between 10000-20000, 32.3 per cent were getting income between 20001-30000 and 22.6 per cent were getting a monthly amount below 10000.

12. Out of the industries, registered industries constitute 51.6 per cent of the sample selected whereas unregistered industries account for 48.4 per cent.
13. With regard to the awareness level of women entrepreneurs of registered and unregistered food processing industrial units towards various financial products, it was seen that Bank deposits (2.262), have the highest awareness level among the women entrepreneurs in unregistered industries and the debit cards (2.408) are the financial product having the highest awareness level among the women entrepreneurs in Registered industries.
14. When awareness level of women entrepreneurs of registered and unregistered food processing industrial units towards various financial services was considered , it was seen that Mutual funds (1.558) are the financial service having the highest awareness level among the women entrepreneurs in registered industries whereas banking services (-1.775) are the financial services having the highest awareness level among the women entrepreneurs in unregistered industries.
15. It was understood that financial planning is the financial term having the highest level of awareness among the women entrepreneurs in registered industries and risk diversification is the financial services having the highest awareness level among the women entrepreneurs in unregistered industries.

5.2.2 *Association of financial knowledge with demographic variables*

1) When association of financial knowledge with age was evaluated, knowledge of financial products,

knowledge of financial services, knowledge of financial terms and knowledge of financial concepts were considered as dependent variables and age as the independent variable. The p values of all the cases were found to be less than 0.05. All the test statistics were found to be statistically significant (**p=0.000< 0.05**) at 5 per cent level pointing to the fact that age is a factor which contributes to the financial knowledge of the respondents. It could be learned that, financial knowledge of the women entrepreneurs in food processing industries taken together differ with their age. When the variables of financial knowledge were taken independently, variation is found to be statistically very significant for all variables in the test of between subjects effects. Individuals belonging to the age group 25 to 35 are found to have lower levels of financial knowledge than respondents who are in the age group 36 to 45.

2) All the test statistics were found to be statistically significant (p=0.000< 0.05) at 5 per cent level pointing to the fact that religion is a factor which contributes to the financial knowledge of the respondents. Variation was found to be statistically very significant for all variables when they were taken independently also since ***all p values are found to be less than 0.05***. Religion based evaluation of financial knowledge revealed that knowledge about financial products and the knowledge about financial concepts are seen to be the more among Hindus whereas knowledge of financial terms and knowledge of financial services are seen to be more among the religious communities other than Hindus, Muslims and Christians.

3) When Marital status of the women entrepreneurs involved in food processing units was examined with financial knowledge levels, all the test statistics were found to be statistically significant ($p=0.000< 0.05$) at 5 per cent level pointing to the fact that marital status is a factor which influences the financial knowledge of respondents. When independent variables were considered, variation was found to be statistically very significant for all variables except in the case of knowledge of financial concepts (**p=0.928>0.05**). It was learned that married individuals are found to have higher mean scores of interconnection with financial knowledge compared to single and separated women entrepreneurs.

5.2.3 Association of financial attitude with demographic variables

1) It was observed that financial attitude of the women entrepreneurs in food processing industries taken together shows that the p value was less than 0.05 pointing to the fact that age is a factor which contributes to the financial attitude of the respondents. When variables of financial attitude were taken independently along with age, variation was found to be statistically very significant for all variables when they were taken independently also since ***all p values are found to be less than 0.05***. Respondents belonging to the age below 25 expressed better financial attitudes than others except in the case of borrowings. Borrowals appeared favourable for respondents aged above 55.

2) It was observed that financial attitude of the women entrepreneurs in food processing industries taken together shows that the p value was less

than 0.05 pointing to the fact that religion is a factor which contributes to the financial attitude of the respondents. When variables of financial attitude were taken independently along with religion, variation was found to be statistically very significant for all variables when they were taken independently also since ***all p values are found to be less than 0.05***.

3) Financial attitude of the women entrepreneurs in food processing industries taken together had p values less than 0.05 indicating that there is an association for financial attitude variables with marital status of the respondents. When the variables were tested discretely, variation was found to be statistically very significant for all variables except in the case of attitude towards investment **(p=0.152> 0.05)** and attitude towards borrowing **(p=0.774> 0.05)**. Married respondents showed more favourable attitude than others except in the case of borrowings.

5.2.4 Association Between Financial Behavior And Demographic Variables

1) With regard to the financial behaviour of the women entrepreneurs in food processing industries, it was seen that when taken together, financial behavior of the respondents had significant association with age of the respondents. When the variables of financial behaviour were considered independently, variation was found to be statistically very significant for all the variables (all p values were less than 0.05).

   Estimated marginal means of the women entrepreneurs in food processing industries indicate that financial behaviour of women entrepreneurs in food processing industries is most favourable for the age group below 25 except in their behaviour towards financial planning (Mean=49.820) and the behavior towards record maintenance (Mean=20.488). Thus it can be concluded that financial behaviour of the women entrepreneurs in food processing industries differ with the age of the entrepreneur taken independently and collectively.

2) When religion of the women entrepreneurs in food processing industries is considered, financial behaviour had association with religion when taken together and the variation was found to be statistically very significant for all variables when the financial behaviour variables were taken independently . Financial behaviour was observed to be more advantageous among the religious communities other than Hindus, Christian and Muslims. Thus, it can be wrapped up by saying that the financial behaviour of the women entrepreneurs in food processing industries differ according their religion when taken independently and when they are taken altogether.

3) Means score of the financial behaviour variables tested among the women entrepreneurs in food processing industries taken together had association with marital status since test statistic gave values which were found to be statistically significant ($p=0.000< 0.05$) at 5 per cent level. When the financial behaviour variables were taken independently, variation is found to be statistically very significant for all variables except for financial planning ($p=0.713>0.05$), record maintenance ($p=0.341>0.05$) and savings ($p=0.086>0.05$). Women entrepreneurs who live separated are found to exhibit higher mean scores of interconnection with all financial behaviours except in the case of

married respondents who exhibit higher mean scores in the case of financial behaviour towards budgeting (Mean=23.365) and financial behaviour towards investments (Mean=29.426). We can end by saying that financial behaviour of the respondents differ according to their marital status when evaluated collectively and independently.

5.2.4 Impact of Financial knowledge on borrowing decisions

1) Significance value of ANOVA for the impact of financial knowledge level on borrowing decisions of women entrepreneurs was found to be less than 0.05. We can thus say that financial knowledge of women entrepreneurs managing food processing industrial units influences their borrowing decisions.

5.2.5 Impact of Financial knowledge on Investment decisions

1) Significance value of ANOVA for the impact of financial knowledge level on borrowing decisions of women entrepreneurs was found to be less than 0.05 . We can thus conclude that investment decisions of the entrepreneur are influenced by the financial knowledge of women entrepreneurs managing food processing industrial units.

5.2.6 Fund utilization

1) "Dividend payment" was identified as the most utilized financial activity in a business (Mean rank 4.13) and investment in current asset as the least utilized financial activity. Chi-square statistic had the value of 54.376 which was seen to be significant at 5 per cent level ($p < 0.05$). We can conclude that the fund utilization activities are

not the same for the women entrepreneurs engaged in food processing industrial units.

2) It was inferred from the study that the food industries engaged in food processing industrial units which are unregistered (**Mean rank 273.17)** are utilizing finance mostly for dividend payment when compared to registered food processing industrial units (**Mean rank 345.50).**

3) Food industries engaged in preservation activities (**Mean rank 208.00**) are utilizing finance mostly for "dividend payment". Chi square value obtained is **84.710** with 4 degrees of freedom, and was seen to be significant at 5 per cent level indicating that there is significant difference in the preference of fund utilization according to the nature of activities being undertaken among the women entrepreneur.

5.2.7 *Problems in the management of finance*

1) Managing cash flows of the organization" is the most important problem in managing the finances (Mean rank 2.71). Chi-square statistic had the value of 1458.409 which is significant at 5 per cent level ($p < 0.05$). It may be decided that there is significant variation among the women entrepreneurs with respect to the problems in managing the finances.

2) Food industries engaged in food processing industrial units which are unregistered (Mean rank 305.83) are facing the highest difficulty in managing cash flows followed by food industrial units which are registered (Mean rank 314.88). p value was found to be more than 0.05 per cent indicating that there is no significant difference in managing the cash flows according to the nature of activities being undertaken.

3) It was observed that food industries engaged in preparation activities (**Mean rank 246.50**) are facing the highest difficulty in managing cash flows. Chi square value obtained is 92.617 with 4 degrees of freedom, and was seen to be significant at 5 per cent level (**p value is less than 0.05**) .Thus we can reach into a conclusion that there is significant difference in the problems according to the nature of activities being undertaken in food processing industrial units.

5.2.8 Relationship Between Financial Knowledge Level and Nature of Activities

1) It was clear from the study that women entrepreneurs managing food industries involved in preparation activities (**Mean rank 197.50)** are having the highest knowledge level about financial products. Chi square value obtained for knowledge about financial products is **131.226** with 4 degrees of freedom, **(p value is less than 0.05)** indicating that that there is significant difference in the knowledge level of financial products according to the nature of activities being undertaken in food processing industrial units.

2) From the study it could be concluded that knowledge level about financial services is the highest for women entrepreneurs managing food industries involved in processing activities (Mean rank 281.75) . Chi square value obtained for knowledge about financial services is 19.256 with 4 degrees of freedom at 5 per cent level of significance (p value is less than 0.05) projecting the fact that there is significant difference in the knowledge level of financial services according to the nature of activities being undertaken in food processing industrial units.

3) Knowledge level about financial terms is the highest for women entrepreneurs managing food industries involved in preparation activities (Mean rank 243.50). Chi square value obtained for knowledge about financial services is 58.908 with 4 degrees of freedom, at 5 per cent level of significance (p value is less than 0.05) pointing out that there is significant difference in the knowledge level of financial terms according to the nature of activities being undertaken in food processing industrial unit.

4) It was learned from the study that knowledge level about financial concepts is the highest for women entrepreneurs managing food industries involved in preparation activities (Mean rank 255.50). Chi square value obtained for knowledge about financial services is 34.431 with 4 degrees of freedom, at 5 per cent level of significance (p value is less than 0.05) indicating that there is significant difference in the knowledge level of financial concepts according to the nature of activities being undertaken in food processing industrial units.

5.2.9 Relationship Between Financial Attitude and Nature of Activities Undertaken

1) Women entrepreneurs managing food industries involved in preparation activities (Mean rank 250.50) are having the most favourable attitude towards budgeting. Chi square value obtained for the attitude towards budgeting is 70.195 with 4 degrees of freedom, and was seen to be significant at 5 per cent level (p value is less than 0.05) demonstrating that there is significant difference in the attitude of women entrepreneurs.

2) It was also found that attitude towards investment is the most favourable for women entrepreneurs managing food industries involved in preparation activities (**Mean rank 263.50**). Chi square value obtained for attitude towards investment is **51.850** with 4 degrees of freedom, and was seen to be significant at 5 per cent level **(p value is less than 0.05).** This shows that there is significant difference in the attitude towards investment among the women entrepreneurs managing food industries in Kerala according to the nature of activities being undertaken.

3) According to the study, attitude towards financial planning is the most favourable for women entrepreneurs managing food industries involved in preparation activities (**Mean rank 239.50**). Chi square value (**55.174**) obtained for attitude towards financial planning was seen to be significant at 5 per cent level **(p value is less than 0.05).** This shows that there is significant difference in the Attitude towards financial planning among the women entrepreneurs managing food industries in Kerala according to the nature of activities being undertaken.

4) It was understood from the analysis that the attitude towards financial record maintenance is the most favourable for women entrepreneurs managing food industries involved in preparation activities (**Mean rank 235.50**). Chi square value obtained for attitude towards financial record maintenance is **55.174** with 4 degrees of freedom, and was seen to be significant at 5 per cent level **(p value is less than 0.05)**. This shows that there is significant difference in the attitude towards financial record maintenance among the women entrepreneurs managing food industries in Kerala

according to the nature of activities being undertaken.

5) Study reveals that the attitude towards financial savings is the most favourable for women entrepreneurs managing food industries involved in preparation activities (**Mean rank 266.50**). Chi square value obtained for attitude towards financial savings is **29.209** with 4 degrees of freedom, and was seen to be significant at 5 per cent level **(p value is less than 0.05)** representing the view that there is significant difference in the attitude towards financial savings among the women entrepreneurs managing food industries in Kerala according to the nature of activities being undertaken.

6) It was inferred from the study that the attitude towards financial borrowings is the most favorable for women entrepreneurs managing food industries involved in preservation activities (**Mean rank 290.50**). Chi square value obtained for attitude towards financial borrowings is **5.761** with 4 degrees of freedom **(p=0.218)** and was seen to be insignificant at 5 per cent level **(p value is more than 0.05)** . This shows that there is no significant difference in the attitude towards financial borrowings among the women entrepreneurs managing food industries in Kerala according to the nature of activities being undertaken.

7) From the study, it is clear that attitude towards utilization of funds is the most favourable for women entrepreneurs managing food industries involved in preservation activities (**Mean rank 268.00**). Chi square value obtained for attitude towards utilization of funds is **12.867** with 4 degrees of freedom **(p=0.012)** and was seen to

be significant at 5 per cent level **(p value is less than 0.05)** indicating that there is no significant difference in the attitude towards utilization of funds among the women entrepreneurs managing food industries in Kerala according to the nature of activities being undertaken.

8) The Kruskal-Wallis Test revealed that the attitude towards spendings is the most favourable for women entrepreneurs managing food industries involved in packaging activities (**Mean rank 218.00**). Chi square value obtained for attitude towards spending of funds is **39.489** with 4 degrees of freedom **(p=0.000)** and was seen to be significant at 5 per cent level **(p value is less than 0.05)** . This shows that there is no significant difference in the attitude towards spending of funds among the women entrepreneurs managing food industries in Kerala according to the nature of activities being undertaken.

5.2.10 Relationship Between Financial Behaviour and Nature of Activities

1. It was understood from the study that women entrepreneurs managing food industries involved in packaging activities **(Mean rank 250.50)** are having the most favourable behaviour towards budgeting. Chi square value obtained for the behaviour towards budgeting is **32.437** with 4 degrees of freedom **(p=0.000)** and was seen to be significant at 5 per cent level **(p value is less than 0.05).** This shows that there is significant difference in the behaviour of women entrepreneurs managing food industries in Kerala towards budgeting according to the nature of activities being undertaken.

2. From the study, it is clear that most suitable behavior towards investment was found among women entrepreneurs managing food industries involved in preparation activities (**Mean rank 294.50**). Chi square value obtained for behaviour towards investment is **8.743** with 4 degrees of freedom **(p=0.068),** and was seen to be insignificant at 5 per cent level **(p value is more than 0.05).** This shows that there is no significant difference in the behaviour towards investment among the women entrepreneurs managing food industries in Kerala according to the nature of activities being undertaken
3. It can be seen that most suitable behavior towards financial savings was found among women entrepreneurs managing food industries involved in conversion activities (**Mean rank 256.50**). Chi square value obtained for behaviour towards financial savings is **47.488** with 4 degrees of freedom **(p=0.000)**, and was seen to be significant at 5 per cent level **(p value is less than 0.05) .** This shows that there is significant difference in the behaviour towards financial savings among the women entrepreneurs managing food industries in Kerala according to the nature of activities being undertaken.
4. Most suitable behavior towards financial borrowings was found among women entrepreneurs managing food industries involved in processing activities (**Mean rank 281.75**). Chi square value obtained for behaviour towards financial savings is **14.866** with 4 degrees of freedom **(p=0.005)** and was seen to be significant at 5 per cent level **(p value is less than 0.05)**. This shows that there is significant difference in the behaviour towards financial borrowings among

the women entrepreneurs managing food industries in Kerala according to the nature of activities being undertaken

5. Most suitable behavior towards towards utilization of funds was found among women entrepreneurs managing food industries involved in packaging activities (**Mean rank 265.50**) Chi square value obtained for behaviour towards utilization of funds is **49.875** with 4 degrees of freedom **(p=0.000)** and was seen to be significant at 5 per cent level **(p value is less than 0.05)** demonstrating the fact that there is no significant difference in the behaviour towards utilization of funds among the women entrepreneurs managing food industries in Kerala according to the nature of activities being undertaken.
6. It was revealed in the study that the most suitable behavior towards spendings was found among women entrepreneurs managing food industries involved in preparation activities (**Mean rank 279.50**). Chi square value obtained for behaviour towards spending of funds is **18.409** with 4 degrees of freedom **(p=0.001)** and was seen to be significant at 5 per cent level **(p value is less than 0.05)** . This shows that there is no significant difference in the behaviour towards spending of funds among the women entrepreneurs managing food industries in Kerala according to the nature of activities being undertaken.

5.2.11 Relationship Between Financial Knowledge Level and Type of Industry

1. Women entrepreneurs of unregistered food industries (**Mean rank 303.83**) have better knowledge level about the various financial products. At 5 per cent level of significance, it

was found that the **p** value was found to be more than 0.05 per cent indicating that there is no significant difference in the knowledge of financial products among the women entrepreneurs of food industry according to the type of industry.

2. It is an indication in the study that women entrepreneurs of unregistered food industries **(Mean rank 265.17)** have better knowledge level about the various financial services. At 5 per cent level of significance, it was found that the **p** value was found to be less than 0.05 per cent indicating that there is significant difference in the knowledge of financial services among the women entrepreneurs of food industry according to the type of industry.
3. Study reveals that women entrepreneurs of unregistered food industries **(Mean rank 285.83)** have better knowledge level about the various financial terms. At 5 per cent level of significance, it was found as the **p** value to be less than 0.05 per cent representing that there is significant difference in the knowledge of financial services among the women entrepreneurs of food industry according to the type ofindustry.
4. It was understood from the figures in the table that being registered and unregistered did not make any change in their knowledge about financial concepts since mean scores obtained did not differ between registered and unregistered units.

5.2.12 Relationship Between Financial Attitude and Nature of Activities

1. From the study, it is clear that registered food processing industrial units **(Mean rank = 293.00)**

managed by women entrepreneurs showed more favourable financial attitude towards budgeting. At 5 per cent level of significance, p value is **0.012**, which is less than **0.05** indicating the presence of significant difference between the two categories under study.

2. In this study, it can be seen that unregistered food processing industrial units **(Mean rank = 302.50)** managed by women entrepreneurs showed more favourable financial attitude towards investments when compared to registered food processing industrial units **(Mean rank = 318.00)**. At 5 per cent level of significance, p has a value **0.281**, which is more than **0.05** indicating insignificant difference between registered and unregistered industries.

3. Unregistered food processing industrial units **(Mean rank = 293.17)** managed by women entrepreneurs showed more favourable financial attitude towards financial planning. At 5 per cent level of significance, p has a value **0.019**, which is less than **0.05** indicating significant difference between registered and unregistered industries in the attitude towards financial planning.

4. It can be understood that, registered food processing industrial units **(Mean rank = 291.13)** exhibit better financial attitude towards record maintenance. P has a value **0.005**, which is less than **0.05** pointing towards significant difference between registered and unregistered industries in the attitude towards record maintenance among the women entrepreneurs of food processing industrial units.

5. With regard to the financial attitude towards Savings, registered food processing industrial units

(Mean rank = 278.00) exhibit favourable attitude. At 5 per cent level of significance, p value is **0.000**, which is less than **0.05** pointing towards significant difference between registered and unregistered industries in the attitude towards Savings in the women entrepreneurs of food processing industrial units.

6. Study clarifies that unregistered food processing industrial units **(Mean rank = 255.83)** exhibit favourable financial attitude towards borrowings. P value has a value **0.000**, which is less than **0.05** indicating significant difference between registered and unregistered industries in the attitude towards borrowings in the women entrepreneurs of food processing industrial units.
7. Analysis of the response reveals that unregistered food processing industrial units **(Mean rank = 290.83)** exhibit favourable financial attitude towards utilization of funds. Since, P value is **0.000**, which is less than **0.05** pointing towards significant difference between registered and unregistered industries in the attitude towards utilization of funds in the women entrepreneurs of food processing industrial units.
8. It was observed that ,unregistered food processing industrial units **(Mean rank = 279.17)** exhibit favourable reviews on the financial attitude towards utilization of funds. At 5 per cent level of significance, p has a value **0.000**, which is less than **0.05** pointing towards significant difference between registered and unregistered industries in the attitude towards spending in the women entrepreneurs of food processing industrial units.

5.2.13 Relationship Between Financial Behaviour and Type of Industry

1. Based on the study, it may be seen that unregistered food processing industrial units **(Mean rank = 294.50)** managed by women entrepreneurs showed more favourable financial behaviour towards budgeting. At 5 per cent level of significance, p value is **0.030**, which is less than **0.05** indicating the presence of significant difference between the two categories under study.
2. In this study, it was seen that unregistered food processing industrial units **(Mean rank = 271.17)** managed by women entrepreneurs showed more favourable financial behaviour towards investments. At 5 per cent level of significance, p has a value **0.000**, which is less than **0.05** indicating significant difference between the attitudes of women entrepreneurs in registered and unregistered food processing units.
3. It could be learned from the study that, unregistered food processing industrial units **(Mean rank = 256.50)** managed by women entrepreneurs showed more favourable financial behaviour towards financial planning. At 5 per cent level of significance, p has a value **0.000**, which is less than **0.05** indicating significant difference between registered and unregistered industries in the behaviour towards financial planning in the women entrepreneurs of food processing industrial units.
4. It was noticed that registered food processing industrial units (**Mean rank = 361.13**) exhibit better financial behaviour towards record maintenance. P has a value 0.005, which is less than 0.05 pointing towards significant difference between

registered and unregistered industries in the behaviour towards record maintenance in the women entrepreneurs of food processing industrial units.

5. It could be understood from the study that unregistered food processing industrial units **(Mean rank = 270.50)** exhibit favourable financial behaviour towards Savings. P has a value **0.000,** which is less than **0.05** pointing towards significant difference between registered and unregistered industries in the behaviour towards Savings in the women entrepreneurs of food processing industrial units.
6. Study revealed that unregistered food processing industrial units **(Mean rank = 241.83)** exhibit favourable financial behaviour towards borrowings. P has a value **0.000**, which is less than **0.05** pointing towards significant difference between registered and unregistered industries in the behaviour towards borrowings in the women entrepreneurs of food processing industrial units.
7. From the study, it was clear that unregistered food processing industrial units **(Mean rank = 265.83)** exhibit favourable financial behaviour towards utilization of funds. P has a value **0.000,** which is less than **0.05** pointing towards significant difference between registered and unregistered industries in the behaviour towards utilization of funds in the women entrepreneurs of food processing industrial units.
8. Based on the study on financial behaviour towards utilization of funds unregistered food processing industrial units **(Mean rank = 250.50)** exhibit favourable reviews on the financial behaviour

towards utilization of funds. P has a value **0.000,** which is less than **0.05** pointing towards significant difference between registered and unregistered industries in the behaviour towards spending in the women entrepreneurs of food processing industrial units.

5.2.14 *Influence of Financial Attitude Towards Financial Behaviour*

1. **25.50** per cent of the variation in financial attitude was observed from the regression. Associated F value **(211.828)** was found to be statistically significant **($p < 0.05$).** We can conclude that the financial behaviour towards budgeting influences the financial attitude towards budgeting among the women entrepreneurs engaged in food processing units.
2. Influence of financial attitude towards investment in the financial behaviour towards investment among the women entrepreneurs was evaluated and **24.60** per cent of the variation in financial attitude towards investment was found among women entrepreneurs in food processing industrial units and that this explanation is statistically valid, as the associated F value **(201.382)** is statistically significant **($p < 0.05$)**. The Beta coefficients are significant as the associated t-values of the regression equation is significant at 5 per cent level of significance **(observed $p < 0.05$)**.
3. It was learned from the analysis of the study that **24.60** per cent of the variation in financial attitude towards financial planning among women entrepreneurs in food processing industrial units is explained by the regression equation and that this explanation is statistically valid, as the associated F value **(267.079)** is statistically

significant **($p < 0.05$)**. The Beta coefficients are significant as the associated t- values of the regression equation is significant at 5 per cent level of significance **(observed $p < 0.05$)**. It means that the financial attitude towards financial planning influences the financial behaviour towards financial planning among the women entrepreneurs engaged in food processing units

4. Analysis of the data collected revealed that **17.20** per cent of the variation in financial attitude towards record maintenance among women entrepreneurs in food processing industrial units is explained by the regression equation and that this explanation is statistically valid, as the associated F value **(128.611)** is statistically significant **($p < 0.05$)**. The Beta coefficients are significant as the associated t- values of the regression equation is significant at 5 per cent level of significance **(observed $p < 0.05$)**. Thus, it is clear that the financial behaviour towards record maintenance is influenced by the financial attitude towards record maintenance among the women entrepreneurs engaged in food processing units.
5. Study reveals about **8.50** per cent of the variation in financial attitude towards savings and that this explanation is statistically valid, as the associated F value **(57.537)** is statistically significant **($p < 0.05$)**. The Beta coefficients are significant as the associated t-values are significant **(observed $p < 0.05$)**. We can conclude that the financial behaviour towards savings influences the financial attitude towards savings among the women entrepreneurs engaged in food processing units.
6. It was seen that, **17.20** per cent of the variation in financial attitude towards borrowings among women entrepreneurs in food processing industrial

units is explained by the regression equation and that this explanation is statistically valid, as the associated F value **(216.593)** is statistically significant **($p < 0.05$)**. The Beta coefficients are significant as the associated t-values of the regression equation is significant at 5 per cent level of significance **(observed $p < 0.05$)**. Thus we know that, financial behaviour towards borrowings is influenced by the financial attitude towards borrowings.

7. Data analyzed portrayed the presence of **11.60** per cent of the variation in financial attitude towards fund utilization among women entrepreneurs in food processing industrial units that is explained by the regression equation and that this explanation is statistically valid, as the associated F value **(80.716)** is statistically significant **($p < 0.05$)**. The Beta coefficients were found to be significant as the associated t-values of the regression equation is significant at 5 per cent level of significance **(observed $p < 0.05$)**. We can hence comprehend that the financial behaviour towards fund utilization is influenced by the financial attitude towards fund utilization among the women entrepreneurs engaged in food processing units.

8. Presence of **42.20** per cent of the variation in financial attitude towards spendings among women entrepreneurs in food processing industrial units is explained by the regression equation and that this explanation is statistically valid, as the associated F value **(451.412)** is statistically significant **($p < 0.05$)**. Figures in the table indicate that the Beta coefficients are significant as the associated t-values of the regression equation is significant at 5 per cent level of significance

(observed $p < 0.05$). It can be concluded that the financial behaviour towards spending is influenced by the financial attitude towards spendings among the women entrepreneurs engaged in food processing units.

5.3 Testing of Hypothesis

1) *$H_0$1: There is no significant relationship between the demographic variables of women entrepreneurs managing food processing industrial units and their financial knowledge level.*

   Relationship of financial knowledge of women entrepreneurs engaged in food processing units with demographic variables like age, religion and marital status was evaluated using MANOVA. It was observed that p values of all the variables were observed to be less than 0.05. Hence null hypothesis was rejected and it can be concluded that there is a significant relationship between demographic variables of the respondents and their financial knowledge level.

2) *$H_0$2: There is no significant relationship between the demographic variables of women entrepreneurs managing food processing industrial units and their financial attitude levels.*

   Relationship of financial attitude of women entrepreneurs engaged in food processing units with demographic variables like age, religion and marital status was evaluated using MANOVA. It was observed that p values of all the variables were less than 0.05. Hence null hypothesis was rejected and it can be concluded that there is a significant relationship between demographic variables of the respondents and their financial attitude level. When the test of between subjects was further carried down, it was noticed that in the case of marital status of the women entrepreneurs engaged in food processing industrial units, it was found that variation was significant for all the variables, except in the case of attitude towards borrowings **(p= 0.774> 0.05)** and attitude towards investment **(p= 0.152> 0.05).**

3) *$H_0$3: There is no significant relationship between the demographic variables of women entrepreneurs managing food processing industrial units and their financial behaviour.*

   Relationship of financial behaviour of women entrepreneurs engaged in food processing units with demographic variables like age, religion and marital status was evaluated using MANOVA. When the variables were considered together, it was observed that p value was less than 0.05. Hence null hypothesis was rejected and it can be concluded that there is a significant relationship between demographic variables of the respondents and their financial behaviour level. When the test of between subjects was further carried down to evaluate further, it was noticed that in the case of, marital status of the women entrepreneurs engaged in food processing industrial units, it was found that variation was significant for all the variables except in the financial behaviour towards financial planning **(p= 0.713> 0.05)**, financial behaviour towards savings **(p= 0.086> 0.05)** and financial behaviour towards record maintenance **(p= 0.341> 0.05).**

4) *$H_0$4: There is no significant impact of financial knowledge level on investment decisions of women entrepreneurs managing food processing industrial units.*

Study of the influence of financial knowledge level on investment decisions was evaluated using regression and it was observed that the significance value of ANOVA for the impact of financial knowledge level on investment decisions of women entrepreneurs was seen to be less than 0.05. Hence null hypothesis was rejected and it was concluded that there is a significant influence of financial knowledge levels on the investment decisions of the entrepreneurs . The beta coefficient of knowledge about financial concepts is found to be positive and significant, as the t values of the beta coefficient were seen to be significant (**observed p<0.05**). Thus, we can say that financial knowledge level has a positive influence on the investment decisions.

5) *$H_0$5: There is no significant impact of financial knowledge level on borrowing decisions of women entrepreneurs managing food processing industrial units.*

Study of the influence of financial knowledge level on borrowing decisions was examined using regression and it was observed that the significance value of ANOVA for the impact of financial knowledge level on borrowing decisions of women entrepreneurs to be less than 0.05. Hence null hypothesis was rejected and it was concluded that there is a significant influence of financial knowledge levels on the borrowing decisions of the entrepreneurs. The beta coefficient of knowledge about financial concepts is found to be significant, as the t values of the beta coefficient are significant (**observed p<0.05**) and positive. Thus, we can say that financial knowledge level of the women entrepreneurs engaged in food processing units has a positive influence on their borrowing decisions.

6) *$H_0$6: There is no significant difference in the utilization of funds among women entrepreneurs engaged in food processing industrial units.*

Friedman test was utilized to analyze the null hypothesis and it was found that the value of Friedman Chi-square was significant at 5 per cent level (value of Chi-square = 54.376 with P = .000 <.05). Therefore, null hypothesis was discarded with a conclusion that the elements for fund utilization were different for the women entrepreneurs engaged in food processing industrial units in Kerala.

7) *$H_0$7: There is no significant effect of financial attitude on financial behaviour of the respondents.*

Study on the influence of financial attitude level on financial behavior of the respondents was evaluated using regression and it was observed that the significance value of ANOVA for the impact of financial attitude level on financial behaviour of women entrepreneurs to be less than 0.05. Hence null hypothesis was rejected and it was concluded that there is a significant influence of financial attitude levels on the financial behaviour of the entrepreneurs. The beta coefficients of financial attitude of the respondents were found to be significant and positive in influencing the financial behavior of the respondents as the t values of the beta coefficient were seen to be significant (observed $p<0.05$). Thus, we can say that financial attitude level has a positive influence on the financial behavior of women entrepreneurs engaged in food processing industrial units.

5.4 Suggestions and Recommendations

The following strategy is recommended for superior financial literacy and financial inclusion in the state of Kerala as well as for the country. These are:

1) Mass based approach:

Financially excluded households should be identified and should be brought in to the financial literacy programs conducted for the masses rather than concentrating all the efforts though the SHG's alone.

2) Focus on Advances To SME's managed by women

Set and boost inner hierarchical and individual credit official staff who will focus on advances to SMEs owned by ladies and track their achievements yearly with respect to loans to women entrepreneurs.

3) Complementing Financial Inclusion and Financial Literacy:

Program of financial inclusion and financial literacy cannot be organized in isolation. If financial inclusion training is carried out in collaboration with the financial literacy training program, it will get a better reach among the beneficiaries for both financial inclusion and financial literacy. Financial inclusion without necessary literacy will not serve the purpose intended.

4) Staggered approach to financial literacy training should be adopted:

Financial literacy trainings should be conducted in multi stages to improve the effectiveness of the trainings. A feedback from the entrepreneurs should also be collected after every stage to gain an understanding about the extent it has satisfied the expected outcome after the training.

5) Reduce the time lag in loan procedures after the training.

Timely credit can serve business better . If funds are not available when required, many opportunities will be missed for the business. Execute effective basic leadership methods to improve the turn-around time in the credit endorsement process, particularly for trained bank customers.

6) Women specific corners in financial institutions

Many of the ladies are having difficulty in interacting with people of the opposite gender. Offer women specific corners in financial institutions or devoted lady financial experts to expand support to ladies entrepreneurs who are considered to have valuable business ideas.

7) Strategies specifically for women entrepreneurs

Women entrepreneurs if developed can support the growth of the society. Support should be extended to the women entrepreneurs in accessing credit, which is a serious issue for the women entrepreneurs. Governments should urge financial institutions to create strategies and systems that will boost their focus for credits to ladies owned SMEs through campaigns to create awareness.

8) Include Women's Associations during strategy formulation

Women associations are collective group of women. Such organizations because of having close contact with the focus group ie, women, will be in a better position to know the requirements and needs of women. Encourage the involvement of representatives from women's associations to decide on the financial and administrative strategy to be followed by government and in extending funds for monetary advancement.

9) Ancestral property in the name of ladies

Patriarchal society keeps all the assets and belongings of the family in the name of male members who are considered superior. Giving the capacity of ladies to claim and use financial resources like bank accounts, ancestral property etc. in their personal capacity rather than depending on family members for collaterals will prompt families to include women in decision making and experiences will improve the financial knowledge of the women entrepreneur.

10) Involvement in policy making

Being dynamic participants for the welfare of the society, Government should include representatives of women entrepreneurs in the policy making bodies of the government. Only women will be able to know the difficulties they face because of gender peculiarities. Women representatives will be able to address the issues in a better manner.

11) Amend laws and attract entrepreneurs

Legal changes favouring women should be developed further. Women are not to be kept within the four walls of the house. They should be left open for changes. Advocate for changes in legislation which create boundaries to the development of SMEs managed by women. Changes in law will motivate more women to try on entrepreneurship.

12) Encourage women entrepreneurs with good ideas to take up loans

Many women find it difficult in accessing finance due to issues like lack of collaterals and inability to repay in the initial years of the business. These issues are preventing women entrepreneurs in growing further.

Potentialities of the business idea as well as her entrepreneurial skills should be taken into account when considering a loan proposal. Bankers should give the necessary support for taking a loan.

13) Customized products

Needs vary from person to person and it is not different for entrepreneurs too. New customized loan products as well as risk evaluation strategies should be developed specifically for lady entrepreneurs when considering a loan application.

14) Innovative financial products

Women business associations should create liason with non-bank partners and financial institutions to develop the innovative SME loan products designed for women-owned SMEs. Women associations should take efforts in creating awareness among the entrepreneurs.

15) Use of more SHG linkages and NABARD Platform:

SHG's are many in number across the state of Kerala. SHG's give a structured platform for giving training on financial literacy and will give better outreach than the other programs which are usually being conducted for the public. SHG's should try to give awareness about banking services and credit linkages with various banks. The resources of NABARD could be utilized in training entrepreneurs of agri-based entrepreneurs and farmers. Food processing industrial units being agri-based should be given training on financial empowerment utilizing the resources of NABARD.

16) Use of audio-visual methods along with lectures:

It would be more beneficial if content for the trainings is given to the audience using audio-visual methods, which will attract the audience better to listen and be attentive. This should be in addition to the classes in the form of lectures to teach about the various financial concepts being followed.

17) Monitoring and timely Follow-up

Monitoring about the quality of the training programs during the session of training and doing the required follow-up to see if things are being practiced as taught in the classes is the need of the hour for better results.

18) Use of local or community trainers:

Training programs can be made more effective with the use of locale trainers for the training. Participants will feel more comfortable and at ease if local dialects are used in the training sessions.

5.5 Conclusion

Financial literacy means possessing a set of knowledge and skills that allow a person to have informed and purposive decisions according to the availability of their financial resources. Developed countries like UK, USA and Japan after realizing the importance of financial literacy for financial management are making efforts to train their citizens. India having huge human capital requires concentration of its efforts to develop the financial literacy for efficient management of finances. People with proper financial literacy will have improved financial decisions and manages finance better than others. So financial literacy training and education is vital for the country's development. Using audio visual mode of teaching, entrepreneurs should be made aware about the various financial techniques to be followed in better management of their restricted funds. Kudumbasrees, SHG's, Asha workers and student volunteers can be utilized in improving the financial skills of the entrepreneur. If financial literacy improves for women entrepreneurs, financial empowerment will take place and improved living conditions for the society will be the result.

5.6 Scope For Further Research

- Governmental policies, strategies and measures to promote financial literacy among women entrepreneurs can be studied in detail.
- Financial literacy among female students after financial education can be premeditated.
- Effectiveness of financial literacy trainings among various categories can be explored.
- Influence of advertisements in promoting financial literacy among various categories of respondents can be studied.

Bibliography

1. Pradip N. Khandwalla: Fourth Eye. Excellence Through Creativity: 1988. Allahabad: Wheeler. 2nd ed., 423 pages. (1991). *Organization Studies*, 12(2), 328–328. https://doi.org/10.1177/017084069101200220
2. Sue Birley, (1989), "Female Entrepreneurs : Are They Really Different?" *Journal of Small Business Management*, Vol. 27, No. 1, (January) 32-37
3. Knapp, J. P. (1991). The benefits of consumer education: A survey report. Yipsilanti, MI: Eastern Michigan University, Consumer Education Center.
4. Penrose, E.T. (1995). The Theory of The Growth of The Firm (3rd edition). *Oxford: Oxford University Press* [with new Foreword by Edith Penrose].
5. Chen, H. and Volpe, R. P., (1998). An analysis of personal financial literacy among college students. *Financial Services Review*, 7 (2), 107-128.
6. Howells, J. (2000). Innovation and Services: New Conceptual Frameworks, *CRIC,Discussion Paper 38* (Manchester: University of Manchester)
7. Volpe, R. P., Kotel, J. E. & Chen, H. (2002). A survey of investment literacy among online

investors. *Financial Counseling and Planning,* 13(1), 1-13.

8. Moore, D. (2003), Survey of Financial Literacy in Washington State: Knowledge, Behavior, Attitudes, and Experiences, *Technical Report* 03–39, Social and Economic Sciences Research Center, Washington State University. Google Scholar
9. Worthington, A. C. (2006). Predicting Financial Literacy in Australia, *Financial Services Review,* 15(1), 59-79.
10. Joo, S.-h., & Grable, J. E. (2004). An Exploratory Framework of the Determinants of Financial Satisfaction. *Journal of Family and Economic Issues,* 25(1), 25-50.
11. Chowdhury, Sanjib and Endres, Megan Lee, Gender Difference and the Formation of Entrepreneurial Self-Efficacy (2005). *Entrepreneurship in a Diverse World,* Vol., 8 pp 2005. Available at SSRN: https://ssrn.com/abstract=1497806
12. Campbell, J. Y. (2006), Household Finance, *NBER Working Paper No. 12149,* Cambridge, MA: National Bureau of Economic Research, Google Scholar
13. Devaney, S., Anong, S., & Whirl, S. (2007). Household savings motives. *Journal of Consumer Affairs,* 41(1), 174-186.
14. "Commissioned by the Australian Government Office for Women in the Department of Families, Community Services and Indigenous Affairs", *Report prepared by Australian government , Financial Literacy among Marginalised Women* (2007), p 54-55.
15. Robert K. and Lisa J., Consumer Financial Literacy and the Impact of Online Banking on the Financial Behavior of Lower-Income Bank Customers, *The Journal of Consumer Affairs,* Vol. 42, No. 2, 2008.

16. Mueller, Stephen & Conway Dato-on, Mary. (2008). Gender-Role Orientation as a Determinant of Entrepreneurial Self-Efficacy. *Journal of Developmental Entrepreneurship* (JDE). 13. 3-20. 10.1142/S108494670800082X.

17. Allen, Kayla and Kinchen, Victoria, Financial Management Practices of College Students (2009). *Global Journal of Business Research,* Vol. 3, No. 1, pp. 105-116, 2009. Available at SSRN: https://ssrn.com/abstract=1555194

18. Mandell, Lewis and Schmid Klein, Linda, The Impact of Financial Literacy Education on Subsequent Financial Behavior (2009). *Journal of Financial Counseling and Planning,* Vol. 20, No. 1, 2009. Available at SSRN: https://ssrn.com/abstract=2224231

19. Huston, S. J. (2010). Measuring financial literacy. *Journal of Consumer Affairs,* 44(2), 296-316. http://dx.doi.org/10.1111/j.1745-6606.2010.01170.x

20. Huston, S.J. (2010b). Determining Financial Literacy: Developing and Refining a Financial Literacy Assessment Instrument. *Consumer Interests Annual,* 56.

21. Norman, A. S. (2010). Importance of financial education in making informed decision on spending, 2(October), 199–207.

22. Oseifuah, E. K. (2010). Financial literacy and youth entrepreneurship in South Africa. *African Journal of Economic and Management Studies,* 1(2), 164-182. doi:10.1108/20400701011073473

23. Xiao, Jing Jian & Shim, Soyeon & Serido, Joyce. (2010). Financial Education, Financial Knowledge and Risky Credit Behavior of College Students. *Working paper* 10.2139/ssrn.1709039.

24. G. Gale, William & Levine, Ruth. (2010). Financial Literacy: What Works? How Could It Be More Effective?. *SSRN Electronic Journal*. 10.2139/ssrn.1758910.

25. Frances M. Amatucci, Daria C. Crawley, (2011) "Financial self efficacy among women entrepreneurs", *International Journal of Gender and Entrepreneurship*, Vol. 3 Issue: 1, pp.23-37, https://doi.org/10.1108/17566261111114962

26. Lusardi, Annamaria & Mitchell, Olivia S., 2011. "Financial literacy around the world: an overview," *Journal of Pension Economics and Finance*, Cambridge University Press, vol. 10(04), pages 497-508, October.

27. Lusardi, Annamaria & Mitchell, Olivia S (2011)"Financial Literacy and Retirement Planning in the United States" *Journal of Pension Economics and Finance*, October 2011, vol. 10(4), pp. 509-525.

28. Andoh, F. K., Nunoo, J., & Darfor, N. K. (2011). Sustaining Small and Medium Enterprises through Financial Service Utilization: Does Financial Literacy Matter? *Journal of Business and Enterprise Development*, 5(1), 74–94.

29. Jusoh, Rosnani & Ziyae, Babak & Asimiran, Soaib & Abd Kadir, Suhaida. (2011). Entrepreneur Training Needs Analysis: Implications On The Entrepreneurial Skills Needed For Successful Entrepreneurs. *International Business & Economics Research Journal (IBER)*, 10. 10.19030/iber.v10i1.933.

30. Barte, R. (2012). Financial Literacy in Microenterprises – The Case of Cebu Fish Vendors. Philippine, *Management Review*, 19, 91-99.

31. Heena K. Bijli (2012) Financial Literacy: An Essential Tool for Empowerment of Women through Micro-finance, *Studies on Home and Community Science*, 6:2, 77-85, DOI: 10.1080/09737189.2012.11885370

32. Kimwolo, a K., Saina, C. K., & Cheserek, G. J. (2012). Effects of Credit Training Skills on Sales Performance among Women Entrepreneurs in Elgeiyo Marakwet County, Kenya. *Journal of Emerging Trends in Economics and Management Sciences, 3*(6), 945–950.

33. Gillen, M. & Loeffler, D.N. (2012) Financial literacy and social work students: Knowledge is power. *Journal of Financial Therapy*, 3 (2), p. 28-38.

34. Graf, R. (2012). Master Thesis Financial Literacy and Financial Behavior in Switzerland, University of St. Gallen, School of Finance.

35. Sobhesh Kumar Agarwalla, Samir Barua, Joshy Jacob and Jayanth R. Varma (2012), A Survey of Financial Literacy among Students, Young Employees and the Retired in India, *IIMA*, study supported by citi foundation, June

36. Attom, B. E. (2013). Cash management practices by micro and small-scale enterprises at Kasoa in the central region of Ghana. *Asian Journal of Business and Management Sciences*, 3(2), 1-12. Retrieved from www.ajbms.org.

37. Ayodele, K. O. (2013). "Demographics, entrepreneurial self-efficacy and locus of control as determinants of adolescents' entrepreneurial intention in Ogun state, Nigeria", *Journal of Educational Research and Studies*, 1(2): 12-16.

38. Ben-Caleb, E., Faboyede, O.S. & Fakile, A.S(2013), Empowering Small and Medium Scale Enterprises

in Nigeria: A Key Poverty Alleviation Strategy, *International Journal of Business and Management Invention,* 2 (5) pp. 06-12.

39. Devi, L. B. (2013). Financial Management In Women Owned Business Enterprises In Manipur (A Case Study Of Imphal West And Thoubal Districts), *International Journal of Social Science & Interdisciplinary Research,* 2(7), 83–89.

40. Sinha, S. B., & Gupta, A. (2013). Financial Inclusion and Financial Literacy/ : A Comparative Study in their interrelation between selected urban and rural areas in the state of West Bengal, *,IOSR Journal of Economics and Finance (IOSR-JEF)* ,67–72.

41. Meta Brown, John Grigsby, Wilbert van der Klaauw, Jaya Wen, Basit Zafar (2013) Financial Education and the Debt Behavior of the Young, *The Review of Financial Studies,* Volume 29, Issue 9, Pages 2490–2522, https://doi.org/10.1093/rfs/hhw006

42. Njoroge, R. M. (2013). Relationship between financial literacy and Entrepreneurial Success in Nairobi County Kenya (*MBA Dissertation,* University of Nairobi).

43. Nwibo, S., & Okorie, A. (2013). Determinants of Entrepreneurship Among Agribusiness Investors, *European Journal of Business and Management, 5*(10), 115–124.

44. Disney, R., & Gathergood, J. (2013). Journ al of Banking & Finance Financial literacy and consumer credit portfolios, *Journal of Banking and Finance,* 37(7), 2246– 2254. https://doi.org/10.1016/j.jbankfin.2013.01.013

45. Ajzerle, Sanja; Brimble, Mark; and Freudenberg, Brett, Is Financial Capability Related to the Effective Use of Debt in Australia?,Australasian Accounting, *Business and Finance Journal,* 7(3), 2013,107-126. doi:10.14453/aabfj.v7i3.7

46. Suchanphin Suwanaphan, 2013. "Personal Financial Literacy of Academic Support-Employee in Chiang Mai University," Active Citizenship by Knowledge Management & Innovation: *Proceedings of the Management, Knowledge and Learning International Conference* 2013, ToKnowPress.

47. Sucuahi, W.T. (2013). Determinants of financial literacy of micro entrepreneurs in Davao city. *International Journal of Accounting Research,* Vol. 1(1), 44-51

48. Nicolini, G., Cude, B. J. and Chatterjee, S. (2013), Financial literacy, *International Journal of Consumer Studies,* 37: 689-705. doi:10.1111/ijcs.12050

49. Taft, M.K., Hosein, Z.Z., Mehrizi, S.M., and Roshan, A. (2013). "The Relation Between Financial Literacy, Financial Well-being and Financial Concern". *International Journal of Bussiness and Management,* Vol. 8 No. 11, pp. 63-75

50. Wise, S. (2013). The Impact of Financial Literacy on New Venture Survival. IJBM *International Journal of Business and Management,* 8(23). doi:10.5539/ijbm.v8n23p30

51. Akande, O., & Oluwaseun, Y. (2014). Influence of budgeting system on Entrepreneurial Business performance: Perspective of Small business Owner in Lagos state Nigeria , *Journal of Business and Management,* 16(6), 58–64. www.iosrjournals.org

52. Chelimo, Joseph Kurwo, and Isaac Ole Sopia, (2014), Effects of Bookkeeping on Growth of Small

and Medium Business Enterprises in Kabarnet Town, Baringo County, Kenya, *International Journal of Science and Research* ,Vol. 3, 432-437.

53. Dahmen, P., & Rodríguez, E. (2014). Financial Literacy and the Success of Small Businesses: An Observation from a Small Business Development Centre. Numeracy, *Scholar Commons*, 7(1). doi:10.5038/1936-4660.7.1.3
54. Fatoki, O. (2014). The Financial Literacy of Micro Enterprises in South Africa, *Journal of Social Science*, Vol 5, No 20, 40(2), 151-158.
55. G., Samkin, E., Pitu, & M., Low. (2014). Identifying the Financial Literacy Skills Necessary to Run a Small New Zealand Business, *E-Journal of Business Education & Scholarship of Teaching*, 8(1), 44-66.
56. Kamal Gupta, Jatinder Kaur(2014) A study of Financial Literacy among Micro Entrepreneurs in District Kangra, *International Journal of Research in Business Management*, 2(2):63-70.
57. Krechovska, M & Tausl Prochazkova, Petra. (2014). Enhancing entrepreneurial education activites: New challenges for SMEs development. *Actual Problems of Economics*. 158. 262-271.
58. Musah, A., & Ibrahim, M. (2014), Record Keeping and the Bottom Line: Exploring the Relationship between Record Keeping and Business Performance among Small and Medium Enterprises (SMEs) in the Tamale Metropolis of Ghana, *Research Journal of Finance and Accounting*, 5(2), 107-117.
59. Xiao, J. J., Chatterjee, S. and Kim, J. (2014), Financial independence of young adults. *International Journal of Consumer Studies*, 38: 394-403. doi:10.1111/ijcs.12106

60. Caroline, A., & Potrich, G. (2015). Determinants of Financial Literacy/ : Analysis of the Influence of Socioeconomic and Demographic Variables *,**, 362–377. https://doi.org/10.1590/1808-057x201501040

61. Brown, E. (2015), *OECD Working Papers on Finance , Insurance and Private Pensions No. 14* Empowering Women Through Financial Awareness and Education Angela Hung, Joanne Yoong, (July).

62. García, M. and Adame, M. (2015) The Characteristics of the Businesses and Entrepreneurs and Their Relationships with the Competitiveness of the SMEs in México. *Open Access Library Journal*, 2, 1-15. doi: 10.4236/oalib.1101555.

63. James Berry, Dean Karlan, M. P. (2015). The impact of financial education for youth., *Tinbergen Institute Discussion Paper*. https://doi.org/10.1016/j.econedurev.2019.101918

64. Titko, J., Ciemleja, G., & Lace, N. (2015). Financial Literacy of Latvian Citizens/ : Preliminary Survey Results. *Procedia - Social and Behavioral Sciences*, 213, 12–17. https://doi.org/10.1016/j.sbspro.2015.11.396

65. Crispus, J., Karanja, N., Mwangi, E., & Nyaanga, P. (2015). Adoption of Modern Management Accounting Techniques in Small and Medium (SMEs) in Developing Countries/ : A Case Study of SMEs in Kenya ., 1–15.

66. Islam, M.M. and Mustaquim, M(2015): Gender Gap in Literacy: A Study of Indian Scenario, in Ismail, M. et al., (eds.), *Life and Living through Newer Spectrum of Geography*, Mohit Publications, Delhi, pp. 188-202.

67. Muraga, K.P., & John, N. (2015), Effects of Financial Literacy on Performance of Youth Led Enterprises: A Case of Equity Group Foundation Training Program in Kiambu County, *International Journal of Social Sciences Management and Entrepreneurship,* 2(1), 218-231.

68. OECD. (2015). New Approaches to SME and Entrepreneurship Financing. In *New Approaches to SME and Entrepreneurship Financing*. https://doi.org/10.1787/9789264240957-en

69. Bediako, Israel Kofi Nyarko, and Matthew Brains Kudo, (2016), Assessing the effects of sound financial statement preparation on the growth of small and medium-scale enterprises, The *International Journal of Business & Management,* 4, 104.

70. Baluja, G. (2016), Financial Literacy Among Women in India/ : A Review, *Pacific Business Review International,* (Vol. 9), October.

71. EndalcachewBayeh (2016), The role of empowering women and achieving gender equality to the sustainable development of Ethiopia, *Pacific Science Review B: Humanities and Social Sciences,* 2 (1), 37-42, https://doi.org/10.1016/j.psrb.2016.09.013

72. Geoffrey Kimunduu, Otieno Erick, Adam Shisia, (2016), *International Journal of Economics Commerce and Management,* Vol. IV, Issue 11, 416-433, UK http://ijecm.co.uk/

73. Lisa Farrell; Tim Fry and Leonora Risse, (2016), The significance of financial self-efficacy in explaining women's personal finance behaviour, *Journal of Economic Psychology,* 54, (C), 85-99

74. Lokhande, M. A. (2016). A Study of Investment Awareness and Pattern of Savings and Investment

of Rural Investors, *Indian Journal of Finance*, Vol IX, Issue 7, July 2015). https://doi.org/10.17010/ /2015/v9i7/72351

75. Trombetta, M. (2016). Accounting And Finance Literacy And Self-Employment/ : An Exploratory Study., pages 1-32, *IE Business School – IE University*, May.

76. Ilmu, J., Josua, R., Yap, C., Komalasari, F., & Hadiansah, I. (2016). The Effect of Financial Literacy and Attitude on Financial Management Behavior and Satisfaction, *International Journal of Administrative Science & Organization*, 23(3).

77. Robert Amoah (2016), "Assessing the Level and Impact of Financial Literacy on African Americans", *A Thesis Report* for Walden University.

78. Stanzin Mantok, (2016) "Role of Women Entrepreneurship in Promoting Women Empowerment", *International Journal of Management and Applied Science (IJMAS)*, pp. 204-207, Volume-2,Issue-9, Special Issue-1

79. Cui, X. (2016). Calisthenics with Words: The Effect of Readability and Investor Sophistication on Investors' Performance Judgment, *International Journal of Financial Studies*, 4(1), 1. doi:10.3390/ ijfs4010001

80. Atkinson, A. (2017), "Financial Education for MSMEs and Potential Entrepreneurs", *OECD Working Papers on Finance*, Insurance and Private Pensions, No. 43, OECD Publishing, Paris,https:/ /doi.org/10.1787/bb2cd70c-en.

81. Da Silva, S., De Faveri, D., Correa, A. and Matsushita, R. (2017) Social Preferences, Financial Literacy and Intertemporal Choice. *Open Access Library Journal* , 4: e3699.

82. Dr. J. Gajendra Naidu(2017). Financial Literacy in India: A Review of Literature, *International Journal of Research in Business Studies and Management*, Volume 4, Issue 6, 2017, pp. 30-32

83. Harsha Vijay Kumar Jariwala (2017). Predicting Financial Literacy Level in Vuca World/ : A Case of Indian Retail Individual Investors, *IOSR journals*, Pages 46-57, May.

84. Ali, Husniyati & Omar, Emi Normalina & Abu Nasir, Hanisah & Osman, Muhamad. (2018). Financial Literacy of Entrepreneurs in the Small and Medium Enterprises, *Proceedings of the 2nd Advances in Business Research International Conference*, pp 31-38. 10.1007/978-981-10-6053-3_4.

85. Asandimitra, N. & Kautsar, A. (2017). Financial Self-Efficacy on Women Entrepreneurs Success, *International Journal of Academic Research in Business and Social Sciences*, 7(11), 293-300.

86. Dr. Vijay Rathee, Ritu Yadav (2017) Role of Women Entrepreneurs in Economic Empowerment of Rural Areas, *International Journal of Emerging Research in Management &Technology*, 9359(12), 1–8.

87. Sezgin, H. F. et.al (2017). Impact of Financial Literacy on Personal Savings/ : A Research on Usak, *Journal of Knowledge Management, Economics and Information Technology*, VII(6), 1–19.

88. Ernest, Negou. (2018). The Role of Bookkeeping on the Survival of Very Small Businesses in the Kumba Municipality, *International Journal of Advanced Engineering, Management and Science*, 4. 713-723. 10.22161/ijaems.4.10.1

89. Venkataraman, R., & Venkatesan, T. (2018). Analysis of Factors Determining Financial Literacy using Structural Equation Modelling #, *Sdmimd*

Journal of management, 19–29. https://doi.org/10.18311/sdmimd/2018/19998

90. Atkinson, A, McKay, S, Collard, S, & Kempson, E. (2007). Levels of Financial Capability in the UK, *Public Money & Management*, Vol. 27, no. 1, pp29-36.http://dx.doi.org/10.1111/j.1467-9302.2007.00552.x

91. Donkers, Bas, and Arthur van Soest. (1999). Subjective Measures of Household Preferences and Financial Decisions, *Journal of Economic Psychology*, 20 (December): 613–642.

92. Gathergood, J. (2012). Self-control, financial literacy and consumer over-indebtedness, *Journal of Economic Psychology*, 33(3), 590– 602.doi:10.1016/j.joep.2011.11.006.

93. Jappelli, Tullio. 2009. Economic Literacy: An International Comparison. *CSEF Working Paper No. 238*, Salerno, Italy: Center for Studies in Economics and Finance.

94. Lusardi, A. and Mitchell, O. (2006). Financial literacy and planning: implications for retirement wellbeing. Pension Research Council, *Working Paper*, The Wharton School.

95. Lusardi, A. and Tufano, P. (2009). Debt literacy, financial experiences, and overindebtedness. National Bureau of Economic Research. *Working paper No. 14808*, doi:10.3386/w14808.

96. Lusardi, A., Mitchell, O. S. and Curtoi, V. (2010). Financial literacy among the young. *Journal of Consumer Affairs*, 44, 358–380.

97. Lusardi, Annamaria, and Olivia Mitchell (2006). Financial Literacy and Planning: Implications for Retirement Wellbeing. Pension Research Council *Working Paper No. 1/2006*. Philadelphia: The Wharton School, University of Pennsylvania.

98. Meng, X, & Mounter, S (2009). Australian Household Debt: A Sectoral-Level Study, *The Asia Pacific Journal of Economics & Business*, Vol. 13, no. 2, pp3

99. Monticone, C (2010). How Much Does Wealth Matter in the Acquisition of Financial Literacy?, *Journal of Consumer Affairs*, vol. 44, no. 2, pp. 403-422. http://dx.doi.org/10.1111/j.1745-6606.2010.01175.x

100. Norvilitis, JM, & Szablicki, PB & Wilson, SD (2003). Factors influencing levels of credit-card debt in college students, Journal of Applied Social Psychology, vol. 33, no. 5, pp. 935-947. http://dx.doi.org/10.1111/j.1559-1816.2003.tb01932.x

101. O'Loughlin, D, & Szmigin, I (2006). I'll always be in debt: Irish and UK student behaviour in a credit led environment, *Journal of Consumer Marketing*, vol. 23, no. 6, pp. 335-343. http://dx.doi.org/10.1108/07363760610701878

102. Sevim, N., Temizel, F. and Sayilir, Ö. (2012). The effects of financial literacy on the borrowing behaviour of Turkish financial consumers. International Journal of Consumer Studies, 573–579. doi:10.1111/j.1470- 6431.2012.01123.x.

103. Ajzerle, Sanja, Brimble, Mark; and Freudenberg, Brett, (2013). Is Financial Capability Related to the Effective Use of Debt in Australia? *Australasian Accounting, Business and Finance Journal*, 7(3), 107-126. doi:10.14453/aabfj.v7i3.7

■■■■